The Uncensored Letters Of A Canteen Girl

by

Katharine Duncan Morse

Double9 BOOKS

The Uncensored Letters Of A Canteen Girl

by Katharine Duncan Morse

ISBN: 978-93-71134-93-4

Published by

DOUBLE 9 BOOKS

2/13-B, Ansari Road
Daryaganj, New Delhi – 110002
info@double9books.com
www.double9books.com
Tel. 011-40042856

ABOUT THE AUTHOR

Katharine Duncan Morse was raised in an environment shaped by intellectual engagement, she developed a strong interest in writing and observation. During the First World War, she volunteered with the American Expeditionary Forces and worked as a canteen worker in France. Her direct contact with soldiers and civilians during this period formed the basis for her later writing. She is best known for her work capturing wartime experiences from a personal perspective, offering insight into the human side of military service and support roles. While detailed records of her broader life and education remain limited, her writing reflects a thoughtful and observant voice shaped by lived experience. Morse's ability to communicate emotional nuance through everyday scenes speaks to her literary sensitivity and awareness of social dynamics. In addition to her wartime reflections, she is believed to have explored other creative forms, possibly including short stories or plays, though few of these works are widely available today. Her contributions provide a valuable lens into the complexities of war, compassion, and endurance. She remains a representative voice for those who served behind the front lines, with her work offering a distinctive perspective on early twentieth-century humanitarian efforts.

CONTENTS

CHAPTER I
BOURMONT—COMPANY A

Bourmont, France, Nov. 24, 1917.

My village has red roofs. When I first came to France and saw that the villages were two kinds; those with red roofs and those with grey, I prayed *le bon Dieu* that mine should be a red-roofed one. Heaven was kind. Every little house in town is covered with rose-colored tiles. We came here yesterday from Paris. Our orders, which were delivered to us in great secrecy, read: Report to Mr. T—, Divisional Secretary, Bourmont, Haute Marne; then followed a schedule of trains. That was all we knew except that some one told us that at Bourmont it had rained steadily all fall.

"It cleared off for several hours once," concluded our informant. "But that was in the middle of the night when nobody was awake to see."

Bourmont is a city set upon a hill, a hill that rises so sharply, so suddenly, that no motor vehicle is allowed to take the straight road up its side, but must follow the roundabout route at the back. Already we have heard tales about our hill; one of them being of a lad belonging to a company of engineers stationed here, who in a spendthrift mood, being disinclined to climb the hill one night after having dined at the café at its foot, bribed an old Frenchman with a fifty franc note to wheel him to the summit in a wheelbarrow. The Frenchman, for whose powers one must have great respect, achieved the feat eventually, the spectators agreeing the ride a bargain at the price.

Two-thirds of the way up the hill on the steep street called grandiosely *Le Faubourg de France* we have our billet, at the home of Monsieur and Madame Chaput. These are an adorable old couple; Madame a stately yet lovably gentle soul, Monsieur le Commandant, a veteran of the Franco-Prussian War and member of the *Légion d'Honneur*. His wonderful old uniforms with their scarlet trousers and gold epaulets rub elbows with my whipcord in the wardrobe.

Outside, the Maison Chaput resembles all the other houses which, built one adjoining another, present a solid grey plaster front on each side of the street. Like all the rest it has two doors, one opening into the house and one into the stable, and like every other house on the street the doors bear little boards with the billeting capacity of house and stable stenciled on them, so many *Hommes*, so many *Off.* (for *Officiers*). It is told how one lad after walking the length of the street exclaimed;

"Gee! Looks as if this were Dippyville. There's one or two off in every house!"

Another boy gazing ruefully at the sign on his billet door, groaned;

"Twelve homes! Why, there ain't one there!"

One stable door nearby wears the legend in large scrawling letters; "Sherman was right." At first the owner was furious at this defacement of his property, but when someone explained the significance of the words to him, he became mollified and even took a pride in them.

"Where are you stopping?" asks one boy of another.

"Me? Oh, at the Hotel de Barn, four manure-heaps straight ahead and two to the right."

The distinguishing feature of the Maison Chaput is the corner-stone. This shows as a white stone tablet at one side of the door. On it is carved "Laid by the hand of Emil Chaput, aged one year. Anno. 1842." It is the same Emil Chaput who with his tiny baby hand "laid" the corner-stone who is now our genial host.

"It is droll," said Madame; "When strangers come to town they must always stop and read the corner-stone. They think the tablet is placed there to mark the birthplace of some famous man."

The Gendarme and I,—Madame has christened G— my companion the Gendarme on account of her vigorous brisk bearing,—live in the *Salle des Assiettes*, at least that is what I have named it, for the walls of the room which evidently in more pretentious days served as a *salle à manger*, are literally covered with the most beautiful old plates. Not being a connoisseur I don't know what their history is nor what might be their value; I only know that they are altogether lovely. The designs are delicious; flowers, insects, birds, little houses, Chinamen fishing in tiny boats, interspersed with spirited representations of the Gallic cock in rose and scarlet. I exclaimed over them to Madame, whereat Monsieur, candle in hand, bustled across the room and called on me to regard one in particular.

"*Ça coute*," he averred proudly, "*quarante francs!*"

Since that moment I have been vaguely uneasy. What if, in a moment of exasperation, I should throw an ink-bottle at the Gendarme's head, and—shatter a plate worth forty francs!

Our room is the third one back. The front room is kitchen, dining and living room. The in-between room is quite bare of furniture, lined all about with panelled cupboards, and quite without light or air except that which filters in through the opened doors. In one of these cupboards Monsieur le Commandant spends his nights. When the hour for retiring comes, he opens a little panelled door and climbs into the hole in the wall thus revealed, leaving the door a crack open after him. When we pass through on our way to breakfast we hurry by the cupboard with averted faces. The family Chaput are not early risers.

Already Madame has taken us into her warm heart. She will be our mother while we are in France, she tells us. Everything about us is of absorbing interest. When the Gendarme exhibited her wardrobe trunk, she was fairly overcome.

"Ah, vive l'Amérique," she cried, clapping her old hands, and, *"Vive l'Amérique!"* again.

Bourmont, it seems, is army Divisional Headquarters. It is also headquarters for this division of the Y. There is a hut here, a warehouse, and headquarters offices, employing a personnel of sixteen or seventeen. By tomorrow the Gendarme and I will know what our work is to be.

Bourmont, November 28.

I have a canteen; the Gendarme, who has had some business training, is to work in the office. My canteen is in Saint Thiebault, the village next door. In the morning I go down the hill, past the grey houses built like steps on either side—some with odd pear trees, their branches trained gridiron-wise flat against the fronts,—over the river Meuse, here a sleepy little stream, to Saint Thiebault. On the way I pass lads in olive drab with whom I exchange a smile and a hello, villagers bare-headed, in sabots, and poilus in what was once horizon blue. In Paris the uniforms were all so beautiful and bright, but here at Bourmont one sees the real hue, faded, discolored, muddy, worn. The soldiers, middle-aged men for the most part, slouch about, occupied with homely, simple tasks, chopping wood and drawing water. One feels there is something painfully improper in the fact that they should be in uniform; they should, each and every one, be propped comfortably in front of their own hearthsides reading *l'Echo de Paris,* in felt slippers while their wooden shoes rest on the sill outside. And yet these very ones, I think as I look at them, may be the defenders of Verdun, the victors of the Marne, the veterans of a hundred battles!

The Bourmontese, who are proud and haughty folk, and call themselves a city though they number only a few hundred souls, look with disdain on the smaller village of Saint Thiebault, *Saint Thiebault des Crapauds* they call it, Saint Thiebault of the Toads. Approaching Saint Thiebault one sees two unmistakable signs of American occupancy; first, a large heap of empty tin cans and then the Stars and Stripes fluttering from a flag pole in the centre of the village. For Saint Thiebault is Regimental Headquarters and it is the boast of the old Colonel that wherever the regiment has gone that flag has gone too. Down the main street of the town I go, past the drinking fountain placarded; "Do not drink, good only for animals," but at which, nevertheless, the doughboys frequently refresh themselves, cheerfully risking death, not to mention a court-martial, in order to get a drink of unmedicated water; and out along the Rue Dieu until I turn off the highway just beyond the village wash-house. The wash-house, known to the French as *la Fontaine,* is a beautiful little building like a tiny stone chapel, with tall arched windows filled with iron grills. Through the centre runs a long oblong pool; at its brim the women kneel to do their scrubbing, handsome peasant wenches many of them, with fresh, high coloring. Often one sees a soldier leaning against the grill, engaged in some attempt at gallantry through the bars. Sometimes one even glimpses a form in olive drab kneeling by the side of one of the peasant girls, he scrubbing his socks, and she her stays, while she gives him a lesson in French and in laundering *à la Française*. When the Americans first came to Saint Thiebault they had only a small-sized guard-house. Then came one historic payday when after months of penury the troops were paid. That night the accommodations at "the brig" proved inadequate and the wash-house had to be requisitioned for the over-flow. This was well enough until the lodgers fell to fighting among themselves and so fell headlong into the pool. Then such a hullabaloo broke loose that the whole camp turned out to see who had been murdered.

Back of the wash-house lies a group of long French barracks, and here lives Company A of the — Regiment, infantry and "regulars." Beyond the mess-hall is the hut, a French *abri* tent with double walls. Ducking under the fly, one finds oneself in a long rectangular canvas room, lighted by a dozen little isinglass windows. The room is filled with folding wooden chairs and long ink-stained tables over which are scattered writing materials, games and well-worn magazines. Opposite the door, at the far end, is the canteen counter, a shelf of books at one side, a victrola and a bulletin board, to which cartoons and clippings are tacked, on the other. Back of the counter on the wall, held in place by safety pins, are the hut's only decorations, four of the gorgeous French war posters brought with me from Paris. There are two stoves resembling umbrella-stands for heating in the main part of the hut and behind the counter another, about the size and shape of a man's derby hat, on which I must make my hot chocolate. For lights at night I am told that occasionally one can procure a few quarts of kerosene and then the lamps that stand underneath the counter are brought out and for a few days we shine; but usually we manage as our ancestors did with candle-light. Our candlesticks form a quaint collection; some are real tin *bourgeois* brought from Paris, some strips of wood, some chewing-gum boxes, while others are empty bottles, "dead soldiers" as the boys call them. As for the bottles, I am particular about the sort that I employ and none of mine are labeled anything but Vittel Water. Others I observe are not so circumspect,—yesterday I chanced in at a canteen in a neighboring village kept by a Y man; on a shelf three "dead soldier" candlesticks stood in a row and their labels read; Champagne, Cognac, Benedictine! For the rest, the hut is equipped with a wheezy old piano, a set of parlor billiards, and a man secretary. It is invariably dense with smoke, part wood and part tobacco, and usually crowded with boys.

The first night after the Chief had taken me over to call at my canteen and I had had one cursory glance at them, I came back feeling that my hut contained the roughest, toughest set of young ruffians that I had ever laid eyes on. The second night I came home and fairly cried myself to sleep over them—they seemed so young, so pitiful and so puzzled underneath their air of bravery, so far away from anything they really understood and everybody that was dear to them. It was Cummings in particular I think who did it for me. He owns to seventeen but I would put fifteen as an outside estimate. A mere boy who hasn't got his growth yet, with soft unformed features and a voice as shrill as a child's, I am sure he ran away from home to go to war just as another lad might have run away to see the circus. Although the regiment is a regular army organization, a large part of the men were raw recruits only last summer, a fact which causes the old-timers, whose service dates from Border days or before, no little regret.

"This Man's Army ain't what it used to be," they complain; "it's getting too mixed."

The "veterans" have a stock saying which they employ to put the youngsters in their places: "Call yourself a soldier do you? Why I've stood parade rest longer than you've been in the army!"

This is sometimes varied, when the speaker happens to be the tough sort, by; "Huh! I've put more time in the guard-house than you have in the army!"

Tonight a boy came up to the counter and asked: "Goin' to serve hot chocolate tonight?"

"Sure thing!"

"Then I guess I won't go out and get drunk."

It's going to be hot chocolate or die in that hut every night after this!

Bourmont, November 31.

I don't like my uniform. I don't like women in uniform anyway. I suppose it is because one is so used to the expression of a woman's personality in dress that when she dons regulation garb she seems to lose so much. And then to really carry off a uniform requires a flair, a dash, a swagger, and such are rarely feminine possessions. The consensus of opinion seems to bear me out.

"Of course I think women in uniforms look very snappy," confided a lad to me today; "but somehow they don't look like women to me!"

"Pas joli," says Monsieur le Commandant severely, referring to my hat. *"Pas joli!"* But when I put on my old blue civilian coat he fairly goes into raptures.

"Be-u-ti-ful!" he ejaculates. "Be-u-ti-ful! *Toilette de ville. Pas toilette de Y. M. C. A.!"*

Besides the suit and cape I had made in Paris, they gave me two canteen aprons, aprons such as French working women wear, voluminous, beplaited, made in Mother Hubbard style. Now there is one point on which I am resolved. They can court martial me, they can send me home, or they can lead me out and shoot me at sunrise, but they cannot make me wear those aprons! What's more, the very first minute that I have to myself I'm going to cut them up and make them into canteen dish-cloths.

Bourmont, December 3.

This French money is the very plague; not because it is French but because it is so flimsy. It may perhaps measure up to the national standards, but it fails utterly to meet American requirements; the difference lying chiefly in the fact that the French don't shoot craps. It comes into the canteen in all stages of disintegration.

"She's kinder feeble. Will she pass?" inquires a lad anxiously.

"With care maybe, and the help of a little sticking plaster," I reply; and getting out the roll of gummed paper kept handily in the cash-drawer, I proceed to patch up the tattered bill.

"Guess this one must have been up to the front; it's all shot to pieces," another lad apologizes; then, at my casual references to shooting craps, grins guiltily. "But say now, ain't it the rottenest money you ever did see?" "The United States ought to teach these Frenchies how to make paper money," remarks a third; while still another adds; "When I'm to home I write to my girl on better paper than that."

Sometimes the bills come in as a mere mass of crumpled tatters; then one must play picture-puzzle piecing it together. Sometimes they are beyond repair; for at times you will receive two halves of different notes pasted neatly together, or at other times one with the corner bearing an essential number lacking. The French banks refuse to pay a cent on their paper money unless it is just so.

"I'm sorry, but that bill's no good," you will occasionally have to tell a boy. Usually he will grin cheerfully as he stuffs it back into his pocket.

"Oh well, I'll pass it along in a crap game."

Then too, the boys have no respect for foreign money and so handle it carelessly with an obvious contempt that is irritating to the French.

"Tain't real money," they declare.

The paper francs and half-francs they call "soap coupons."

"Why, you might just as well be spendin' the label off a stick o' chewin' gum!" they jeer.

Next to the paper money that comes to pieces in their fingers, the boys detest the big one and two cent coppers. Known to the navy as "bunker-plates," in the army they pass as "clackers." "You get a pocket-full o' them things and you think you've got some money, and all the time it ain't more than ten cents altogether," they grumble.

"I can't be bothered carryin' that stuff around," they declare when I beg them to pay me in coppers. "I always throw 'em away or give 'em to the kids." A prejudice which greatly complicated the matter of making change until I had an inspiration. Now I give them their small change in boxes of matches or sticks of chewing gum.

Then there is the annoyance of the local money. Since the war, the cities of France have taken to issuing their own paper francs and half-francs. We accept all this local money in the canteens and send it to Paris to be redeemed. But the French tradespeople in general refuse to honor these bills except in the city that issues them or its immediate vicinity. Many a puzzled doughboy has been driven to indignant protest or even to "chucking the stuff away" in his exasperated disgust when told by the shopkeepers that his paper money was *pas bon*. But the grievance is not quite all on one side: no small amount of worthless Mexican money, brought over by Border veterans, I am told, was palmed off on shopkeepers at the port when the Americans first landed!

In contrast to their disdain for this foreign currency the boys cherish to a degree that is half funny, half pathetic, any specimens of "real money" that they are lucky enough to possess.

"Say, I had an American dollar bill in my hand the other day,—I felt just as if the old flag was waving over me!" And another lad; "Saw a U. S. Dollar bill today. Oh boy! but it looked a mile long to me!"

If anyone displays an American greenback at the counter a little riot is sure to ensue. All the boys nearby crowd about, feast their eyes on it, touch it, pat it, kiss it even.

"Lemme see!" "Ain't she a beauty?" "That's the real stuff!" "Say, how much will you sell her for?"

Even the half-dollars, quarters and dimes are precious.

"You don't get that one," they say as they pull a handful of change from their pockets. "That's my lucky piece. I'm savin' that there little ol' nickel to spend on Broadway."

French money, Belgian money, Swiss money, English money, Spanish money, Italian money, Greek money, Canadian money, Luxembourg money, Indo-Chinese money, money from Argentine Republic, and yesterday a German mark even, all come across the counter and go into the till without comment. But when any American money comes in I always feel badly over it. For, be it a crisp five dollar bill, an eagle quarter or only a buffalo nickel I know it signifies just one thing,—bankruptcy.

Bourmont, December 7.

To be a corporal in the Ninth Infantry, it is said, a man must be able to speak eight languages, one for each soldier in his squad. The same could be said with almost equal truth of our regiment. I don't know whether it is this mixture of many nationalities that gives my family its flavour; be that as it may, Company A has more color, more character, more individuality to the square inch than I had dreamed any such group could possess. And they are so funny, so engaging in their infinite variety and their child-like naivete!

First there are Gatts and Maggioni; Gatts, lean, tall, honest-eyed, with a grin that won't come off and a quaint streak of humour,—Gatts who looks pure Yankee, but is, if the truth were told, three-quarters German,—Gatts who hangs about my counter hour after hour; and by his side sticks little Maggioni, who told the recruiting officer that he was seventeen but whose head just tops the canteen shelf, and who looks, with his pink cheeks and his great dark eyes, like nothing in the world but an Italian cupid in the sulks. The two have struck up the oddest comradeship.

"Me an' Gatts, we're goin 'to stick side by side," explains Maggioni, "an' if I see a crowd o' Germans pilin' onto him, why I'll just go right after 'em, an' if too many of 'em come for me ter oncet, why Gatts here, he'll just lay right into 'em."

And Gatts nods, looking down at Maggioni with a parent's indulgent eye.

"He thinks he's a tough guy for sich a little feller," he comments reflectively; "but he's the only one in the regiment that knows it."

"You all think I'm mighty little!" snaps the cupid. "When I joined at Syracuse everybody said to me 'Baby, where'd you leave your cradle?' But lemme tell you, I've growed since I've been in the army!"

"Waal I do believe there's one part of him that's growed;" Gatts is very solemn.

"What's that?" I ask.

"His feet."

Private Gatts has promised me one of the Kaiser's ears!

Then there is Brady, "Devil Brady" the little black Irish coal-miner from Oklahoma, who spends his days trying to get put in the guard-house, so he won't have to drill.

"I'm plumb disgusted," he confided to me today. "I never worked so hard in my life as I did the other night gettin' drunk, an' then the guard was so much drunker than I was, I had to carry him to the guard-house. I thought sure they'd give me thirty days at least, but they only kept me twenty-four hours and then out!"

"Hard luck," I sympathized.

"I just knew how it would be," he mourned. "It was Friday the thirteenth when I joined the army; there were just thirteen of us fellers, and the thirteenth was a nigger."

He tells me the most wonderful yarns about the miners and their pet rats, about explosions and disasters and rescue parties. Last night he told me the story of one mine-horror that will stick in my memory.

"And we shoveled the last three men and a mule into one bag," he finished.

Now and then I catch a glimpse of Jenicho the Russian giant, but he is very shy. A huge lumbering fellow, sluggish, and seemingly stupid, with little pig eyes that are quite lost to sight when he smiles, Jenicho is the butt of the Company. When he joined the regiment last summer, they tell me, he knew no word of English. The first phrase that he acquired was; "You no bodder me." For the boys can't resist the temptation to plague Jenicho, and though his strength is such that if he once should get his hands on his tormentors he could break them into bits, he is so slow withal that they always can elude him. Not long ago Jenicho was walking post one night when the Officer of the Day hailed him and announced himself. To which Jenicho lustily responded; "Me no give damn. Me walk post, gun loaded, bay'net fixed. You no bodder me. Me shoot!" And the Officer of the Day discreetly walked on.

Then there is little Philip R. who plays our decrepit old piano quite brilliantly by ear, and who is, he tells me, half Greek and half Egyptian. Philip R. is the pet of a French family in one of the neighboring villages. He stopped at a house to ask for a drink of water when out walking one day.

Madame asked him in, pressed him to stay to supper. The family made much of him, and all because forsooth he was the first "American" they had ever seen. Since then he has been a constant welcome visitor.

There is St. Mary too. If you can conceive of a cherub eating watermelon you have a perfect picture of St. Mary. St. Mary converses entirely in words of one syllable and very few at that. He makes smiles serve for speech. St. Mary loses everything he owns; not long ago he lost his overcoat, now he has lost his bayonet. Yet St. Mary is the best natured boy in the company; he needs to be. When St. Mary helps me stir the chocolate it seems as if half the company lined up on the other side of the counter to shout; "St. Mary! Take your dirty hands out er that there chocolate!" and St. Mary never says a word but grins until his eyes are nothing but little slits and ducks his head until only the curls on top are visible.

"St. Mary, he's kind o' simple," explains Private Gatts. "But there ain't anybody in camp that's got a better heart."

And there is Bruno, Angelo Bruno, a little grinning goblin of a man, but strong, they say, as a gorilla. Bruno gives the non-coms no end of trouble; he's a "tough nut to manage." Whenever he is told to do anything that does not suit his tastes, he merely shrugs his shoulders, "No capish," and that's the end of it. The other day while on guard he was interrogated by the Officer of the Day.

"What's your name?"

"Bruno."

"What are your general orders?"

"Angelo."

The Officer gasped, thought he would try again. "What are your special orders?"

Bruno saw a light. "They're ina my pock!"

When I first came to Saint Thiebault I was puzzled by the silver half-francs in my cash drawer which were bent in the middle, some of them so far as almost to form a right-angle. Then the boys explained. Bruno was once a strong man in a circus sideshow. He did things with his teeth. The crooked half-francs were the results of his exhibiting his prowess to the boys. So now when damaged half-francs appear I know that our little Angelo has been trying his teeth again. At present our social intercourse with Bruno is limited. He is serving thirty days in the guard-house. But every day or two he slips into the hut to do his shopping, the kind-hearted guard standing at the door, as he does so, a sheepish look on his face. If there is one military duty which the doughboy hates above all others, it is this job of "chasing prisoners," and when you meet a file of guard-house habitués escorted by a rifle in the rear, it is invariably the guard, and not the prisoners, who looks the culprit! The interest of Bruno's visits lies largely in seeing what is his latest acquisition in the way of jewelry. For Bruno has a pretty taste for finery and enlivens the dull evenings of his captivity by winning away the ornaments of his fellow prisoners. Already he has come into the canteen decked out with seven large rings and a fat watch and chain. Today he appeared with his latest prize, a pair of gold-rimmed eye glasses. They are hideously unbecoming, they pinch his nose so that it hurts, moreover he can't more than half see out of them, and yet it is quite evident those eyeglasses are the pride of his heart.

Last week our Secretary conceived a big idea. He would educate A Company. He would teach them to read, write and speak English. He started a class. On the first night there was a large crowd, eager and interested; the second night there were six, the pupils when sought out complaining they were "tired" or "busy;" the third night there was Saint Mary who made one; the fourth night the class died an easy death. I am afraid Company A is going to continue uneducated. As Brady said:

"There were just two things I learned in school; one was to throw a spit ball, the other was to bend a pin convenient for somebody to sit on." And it looks as if it would have to go at that.

"Why, those birds don't even understand their own names," complain the officers; "except on payday, and then they'll answer no matter *how* you pronounce them."

Bourmont, December 9.

There is something queer about me. I don't mind the mud, I don't mind the rain, I don't mind the hill, I don't even mind the mess. Of course I admit that the food isn't quite what one is used to, and the surroundings are a trifle unsavoury, but it is, after all, so much better than the state of semi-starvation that I was led to half anticipate, that I for one am quite content.

Our mess is held at the house of an old couple who live a little way above our billet on the hill. The house was differentiated from the others in the row by a spindling and discouraged tree which stood in a green tub outside; as this was the only tree in front of a house on the whole street it has always been easy to pick out our otherwise undistinguished entrance. Last night however, the weather waxing colder, the tree moved indoors. This morning the whole Y. personnel wandered distractedly up and down the hill trying to identify the mess-house door, until some kindly villagers, sensing the situation, came out on their front steps and pointed us to the place.

The house, like most of the village dwellings, consists, downstairs, of just two rooms. In the front room the family cooks, eats and spends its days. In the back room the family sleeps, and here we have our mess. The drawback of this arrangement is that one has to pass through the kitchen in order to reach the dining-room and this is likely to spoil one's pleasure in the meal that follows. As for me, I go on the principle that what one doesn't know won't take one's appetite away, and so hurry through the kitchen with one eye shut and the other fixed on the door ahead of me.

Said my right-hand neighbor to my left-hand neighbor at supper the other day, as he offered him the *pièce de résistance* of the meal:

"You aren't taking rice tonight?"

"Thanks no. Saw the old lady picking 'em out this noon."

"That's nothing. I saw the old man picking 'em out of the beans yesterday."

But why should people come to war if they are going to be so squeamish?

A few days ago one rash soul among us conceived a hankering for salad. She went to Madame and, being ignorant of the French word, demanded simply.

"*Avez-vous* lettice?"

Madame shook her head uncomprehending, but finally as the words were repeated a light dawned.

"*Ah oui, oui, oui!*"

She turned and hurried upstairs, descending triumphantly a moment later with a large bundle of old letters! In just what form she expected us to have them served I have not yet been able to ascertain.

The mess-room is so crowded that to reach a seat often requires considerable manœuvering. In one corner stands an ancient dressmaker's dummy—by popular vote awarded as sweetheart to the most bashful man at table; in the corner opposite is the bed of Madame and Monsieur. The men who get up for early breakfast, swallow their bread and jam and coffee with Monsieur watching from his couch of ease. Today Madame was indisposed and when we came to supper we found that she had retired already. All through the meal she lay there, under the red feather-bed, looking like a dingy, weazened old corpse, staring at the ceiling, her mouth wide open.

For the last few days we have had a visiting clergyman with us. To all appearances a meek and long-suffering little man, he has been giving special revivalistic discourses at the huts and eating at our mess. This morning he was asked to say grace. In the middle of a long and earnest exhortation I was startled to hear these words: "Oh Lord, Thou knowest we are apt to grow lean and to starve in Thy service!" I fairly had to stuff one of the one franc canteen handkerchiefs, which serve as napkins at the mess, into my mouth to keep from laughing.

Bourmont, December 12.

In Paris a man who lectured to us said: "Get the fellows who have influence with you, and you can swing the crowd." Sometimes I think that if Pat were our enemy instead of our friend we might almost as well shut up the hut. For Pat the sharp-shooter, Pat the dare-devil, Pat, who in company phrase "has Harry Lauder and George Cohen stopped in a hundred places," Pat the happy-go-lucky adventurer is one of the leading spirits in Company A. He has served, it seems, already in the war with the Canadian army.

"But how did you get out of it?" I asked.

Whereupon Pat regaled me with a wonderful rigmarole involving an extraordinary case—his own—of shell-shock out of which I could make neither head nor tail. Later, from one of the Secretaries who had been at Saint Thiebault before I came, I learned the truth. When America had declared war, Pat had deserted from the Canadian in order to enlist in the American army. Pat had showed him a letter from one of his old-time friends; it ended:

"Of course I wouldn't think of splitting on an old pal like you, Pat, but I do need twenty dollars like hell."

"What did you do?" asked the Secretary.

"Sure an' I sent him the money," grinned Pat.

Shortly after I first became acquainted with him, Pat, who is naturally gallant, with a tongue inclined to blarney, extracted a promise from me. Some day, after the war, if we should happen to meet, say, strolling down Fifth Avenue, Pat "dressed in a nice blue serge suit" is going to "take me away from the other feller" and take me out to dinner. It was after solemly pledging my word to this agreement that I learned that Pat had formerly been a saloon keeper and had had an extensive police-court record. Immediately I began to hope that Pat would forget that post-war party, but not he. Instead, he is constantly reminding me of it, always before an audience, dwelling on it and elaborating it, until now I find it has grown from a mere dinner, to dinner, the theatre and a dance!

Lithe, wiry, lean-faced with close-cropped hair, pale blue gimlet eyes and an almost unvarying expression of intense seriousness on his face, Pat, when present, is the life of the hut. Forever at his clowning, you would never dream from his demeanour that Pat's domestic affairs are in a state little short of catastrophic. His wife, according to her photograph a handsome, sullen, passionate type, half Mexican, ran away about a year ago, taking with her all his money that happened to be handy, together with his new automobile. Encountering some of Pat's friends, she had explained her apparently care-free single state by telling them that Pat was dead. Now she has discovered that Pat is in France, she is all for reconciliation. She has written him a letter in which she addresses him as her dear husband about six times to each sheet, informing him that she needs money, and inquiring of him what he wished her to do with his clothes.

"What did you answer?" I asked, for Pat, who must always share his correspondence, had shown me the letter.

"I told her," grinned Pat, "she cu'd keep the clothes and maybe she'd find another man to fit 'em."

But there is another and more serious side to the matter. It seems that the lady in the case has written to the Captain of A Company, requesting him to forward a large proportion of Pat's pay to his deserving and indigent wife. Whether or not this will be done is still uncertain. Pat refuses to discuss the possibilities, but from the glint in his eyes I have a premonition that if next pay day Pat finds any considerable deduction made from his pay, that that night one wild Irishman will run amuck in Saint Thiebault.

Occasionally in the midst of Pat's racy discourses I overhear things not meant for my ears, such as his remarking how in Rochester once he "went on a seven day's pickle in company with a female dreadnut." But usually he is very careful to only "pull gentle stuff" in my hearing. The other day he delivered himself of a wonderful dissertation on the deceitfulness of pious people, ending with this gem;

"So whenever I see one of these guys comin' towards me with a gold crown on his bean, looking' as if he couldn't sin if he had to, why I nip tight on to my pocketbook and I cross to the other side of the street!"

Today Pat came into the canteen with a newspaper clipping and a letter to show me. The letter was from the Chief of Police of K—, one of the many cities in which Pat has resided during his short but crowded life, the clipping from the K— Daily Sheet. The clipping was comprised of a letter which Pat had written to the Chief of Police giving in humorous phrase his version of life in France and an accompanying paragraph stating that though the writer had given the police force no little anxiety during his residence in K—, still he had been in spite of all, a good-hearted and likable rascal, and now that he had gone to war for his country, bygones should be bygones and K— must be proud of him. The letter from the Chief was in much the same vein.

"Yes," ruminated Pat; "I kept the old feller pretty busy, though me an' him were friends just the same. But it sure would get the old man's goat, just after he'd had me up and fined me, to come home and see me settin' at his dinner-table alongside of his pretty daughter."

Bourmont, December 14.

Because it took too much time right in the most important part of the day to climb Bourmont Hill for mess at night, I have arranged to take my suppers with two little old ladies here in Saint Thiebault. The suppers are to consist of a bowl of cocoa and a slice of bread with jam. The little ladies supply the bread and milk for the cocoa and I supply the rest, paying them one franc a day.

At half-past five I put on my things, light my little candle-lantern and set forth. The boys, coming in after mess, will be crowding the hut; a chorus of anxious voices queries.

"You're comin' back sure, ain't you?"

And, "What time is that hot chocolate goin' to be ready?"

I pick my way down the slippery duck-boards to the highway. Trudging along the muddy road, friendly voices hail me from the dark. I am known by the little light I carry. At number two Rue Dieu I rap and enter, trying desperately to leave some of the mud from my boots on the door-step, for in this land of wooden shoes scrapers are as unknown as they are unnecessary. Once inside I have to fairly strain my eyes in order to be able to see anything, for all the light in the room is supplied by the embers on the hearth and one tiny gasolene lamp with a flame not much bigger than the point of a lead pencil. Kerosene is unobtainable for civilian use; the price of candles is prohibitive.

"C'est la guerre. Cest la misère," say the little old ladies. "One must sit in the dark—*"Cest triste comme ça."*

My candle doubles the illumination, yet in spite of that, so strong is the instinct for economy, they will not rest easy until they have blown it out.

The little old ladies are cousins. The elder of the two, "Madame," is lame and has snow-white hair. She sits by the fire always in the self-same spot. The younger, "Mademoiselle," is a tiny dwarfish creature with a back that is not quite straight. Over her dark dress she wears a jaunty little scarlet apron sewn with black polka dots. I am grateful for that apron; it makes the one bit of color in the sombre room.

I sit in front of the fire at the round table and sip my chocolate. The table has an oil-cloth cover on which is printed a map of France, so as I eat my supper I can take a lesson in geography. It is a pre-war tablecloth I fancy; over at one edge shows a slice of Germany. The little old ladies point to that side of the table with scorn, *"Les sales Bodies sont là!"* they explain.

I wonder that it doesn't give them heart-burn to look down and see the captive and devastated districts of France lying beneath their tea cups.

Think of setting your salt-cellar on the city of Lille or your mustard pot on the sacred citadel of Verdun!

As I sup I endeavour to converse politely, but as my French is little more than camouflage, this is a dubious proceeding. Whenever I prove particularly stupid, out of the corner of my eye I catch Madame shaking her old head at Mademoiselle despairingly.

"Elle ne comprend pas!" she murmurs sotto voce, pityingly; *"elle ne comprend pas!"*

At odd times they turn an honest penny by doing a little sewing for the villagers. But life is very difficult these days: the prices of everything have gone so high. Why, wooden shoes that cost five francs before the war now fetch fifteen!

Tonight I noticed an item in a Parisian Journal lying by my plate. It was to the effect that at the Madeleine that day Mlle. X had married Lieut. Z., a veteran of the war who had lost both arms and both legs. I showed it to the little ladies.

"Ah oui!" sighed Mademoiselle with a shiver. *"Elle a beaucoup de courage, celle-là!"*

And Madame shook her white head and echoed. *"Oui, elle a beaucoup de courage!"*

Upstairs an American officer is billeted. I fancy his presence supplies a certain dash of romance to the little old ladies' lives. The Americans are nice, they say, and make little noise in the village; when the Russians were here it was different.

"It will be lonely when the Americans are gone," sighs Mademoiselle. "The houses will seem empty."

Bourmont, December 18.

Yesterday I explored the top of Bourmont Hill. It is here that the Quality Folk live, and here are some stately old houses with beautiful carved doorways and even an occasional gargoyle. Here too the general commanding the Division lives, and I have often observed with glee corpulent colonels and rotund majors puffing and blowing and growing red in the face as they climbed the hill to Headquarters. At the top of the hill there are two churches. Some two weeks ago, it is whispered, a spy was caught signaling from the tower of Notre Dame. His signals, it is said, were flashed to another spy stationed on the hills to the east, who in turn sent the messages on to the lines. The Curé of Notre Dame is being held under suspicion of complicity.

From Notre Dame an avenue bordered by magnificent old trees sweeps around to the Calvary, a tall wooden cross surmounting a curious structure of rough stone, ringed about with shallow steps—the Mecca of many pilgrimages. Beyond the Calvary one comes to the Mystery of Bourmont. A faded sign declares *Défense d'entrée*, but one looks the other way and slips by. For once past the gate you are in an atmosphere of enchantment. No one seems to know just what it is, nor how it came about; I can get no intelligent explanation from Madame or Monsieur. To me it seems like the forgotten playground of an old mad king in some fantastic legend. For here among the trees are stone stairs, walls and terraces, and, cut in the curiously cleft rocks, are niches and tunnelled passage-ways, all mantled over now with green moss and ivy, the whole making one think of a dream garden out of Mæterlinck.

Coming down Bourmont Hill afterwards I was startled by the beating of a drum; looking back I saw a woman, bare-headed, her blue apron fluttering in the wind, descending the street after me; from her shoulders was slung the drum which she was beating with a martial vim. It was the town-crier, *le tambour* as the French put it. Arrived at an appropriate spot, she stopped, pulled out a paper, cried "*Avis!*" and began to read in a rapid high official monotone. The wash-house was to be closed between two and four o'clock the following afternoon on account of the new water system the Americans were installing. Certain requisitions of grain were to be levied.... The villagers were notified to call at the Mayory for their bread cards, without which, after such a date, no bread could be obtained.... One or two women came to the doors of the houses and listened. She took no notice of them. The reading over, she rolled the paper up with a quick decisive gesture, and resumed her march, the sharp rub-a-dub-dub of her drum pursuing me all the way to Saint Thiebault.

Of late the air has become fairly vibrant with disquieting rumours: one does not know what to believe, what to reject.

The Germans are massing for a gigantic drive on Nancy. In three weeks, some say, the offensive is to begin; three days, say others. Nancy is to be another Verdun. If they break through they will pass this way. The American troops are being withdrawn from this neighborhood: any day the order may come for us to leave. At Paris the political situation is dark. Some people even fear a popular uprising against the government. I hinted at this to Monsieur, he shook his old head hopelessly. But yes, things were in a bad way. Now if France only had *Veelson* at her head! France and *Veelson*! His gesture indicated the grandeur of such a contingency. As it was, France lacked a leader. And underneath all this runs another rumour, still darker, still more disquieting. The French, the gallant French, they say, are "laying down." They are ready to make peace at any price. They are played out, sick to death of it all!

"Forty-two months in the trenches!" cried a sergeant *en-permission* last night; "It is enough! I am through. Let the Americans do it!"

And this feeling, they tell us, is wide-spread. The people see our soldiers day after day, in the training camps, inactive. "What are they here for?" they are asking. "Why don't they fight? Are they going to wait until it is all over?"

Will our soldiers, half-trained as they are, and a mere handful, be forced, to satisfy them, into the trenches?

In the canteen I look into the boys' faces and smile, but my heart turns sick within me.

Bourmont, December 20.

Such a strange, incredible thing has happened,—a thing that has upset all my preconceived ideas of human nature. It began with Malotzzi. Malotzzi as his name betrays is a "wop;" he is also the smallest fellow in the company which contains many small men. Nor is he only small, but with his thin olive-tinted face and his slender body, he looks so delicate, so ethereal that you feel a breath of wind might fairly blow him away. To the company he is "a good kid, quiet, never makes any trouble." To me he has always seemed an elfin, changeling creature, a strayed pixie, whose impishness has turned to gentleness. Child of the tenements that he is, he is possessed of the most exquisite old-fashioned courtesy that I have ever yet encountered; and he has the starriest eyes of any mortal born.

Not long ago he came to the counter to show me a post-card from his sweetheart. It had an ugly picture of a red brick city block upon it, and the message scrawled in an unformed hand beneath contained little except the simple declaration that when he came home she would go with him to the photographer's over the candy store at the corner and they would have their pictures taken together. Yet no flaming and lyric love-letter could have rendered him more naively proud. Malotzzi with a sweetheart! It was absurd, he was nothing but a child! I can well believe that Malotzzi wouldn't make a very "snappy" soldier.

This afternoon when the company was out for drill, a certain Second Lieutenant discovered that Malotzzi hadn't got his pack rolled up right. This was not the first time he had offended in this manner. The Lieutenant had warned him. He was angry. He took Malotzzi over to the bath-house, stripped off his blouse, tied his hands so he couldn't struggle, and beat him with a gunstrap until he fainted.

The story flashed around the camp. When I came back from supper I found the boys at white-heat with indignation. They fairly seethed with anger. I think if the Lieutenant had happened in, they might have killed him.

Presently a little crowd carried Malotzzi in. They rolled back his sleeves and showed me the great purple welts upon his arms. His back was all like that, they said. He had to be held up in order to keep his feet.

"You had better take him to the hospital," I told them.

They carried him out again. He is at the hospital now, where he is likely to stay for some time. His lungs are delicate and the beating caused congestion. The medical officer made a report and the Lieutenant has been placed under arrest.

I have never met the Lieutenant to know him, but curiously, the Secretary, who messes with the officers, asserts that of all the men there this Lieutenant has always appeared as the most clean-spoken, the most cultured, the most gentlemanly. And the boys have always considered him a very decent sort. The whole thing is absolutely and blankly incomprehensible to me. There is one explanation the boys offer; which is that the Lieutenant, having a yellow streak, has lost his nerve at the prospect of going to the front, and has done this as a desperate expedient, in the hope of being dishonorably discharged. The only other possible explanation which I can come upon is that the Lieutenant has a German name.

Bourmont, December 23.

The burning question that is on every lip: Will the Christmas turkeys come?

We had been promised turkey. What's more I had been promised some of that turkey too, at Company A's mess table. Now uncertainty holds us in torment. Every sort of a rumor is rife. Some darkly insinuate that neighboring organizations have sidetracked those turkeys. Others declare that the turkeys, having been smuggled in by night, are now actually in camp among us.

"Huh!" snorts my friend the Tall Kentuckian. "Funny turkeys they have in this army! I done heard those turkeys had four legs and a pair of horns!"

Of course Christmas won't be Christmas without the turkeys, but anyway we have done our best to bring Christmas into the hut. The question of Christmas trees was taken up in the Bourmont office some days ago. An application was made to the Mayor; the Mayor referred the matter to the representative of the Bureau of Forestry. The Bureau of Forestry proved to be a good scout. He ruminated a while, "Mademoiselle," said he, "this matter is so tied up with red tape, that if one were to unwind it all, it would be New Year's before you got your tree. My advice is that you select your tree, wait until after dark, then go out, cut it down close to the ground, and cover the place carefully with snow."

Tonight when the subject of Christmas trees came up in the canteen I repeated this anecdote to the boys. It was then growing dusky. Several boys immediately disappeared. In an hour they were back again, dragging not one, but two beautiful hemlocks. We set up the more perfect one, and cut the other up for trimmings. With flags, paper festoons, Japanese lanterns, tinsel which the French call "angel's hair," and tree ornaments the hut was transformed in a twinkling as if by magic. Now it is no longer a muddy-floored tent, but a green bower threaded with myriad bits of bright color, and I have really never seen anything of the sort that was any prettier.

Yesterday several cases of free tobacco from the Sun Tobacco Fund arrived in camp. The boys in the orderly room opened the cases last night and hunted through and through them, trying to find packages which bore the names of unmarried lady donors. Unfortunately the Misses who contributed were few and far between, but hope dies hard.

"Say, mightn't Asa be a girl?" the lads are asking me eagerly today.

"Lucien ain't a man's name, is it?"

Enclosed in each package is a postal-card on which one may, if so inclined, return thanks to the giver. The boys who are taking the trouble to write are doing it frankly with the hope that this may encourage the recipient to repetition. How to tactfully suggest this without seeming greedy is a problem whose delicacy proves difficult.

"You tell me how to say it," they tease.

"Say, won't you write it for me, please ma'am?"

I saw one postal-card accomplished after an evening of concentrated effort; "Your precious and admired gift," it began.

Already Santa Claus in the person of Mr. Gatts has presented me with a beautiful white silk apron embroidered with large bunches of life-like violets.

Bourmont, Christmas Day.

Joyeux Noël!

As I came in last night there was a great log burning on the hearth.

"C'est la bouche de Noël," said Madame and explained how it would burn all night, then Christmas morning she would take the little end that was left and put it away in the loft until the next Christmas: it would protect the house from lightning; it was a very ancient custom.

Back in the *Salle des Assiettes* I found our table spread as for a little fête with a wonderful cake and a bottle tied up with a bouquet of chrysanthemums and long ribbon streamers of red white and blue. I was so innocent that I supposed at first that the chrysanthemums were in the bottle, an improvised vase, but Madame quickly enlightened me: *"C'est le vin blanc,"* she explained to my embarrassment.

The Gendarme and I took counsel together as to how we could best express our feelings on this occasion toward the Family Chaput, the household having been increased over night by the arrival of the married daughter and her small boy and girl. After various projects had been considered and abandoned, we finally took the little stand from our room, dressed it with evergreen and tinsel, then heaped it with nuts, candies, chocolate bars, and little jars of jam all from the canteen, together with a few small toys, and carried it in and placed it in front of the hearth. The family appeared delighted. We observed, however, that after the first toot, baby Max's whistle was swiftly and silently confiscated. Later when *La Petite*, the little maid-of-all-work who takes care of our rooms, came in, we had a few trinkets dug from the depths of our trunks to bestow on her. Later still I carried chocolates and *confiture* to my little old ladies of the Rue Dieu.

This Christmas day I fancy will be long remembered by the inhabitants of this part of France; for in every one of the villages about, our soldiers have given the French children a Christmas tree. I went to see the tree at Saint Thiebault. The ancient church, its chill interior ablaze with light, was crowded with villagers all dressed in their fête day best. The old people were just as excited and eager as the children; not one had ever seen a Christmas tree before. They stood on the pews in order to get a better view. The tree which was very large and beautiful stood just outside the altar rail. It bore a gift for every child in Saint Thiebault. While the tree was slowly being unburdened of its load, the band-master's choir, high up in the choir-loft, sang an accompaniment. Some of the selections were of a sacred character, others frankly secular, such as Drink To Me Only With Thine Eyes; but as one of the choristers remarked;

"As long as we sing them slow and solemn the Frenchies won't know the difference."

After the Christmas tree I went around to the little local hospital to take some gifts to the patients. There were half a dozen of them lying on cots in the bare barracks room, a dreary set in a drearier setting. In one corner lay a boy who muttered incoherently. He had just been brought in, they told me, and was very ill: the doctors were puzzled to know what was the matter with him. I left some little gifts for him when he should be better.

It was half-past four when I reached the hut. Suddenly it popped into my head that we ought to have a Santa Claus. At half-past six Santa walked in through the door. It was Pat in a big red nose, a red peaked cap, much white cotton-batting beard and whiskers, rubber boots, the Chief's fur coat, covered over for the night with turkey-red bunting, and a fat pack slung over one shoulder. I had just dressed him in the mess hall, and for an impromptu Santa Claus, I flatter myself he was quite effective. The boys whooped. When they discovered who it was behind that nose, they yelped like terriers.

"Ain't he the beauty! Oh you whiskers! Say Pat, kiss me quick!"

We got Santa safely behind the counter and then opened the pack. It was full of foolish little things; tricks, puzzles, games, mottoes, whistles, tin trumpets, paper "hummers". The boys went wild. It was the musical instruments that made the hit. For two hours that hut shrieked pandemonium. Every last man in the company tootled and squawked as if his life depended on it, and every last one of them was tootling a different tune.

"C'est des grands gosses!" Truly, as Madame Chaput says, they're nothing after all but so many big little boys.

After the stuff was distributed the Secretary and I invited the boys to partake of hot chocolate and sandwiches. But to our disappointment they only took a languid interest in the treat. Instead of the five and six cups apiece which many often swallow, not one of them consumed more than a cup and three-quarters. Too late we realized; they had already gorged themselves on the contents of their Christmas boxes from home.

Reports coming in from the village stated that one American Christmas custom had made a strong appeal to the feminine portion at least of the population. Quantities of mistletoe grow hereabouts. The French, although averring that it brings good-luck, consider it a pest and let it go at that. It took the American doughboys to enlighten the *Mademoiselles* as to its Anglo-Saxon significance. It would be curious, I have been thinking, if the adoption of this ancient privilege should prove one of the lasting evidences of the American troops in France!

As I left the canteen I learned that the boy who had been so sick at the hospital was dead.

Bourmont, December 26.

Last night was a wild night in the barracks. This morning the hut was full of echoes of it. Company A indeed wore a jaded look. They had had very little sleep it was explained. And it was all on account of the Christmas hummers.

"I ain't got nothin' against you people, but I shore don't think you gave A Company a square deal," remarked my friend the Tall Kentuckian as he lit his cigarette at the counter.

"Why, didn't you like the present that Santa Claus brought you?" I teased.

"Huh! I would shore have singed the ol' gentleman's whiskers for him last night if I could have caught him!" He went on to explain; "We'd just get settled down good to sleep when some guy or other would start up a-squawkin' on one of them things. An' Sergeant —, well he'd had just enough to make him fightin' mad, an' he shore would rare around that there barracks tryin' to find them fellers. Why, half the corporals in the outfit was marchin' up and down the place most all the night long, shyin' hob-nailed shoes in what they guessed was the direction of them noises."

I began to discern what a night of terror it had been.

"Yes suh!" declared the Kentuckian. "There was one feller with a hummer we couldn't get. He kept blowin' Tipperary. He must have blowed it for two hours steady, on an' off. I guess he had every last hob-nailed shoe in the hull barracks throwed at him."

Nor is this all. It seems I have committed a ghastly *faux pas*. I have gotten the Y. in dreadfully dutch with the officers. It is all along of the Christmas calendars. The Christmas calendars arrived at the canteen just the day before Christmas. They were designed to be sold to the boys for five cents apiece in order that they might have something to send to the folks at home as a Christmas greeting. But since they reached us so very late the Secretary and I decided we didn't have the face to put them on sale.

"Let's give them away," I suggested, and on his agreeing, laid them in heaps on the counter and invited the boys to help themselves. The boys weren't bashful. They helped themselves with enthusiasm and zeal. They came back for more and more. For the rest of the day no one did a thing at the hut but sit at the tables and address envelopes. One boy, I learned later, sent off as many as thirty-five. I was awfully pleased to have the boys appreciate the calendars so. And I never once for a moment thought of the censors; but presently I heard from them. The company censors, two of the younger lieutenants, had been looking forward, it seems, to some leisurely care-free hours at Christmas. When the stacks of calendars started coming in they saw their holiday vanish into thin air, nay more, they saw themselves sitting up nights for weeks to come censoring those precious calendars. And they were swearing, raving mad. They were going to run the Y. out of the town! They were going to shut down the hut! Finally they compromised the matter with their consciences by censoring half and chucking the other half into the stove. But even then they couldn't stop fussing and fuming over it. Tonight just to top the matter off, we received a sharp reprimand from the Business Manager at Bourmont for being so extravagant as to give the calendars away, unauthorized. Was there ever such a tragedy of good intentions?

Bourmont, December 27.

Today we buried the lad who died on Christmas night. I had never seen a military funeral before and I had never dreamed that such a ceremony could be so thrillingly beautiful.

The company formed at three o'clock in the road in front of the canteen, then filed slowly through the streets of the little grey age-old village. The band marching at the head of the procession played the *Marche Funèbre* of Chopin. After the band came the officers of the company and then the firing squad of eight sharp-shooters, followed by an ambulance carrying the boy's coffin covered with a great flag. Behind, marched the whole of Company A and after them crowded a throng of villagers. All the men in town, with the innate respect that the French have for death, stood uncovered as we passed, while many of the women watched with tears streaming down their faces.

We passed through the village and down the road to the little grey-walled cemetery, ringed around with evergreens and now deep in freshly fallen snow. All about stretched virgin shining snowfields and over them to the east rose Bourmont like a dream city, etched as delicately as by a silver-point against the soft dove-colored sky.

The majestic phrases of the Catholic burial service rang out clearly on the frosty air:

Eternal rest grant him, O Lord,

And let perpetual light shine upon him!

The coffin with the great flag burning in blue and scarlet was lowered into the grave. Slowly, with perfect expression, a bugler blew the poignant, unforgettable notes of Taps. The rifles of the firing squad cracked sharply; three volleys, it was over.

"Will they leave him there?" An old Frenchwoman asked one of the boys afterwards.

"'Till the war is over, then likely they will send him home."

"But why? He won't be lonely here. There will always be some one to put flowers on his grave."

Tonight I was talking to the Supply Sergeant about the lad.

"I think he died of a broken heart as much as anything," he told me. "They wouldn't let his mother see him at the dock when we sailed. She came to say good-bye but it was against the rules. He never could get over that; he kept brooding all the time and fretting for her. I read some of her letters to him. They seemed more like a sweetheart's than a mother's."

The doctors, however, diagnosed his disease as spinal meningitis. They have ordered the barracks in which he slept to be quarantined. Already a half a dozen boys in quarantine have taken to their beds, but this we hope is largely due to over-stimulated imaginations. Even if the disease doesn't spread, however, I am wondering what will become of ninety-seven lively boys bottled up for two weeks in one barracks. Already various ones have eluded the guard and come sneaking furtively into the canteen to buy their cigarettes and chocolates. Whenever one of these unfortunates is recognized a regular howl goes up all over the hut.

"Outside! You're one of the crumby ones!" they jeer, or; "Convict! Get back to your cell!"

Bourmont, December 28.

The worst of my job is playing dragon to the French children. In view of the fact that if allowed in the hut at all they swarm in, in such numbers as to fairly overrun it, and pester the boys with their insatiable appeals for "goom" and chocolate, it has seemed best to make a strict rule against their admission. (Besides which I don't approve of giving them gum, for in the face of anything one can do or say they will insist on swallowing it, which is, I'm sure, not at all good for their tummies!) But in spite of this prohibition the place holds an irresistible attraction for them. At night one can often see their faces pressed flat against the isinglass windows as they peer inside; while chiefly on Saturday and Sunday afternoons they will slip slyly in, and then if the dragon isn't on the jump to explain to each and every one in her very best French, that she is so sorry but it really is forbidden, why in a twinkling the hut becomes full of them. And they are so picturesque, so appealing, so full of shy wonder at the gramophone with the wheel that "marches by itself" that it is very hard to turn them out.

Since Christmas I have been kept busy by a tiny tad of a ragamuffin with a funny round cropped black head and a face as solemnly expressionless as a little carved Buddha. He slips in among the tables and he is positively too small to be seen. The Christmas tree with its shining ornaments is his stealthy objective. In vain I explain matters politely to him; without a sound, without the hint of a flicker in his little beady black eyes, he turns and clumps out in his ridiculous *sabots*, only to presently slip in again. And now it seems he has lain low and sagaciously observed my habits; for returning to the hut after mess this noon, I met him trudging along the Rue Dieu, his eyes encountering mine blandly without embarrassment, his absurd little figure bulging all over with purloined Christmas tree ornaments. In the hut I found our poor tree stripped to a height of four feet from the floor of all its finery.

These last few evenings the hut has been given over to writing Christmas thank-you letters home. The official writer of love letters for the company has been working overtime; not that his clients cannot write themselves, but because they feel he is more able to do justice to the subject.

Every night now I see him sitting out in front of the counter, his Jewish profile bent low over the table as he covers sheet after sheet with his fine and fanciful handwriting, while next him perches anxiously the interested party, watching developments and occasionally proffering a suggestion. When it is done they must bring it to me for my approval.

"That's a real classy letter, ain't it?" the lover will query proudly and I assure him that it is indeed.

"When she gets that, I bet she'll come across with that sweater she told me she was makin' for me, all right!"

"Say do you think that ought to be good for a *cartoon* of cigarettes?" another one inquires.

Of course there are many who, no matter what the effort, prefer to write their own. Sometimes when cleaning up the canteen tables I come upon specimens of such, first drafts discarded on account of blots. One such love letter, classic in its brevity, picked up the other day, ran:

> Dear Sweetheart,
>
> I am writing you a few interesting lines which I hope will be the same to you wishing you a merry Xmas and a happy New Year
>
> Your loving friend
>
> Pvt. —

Of late I have been moved to speculate wonderingly on the mental processes of the American public. I have been going through the stacks of magazines in the warehouse sent from the States for one cent per to provide amusement for the doughboys' leisure moments. Among the rest I found the Upholsterer's Monthly, The Hardware Dealer's Journal, The Mother's Magazine, Fancy Work and The Modern Needleworker. I showed some of these prizes to one of the boys; "Gee, but that's the kind of snappy stuff to send a feller over the top!" was his comment. That numbers of the Undertaker's Journal have also been discovered among the donations from home I have heard asserted on excellent authority, but as yet I have not personally come across any.

Just as we were closing tonight, Pat came up to the counter, solemnly leaned across it:

"Have you seen the new shoes they're issuin'? he demanded. "They've got pitchers on them so a feller can't see his own feet!"

Bourmont, January 2, 1918.

Once a week our peripatetic movie-machine makes its appearance among us. Louis, the sixteen year old French operator, unpacks the big cases, sets up the apparatus, and, if our luck holds, we have a show. Owing to the short range of the little machine the screen must be hung in the middle of the hut. This means that half the audience must view the pictures from the back, the essential difference being that the lettering is then reversed; "The Jewish Picture Show," the boys call this. But then as half of us can't read anyway, why should we mind?

The joy of the show lies in the audience. Just as soon as the lights are put out the fun begins: "Everbody watch their pocketbooks!" goes up the shout and from that moment we are never still.

The curly-headed heroine makes her coquettish entrance.

"Ooo la la! Oooo la la!" rises the enthusiastic welcome.

A bottle is displayed; "Cognac!" the yell shakes the roof.

The neglected wife begins to waver in response to the tempter's wiles; "Now don't forget your general orders, little lady!" admonishes an earnest voice.

Lovers indulge in a prolonged embrace; "Aw quit! Quit it! Yer make me homesick!" goes up the agonized appeal.

The enraptured lover stands registering ecstasy; "Hit him again, he's coming to!" comes the derisive shout.

And so it goes. The actors aren't on the screen, they're in the house, and truly there isn't a dull moment on the programme!

Last night, however, instead of the joyous chorus of running comment a subdued and decorous silence reigned, broken only by a few half-hearted sallies. What was the matter? I racked my brain to find the cause. All the joy had gone from the show. The evening was stale, flat and unprofitable. When the lights were lit again the mystery was immediately made plain. At one end of the counter stood an officer. I wonder if he dreamed what a spoil-sport he had been?

Once a week also a lady comes from the Bourmont office to give us a French lesson; not that Company A betrays any burning desire to learn to *parlez-vous,* but just that it seems obviously the proper thing to do under the circumstances, so French they must be taught willy-nilly. There were two lessons to be sure in which they took a degree of interest; the lesson about buying and counting money, and the lesson about food and drink. But when they had once learned to ask the price of things and to understand the answer, and had learned the words for eggs, bread, butter, beer, ham, beefsteak, chicken and French fried potatoes, their interest lapsed until it became positive boredom. Of late it has seemed to me that it was only the boys with French blood that learned anything and they, of course, knew it all already.

For entertainment Company A can upon occasion furnish its own show. This was demonstrated by an impromptu programme staged in the hut the other night; there's no use we have discovered in planning things beforehand, if one does, as sure as fate, all the star performers "catch guard" that day! Pat by request acted as stage-manager and master of ceremonies. To stimulate the artists we announced prizes.

Private Dostal opened the programme; a large red-faced lad with a bland and simple cast of countenance, he is the comic balladist of the company. His first contribution was a selection popularly known among us as *Beside the dyin' boxcar, the empty hobo lay,* a piece with a vast number of verses in which the dying hobo repents an ill-spent life, only, in the last line, to "jump up and hop the train." For an encore we had *Papa Eating Noodle Soup* which could best be described as a "gleesome, gluesome" recitative, the chorus of each of numerous verses consisting of a realistic imitation of Papa partaking of the Soup. Mr. Gatts gave us a jig. Then Bruno who, as the boys say; "Could sing pretty good, only he don't sing nothin' but wop," favored us with *Oh Maria,* prefacing his performance with the earnest admonition, "No laffin! nobody!" and after that with an Italian folk dance in which he looked more like a grotesque little punchinello than ever. Our light-weight boxing champion then gave us *Love's Old Sweet Song* and the heavy-weight champion popularly known as *Magulligan,* together with Mr. Bruno rendered *Bye low my Baby,* antiphonal fashion. The last number was furnished by a poilu who had wandered in, in company with one of the boys. He sang a long dramatic ballad, entitled *The Last Cuirassier,* depicting some incident in the Franco-Prussian War. Just what the boys made of it I don't know, but to me it was intensely thrilling, not on account of the words for I couldn't catch them, but on account of the fervor, the imaginative sympathy, the martial spirit which that old fellow in his faded trench coat threw into his tones.

When the show was over Pat stood up on the counter and announced that as long as all the performances had been of such superlative merit, it was impossible for the judges to decide between them. So we handed out a couple of packages of "smoking" to each one of the artists, and everybody was satisfied.

Once too we had a party, an athletic stunt party. There were potato-races and sack-races, string-eating contests, three-legged and obstacle-races; but the sensational, the crowning event was, of course, the pie-race. The pies which were of French manufacture had only been arranged after difficulties: consulting the *boulangère* at Bourmont I had discovered that the calendar now only allows two pie-days per week, Sunday and Wednesday; since the party was to be Friday, pie was unlawful, unless—and here the law, like all good laws allowed a loop-hole—unless the pie be made with commissary flour! The pie-race was the "dark horse" on the programme. Fearing that if the boys learned beforehand of the prospective pie not only would we be mobbed by would-be contestants but also that their interest in the rest of the programme would suffer, we had kept the pie-race a profound secret. Smuggled in when the hut was empty those pies had reposed serenely under the counter all afternoon and contrary to my fears not a boy had sniffed them! When the proper moment came the pies were placed on a board in the middle of the floor, the contestants, of whom Pat was one, knelt with their hands tied behind them. At the word *go!* they fell to. The hut howled. Then it was discovered that Corporal G. laboured under a cruel handicap; *his* pie was a cherry pie and every cherry had a stone in it. Half-way through his pie, Pat, jerking one hand loose, seized a large piece, plastered it on the head of his opponent opposite; the race ended in a riot. Strangely enough, when peace was restored not a trace of pie could be found anywhere,—nowhere, that is, except in the back hair of the contestants.

Bourmont, January 6.

Now I know how the prince in the fairy tale felt when he was bidden to climb the mountain of glass. For Bourmont Hill is sheeted with ice, and it is fairly as much as one's life is worth to attempt to go up or down. Every morning I stand and look at that dizzying slide aghast, and wonder if I may possibly reach the foot alive; then assistance comes, sometimes in the shape of a French lad in *sabots*, sometimes as a stalwart doughboy with a sharp-pointed staff, and together the two of us go slipping, slithering down the hill-side. In the middle of the road yelling doughboys, seated on cakes of ice, whiz by at a mad rate of speed; long before they reach the bottom of the slope, the ice-cake splinters into bits, but the doughboy shoots on downward, sprawling, spinning like a top, while you hold your breath and gape to see that his neck isn't broken. For the French people all this supplies the sensation of a life-time; they crowd their front doors and their front yards laughing, shrieking warning or encouragement, as they watch the progress of the mad Americans up and down the hill.

"If one could only have a movie of Bourmont Hill on a day like this!" sighs the Gendarme.

The other day I encountered a sergeant of engineers on the hill-side.

"You ought to have a sled, Little Girl," he told me.

"Well why don't the engineers make me one?" I unthinkingly retorted.

"Sure and they will!" he answered.

Since then I have gone in terror. If the sergeant should have that sled made for me, as he likely will, why I shall have to use it. And as for starting down Bourmont Hill on a sled, I would just as soon attempt Niagara in a barrel.

Ever since Christmas it has been cold, bitter cold. At the canteen I wash my chocolate cups with the dishpan on the stove in order to keep the water fluid; hanging the dish-cloth up to dry at the corner of the counter, in a few minutes I find it stiff with ice. At night the ink-bottles freeze and then burst, spreading black ruin all around them. What to do with the still unfrozen ones is a vexing problem; I might I suppose take them home each night with me and sleep with them underneath my pillow. In the little umbrella-stand stoves the green wood, which comes in so freshly cut, that the logs have ivy still unwithered twined around them, simply will not burn, and the stoves will smoke, *mon Dieu*, how they will smoke! Every time the wind blows, the stove-pipes, secured shakily by the canvas walls, become disjointed, parting company with the stoves, and then the clouds pour forth as if we housed a captive Etna.

In the barracks the boys tell me their shoes freeze to the floor over night. They have taken to sleeping two in one bunk for the sake of warmth. Blanket-stealing has been elevated to the rank of a deadly crime. Even the problem of keeping warm by day is an acute one. The boys who have money to burn are spending it to purchase extravagantly priced fur-lined gloves. The boys who can't afford them, wait until they see somebody lay a pair down.

The taking of baths has become an act of heroism.

"Took a bath today," growls a lad. "Think I ought to get a service stripe for that."

While another boy grins; "Gee but I'm feelin' rich! Took a bath today and found two pair o'socks and three shirts I didn't know I had!"

"Now ain't you sorry you cut off the bottom of your coat!" a long-coated doughboy taunts an abbreviated one. "I told you not to. First, you're out of luck at Reveille 'cause the Top Kick can see you ain't got no leggin's on. An' now before you know it, you'll be havin' chilblains in your knees."

"You should worry," growls back the short-coated one. "I couldn't stand that thing flappin' 'round my feet no longer. An' most of the other guys done it too."

Which is true. Before this cold spell set in, half the boys in the company had taken a slice off the bottom of their overcoats, a procedure which leads to an odd effect *en masse* as each has chosen his own length which means everything from knees to ankles, and drives the exasparated Loots to demanding; "D'you want to know what you look like? Well, you look like *hell!*"

In the village streets snow-ball fights are in order. As soon as the boys start an offensive, all the inhabitants of the *Faubourg de France* run out and put up their shutters. Better to sit in the dark while the battle rages than to risk a pane of precious window-glass! Yesterday out at Iloud the boys caught the Y Secretary, a meek and mild little man, in the road and started to give him a thorough pelting. He ran for the hut, they chased him, he gained his refuge, locked the door after him; they proceeded to heap about half a ton of snow against it, making it immovable. The unhappy man had to remove a window frame and crawl out through the opening, then spend the rest of the afternoon digging out his hut door.

Here at our billet our little pea-green porcelain stove with the lavender thistles growing over it has proved to be more ornamental then useful. Since the Gendarme is one of your naturally efficient souls, I feel that such practical details as building fires belong to her. If she wishes to coax and cozen the wretched thing for an hour on end, well and good. As for me I prefer to go and hug the cook stove in Madame's parlor. French fires don't burn the way American fires do, I tell Madame. But to her the matter is quite simple. The stove, she says, doesn't understand English.

Today I met the sergeant of engineers. Some imp impelled me to question jovially;

"Where's that sled you promised me?"

"It's almost done." My knees went weak beneath me.

Tonight I confided my apprehensions to the Gendarme. She looked at me with an unpitying eye.

"The more goose you, for encouraging him," was her cold comfort. "What are you going to do about it?"

"I'm going to pray for a thaw," I told her.

Bourmont, January 8.

Life at the Maison Chaput doesn't flow quite so peacefully these days as it did before Christmas. The disturbing factor is four-year old Max, left by his mother to visit his grandparents. Max is a spoiled child according to the Chaput point of view. He is expected to walk a chalk line with his little red felt toes, and failing this, he is spanked early and often. It is unlucky for him that the fagots by the hearth afford a continual supply of handy switches.

"The little Jesus will never bring you anything again at Christmas," warns Grandmamma; "never again! And neither will the *Père Nicolas*!" Then she appeals to me; "All the little children in America are always well-behaved, are they not?"

"But yes, certainly!" I reply, avoiding Max's eye.

Coming home in the evening I often stop on my way back to the chilly *Salle des Assiettes,* in response to an urgent invitation, to warm myself at the fireplace. Old Monsieur will be sitting on one side of the hearth and I on the other, while Baby Max toasts his toes in their scarlet slippers on a stool between us. Sometimes they will sing for me. Monsieur had a fine voice when he was young and even now he sings with a delightful air, a sort of indescribable old gallantry that is a joy to me. When he and Max sing together the effect is irresistible.

"Now we will sing *Le Drapeau de la France,*" cries Monsieur. "We must stand for this!" And Monsieur in his gay red neck cloth and little Max in his blue checked pinafore stand up before the fire and sing with their hearts in the words "*Saluons le drapeau de la France.*" When they come to that line, Monsieur le Commandant veteran of 1870 and baby Max salute together.

Then, "*Vive la France!*" I cry, and "*Vive la France!*" they echo.

When new troops pass through town Max must always run to the door to cry "*Bonjour les Américans!*" a salutation which is often followed I fear by a request for cigarettes, for Max, baby that he is, enjoys a smoke, much to his grandparents' amusement.

Among the china-ware at the Maison Chaput there is a funny little jug which the Gendarme and I use for fetching hot water. It is made in the shape of a fat frog with a blue waistcoat and a pipe in one of his webbed feet. I had thought it was the famous frog who would a-wooing go, but Monsieur has his own explanation. It is the original St. Thiebault toad he declares, to tease me. Every time I come to draw a little hot water from the stove he must crack the self-same joke.

"*C'est le crapaud de Saint Thiebault,*" he cries and baby Max pipes up; "*Il a soif!*"

Yesterday as I was passing through the front room on my way to the canteen Monsieur stopped me to draw me into conversation. There were several neighbors present. They gathered in a ring around me. I could see they had some weighty question to put to me. After a moment's hesitation it came out:

"*Pourquoi,*" they demanded, "*pourquoi,* does the American soldier blow his nose with his fingers?"

I stared, taken aback. In order to make their meaning quite clear they illustrated with expressive gestures.

"Why," I stammered, "does the poilu never do such a thing?"

"But never!" they declared in chorus. "The poilu always uses his handkerchief!" And again they illustrated in pantomime.

I labored to explain; the French climate had given the boys colds, and the question of laundry and clean handkerchiefs presented difficulties....

"But," declared old Monsieur sagely, "in America I have heard it is the custom. There all the *haut monde*, it is said, lawyers, doctors, ministers, statesmen, blow their noses in that manner!"

This was too much. I hurried from the room.

This morning Monsieur accused me of being a coquette. Hotly I denied the charge. But why then, he rejoined triumphantly, had I asked for a looking-glass in my bed-room?

Bourmont, January 9.

Company A is going to China! Somebody heard somebody say that somebody told him that the Chaplain had said so. The boys are all excitement over the idea.

"Won't that be jolly! You'll all be coming home with little shiny pigtails hanging down your backs!" I tease them.

"Yes sir! an' we'll learn to eat our chow with chopsticks!" I have solemnly promised the boys that if Company A goes to China I will go too. What's more I will learn to make Chop Suey for them. I have always wanted to visit China.

Thus does the army rumor make sport of us. Reports of this sort incessantly spring up among us, flourish for a day, to be forgotten on the morrow. It is just a sign I suppose of the restlessness that is rife among the boys, the nostalgia, the rebellion at the grinding monotony of their lives. Half the men in the company, it seems, have gone to their officers begging to be transferred into one of the two divisions that have already been in the lines.

"I'm sick o' this kind o' life; what I came over here for was to fight," they growl.

In the canteen they look at the French National Loan poster which has the Statue of Liberty on it, and speculate as to their chances of ever seeing her again.

"Oh boy! but I bet there'll be some noise on board ship when we catch sight o' that ol' gal again!"

"They wouldn't be breakin' my heart if they gave out orders tonight to start for home termorrer." The chorus groans assent. "No sir!" speaks up Private Gatts, "I don't want to go home until I've killed some of them Germans."

"Aw, come off," rises the incredulous jeer; "you know, if they'd let you, you'd start out to walk to Saint Nazaire tonight if you had to carry your full pack an' your rife an' your extra shoes."

To beguile the tedium they indulge in what appears to be, next to crap-shooting, the most popular indoor sport of the A. E. F.—mustache raising. I don't believe there's a man in the company outside of Cummings and Maggioni who hasn't tried his luck at it. Sometimes it seems as though an epidemic of young mustaches will break out overnight as it were. The second lieutenants jeer and witticize in vain. There is one squad who have solemnly pledged themselves to remain mustachioed until they "can the Kaiser;" but for the most part, the little "Charlies" are fleeting affairs that come and go according to their owner's whim. This makes it quite confusing for me, because no sooner have I got to know a lad with a mustache by sight, than he shaves it off and alters his appearance so that I have to learn him all over again. But even the excitement of raising a mustache and having your picture taken and sending it back home to your best girl and then waiting to hear what she will say about it, affords only a brief diversion. And when that is done, we are face to face again with the stark sheer stupidity of drilling and hiking, hiking and drilling, day after day, week in and week out, in the slush, the mud, and the rain.

"Another day, another dollar," remarks my friend Mr. Brady with philosophic resignation as he comes in from walking post at night, "Betsy the Toad-sticker," as he familiarly terms his rifle, over his shoulder.

"I sure was strong on the patriotic stuff when I enlisted," mourns a lad cast in a less stoic mould, "but since I got over here I'll tell the world my patriotism is all shot to pieces."

"Who called this here land *Sunny France,* I'd like to know?" is the indignant question which someone is bound to propose at least once a day.

"I've only seen the sun twice since I've been here," complained one lad, "and then it was kind of mildewed."

"It stopped raining for three hours the other day," remarked another, "an' I wrote home to my folks an' told 'em what a long dry spell we'd been having."

Altogether we are inclined to take a very pessimistic view at present of our surroundings.

"This land is a thousand years behind the times," is the reiterated comment, and who can blame them, having seen nothing of France but these tiny primitive mud-and-muck villages? "It ain't worth fightin' for. Why if I owned this country I'd give it to the Germans and apologize to 'em."

"It ain't the country, it's the people in it," asserted another lad darkly.

While the Tall Kentuckian declared, "When I came to France, the height of my ambition was to kill a German. Now the height of my ambition is to kill a Frenchman."

What can one say to them? I try fatuously to comfort by reminding them of the good time coming when we all get home again. I paint rosy pictures of a grand parade of the division up Fifth Avenue, but they are sceptical.

"Huh! That won't be for us! All the fuss will be for the National Guard and the draft guys. The reg'lars don't never get no credit."

Then someone will start to hum the song which goes;

"O why didn't I wait to be drafted?

Why didn't I wait to be cheered?"

"Well I'll tell the world that you deserve the credit!"

Anyway Company A has settled one point: if they ever march up Fifth Avenue I am to march with them.

Bourmont, January 11.

The "convicts" are out of quarantine, and none the worse it seems for the experience. Yet my family is still depleted. Forty boys from the company have been sent out on a wood-chopping detail. Detachments from each of the four companies in rotation are being sent out into the forest to cut fuel for the use of the First Battalion and now it is our turn.

The boys, we learn, are billeted in a twelfth century fortress in a tiny village at the forest's edge. From time to time some of them hike the four miles in to Saint Thiebault after the day's work is done, in order to get a cup of hot chocolate and to tease a candle out of me. For the chateau boasts none of the modern luxuries of heat and light.

"What do you do in the evenings?" I asked Mr. Gatts.

"Sit in the *café*. It's the only place there is to go."

"I'm sorry."

"Well you needn't worry about the boys drinkin'. They ain't none of them got no money. All they can do is to sit and watch the Frenchies."

Indeed such a long time has passed since our last payday that the whole company is feeling the pinch of poverty. Canteen sales have narrowed down to the three essentials; chocolate, cigarettes and chewing gum. I am running accounts on my personal responsibility, giving them "jawbone" as the boys say, a proceeding at which our Secretary looks with a disapproving eye. To be sure the air is full of rumours of impending payday but meanwhile there is no disguising the fact that the great majority is "dead broke."

Says Sergeant X to Sergeant Z, a boy with a curious cast of countenance; "Say, Bill, do you remember the time I paid ten cents to see you in a cage at Barnum's? Well I want that dime back now."

Another lad in answer to the appeal of "got a cent?" replies with feeling; "One cent? Why man, if I had a cent I'd go to Paris!"

They have court-martialed the lieutenant who beat Malotzzi. His punishment is to be transferred to another regiment.

Bourmont, January 14.

Madame is sick and I am worried. It isn't so much that she is dangerously ill as that she is dangerously old. She lies in the big blue room upstairs, looking like a patient aged Madonna, without a fire, and with no one to look after her. Monsieur it seems has made up his mind to her demise and piously resigned himself. I called in an army doctor.

"She's pretty low," he said, "but it isn't medicine she needs so much as nursing."

I informed Monsieur. He must get a woman to come in and take care of her. But there was no such woman. He must try to find one. But no, it was impossible! "Well at least, you can make a fire in her room," I told him. As for *La Petite,* she has proved herself a broken reed. Lacking Madame's rigid eyes upon her, she has become lazy and negligent. Moreover she is indubitably in love with some doughty doughboy, the proof being that she spends the time when she should be gathering the harvest of dust from the *Salle des Assiettes* in copying English phrases from our books on to the Gendarme's pink blotting-paper. Yesterday we found "Welcome Americans" scrawled all over it. Meanwhile Monsieur seems to consider himself as qualifying for a martyr's crown because he gets his own meals and washes his own dishes. *"Mais, regardez Mademoiselle!"* he calls to me as I pass through the living-room, and flourishes the dish-cloth at me with a tragic air. So between excursions to the canteen I am trying to play nurse to Madame, and a pretty poor one I make, I fear. Worse still, I must act as interpreter for the Doctor, whose French is absolutely nil, at every visit and since my scanty stock of French phrases hardly includes a sick-room vocabulary I am often absolutely at a loss. But we muddle through somehow and the Doctor gets his reward when we stop to speak to Monsieur in the front-room afterwards, for then Monsieur must bring out a bottle of champagne and together they sit in front of the fire and toast each other.

Yesterday the Doctor prescribed fresh eggs. I told Monsieur. But there were none in Bourmont he declared.

"Very well," I said, "then I'll get them."

I started out to search. I knew of course that eggs in France these days were difficult. In some places the Americans have been forbidden, on account of the scarcity, to buy either eggs or chickens; a ruling which officers have been known to evade by the simple expedient of renting laying hens. But no such prohibition exists at present in Saint Thiebault. Just the other day a lad told me he had consumed twelve fried eggs at one sitting.

"Yes and Corporal G. ate more than I did."

"How many did he eat?"

"Oh, just thirteen."

"No wonder," I observed, "that the French talk about *la famine*!" I started a house-to-house canvas of Saint Thiebault only to be met by a shake of the head and "*Pas des oeufs*" everywhere I went. Finally back at the canteen I put the question in despair to the boys. "Have you been to the tobacco shop?" they inquired. So to the tobacco shop I hurried and sure enough there they were, all one wanted at the rate of seven francs a dozen.

Last night Madame had an egg-nogg and this morning an omelette. Now the Doctor says that she is better.

Bourmont, January 17.

If my fairy god-mother should lend me her magic wand, the very first thing I would wish for would be a dinner, a real dinner just like Mother used to cook, for Company A. It would start with turkey and cranberry sauce and end with several kinds of pie, ice-cream and chocolate layer cake. There would be no soup on the menu. Such a meal I am sure would do more to raise the morale of Company A than the news of a smashing allied victory. It is the everlasting sameness, the perpetual reiteration of a certain few articles of food, I suppose, that makes the boys' "chow" so depressing.

"I've eaten so much bacon since I've been in the army," remarked one boy mournfully," that I'm ashamed to look a pig in the face."

There is one question which the whole A. E. F. would like to have answered. They've "got the bacon," but what became of the ham?

Far more hated than the bacon, however, is the "slum," a word which Pat informs me is derived from the "slumgullion" of the hobo. It is this "slum" that gives the doughboy his horror of anything like soup.

"When I get back to New York," said a lad to me the other day, "I'm going to go into a real swell hotel and order a big dish o' slum. Then I'm going to order a regular dinner, beefsteak and oysters and all the fixings, and then I'm going to sit and laugh at the slum."

Pat came in with a whoop after dinner yesterday. "We had a change today," he sang out, "they put a pickle in the beans!" This noon he bounced in again. "We had a change today," he shouted, "they cut the beans lengthwise instead of cuttin' them acrosst."

I made a fatal error. "Don't you like beans?" I asked. "Why I'm very fond of them. I wish they'd give them to us at our mess once in a while."

Pat looked at me with his sharp eyes narrowing. "D'you mean it?"

"Why of course I do!"

He turned and walked out of the hut. Two minutes later he returned with a hunk of bread and a mess-kit brimfull of beans; he laid them on the counter in front of me. I gasped but did my best to rise to the occasion. I was delighted to see those beans, I assured him. I had just been starting out to go to mess; a little bird had told me they were to have roast pork, French fries, and peach pie for dinner, but now I would stay at the hut and eat beans instead. Then I tasted the beans. They were as hard as bullets, they stuck in my throat; I had never known anything could be quite so awful. But Pat's eyes were upon me. There was nothing for it but to swallow those beans. So swallow them I did, every last one, and there were positively at least a thousand. Then I washed the mess-kit and returned it to friend Pat with effusive thanks. At least, I complimented myself, I had been game. Tonight, just as I was starting out for my supper of toast and chocolate with the little old ladies of the Rue Dieu, Pat suddenly appeared on the other side of the counter.

"We had 'em again tonight," he announced joyfully, "and I thought since you were so fond of 'em,"—he pushed another mess-kit full of beans across the counter. I glared at him. I had vainly been trying to recover from the dinner beans all afternoon.

"Take those things away," I snapped, "I don't want to lay eyes on another bean as long as ever I live!" Pat had called my bluff.

For the last week Company A has had guests in the mess-hall. Several French soldiers have been sent here to instruct the boys in some special drill; it was arranged that they eat and sleep with the Americans. Dreary as the boys find their chow, it proved a treat to the poilus who evidently spread the news of their good fortune among their friends in the vicinity, for day by day the number of Frenchmen messing with Company A was mysteriously increased.

"Yes sir!" the indignant Mess Sergeant declared to me. "They started in with five and now they've grown to be fifteen. I can't tell one from t'other because all these frogs look alike to me, and they know as how I can't sling their lingo. That's a nice thing for them to be putting over on me!"

But yesterday he got his chance to get even. He caught one of the Frenchmen putting a piece of bread in his pocket. It is of course a military offense to carry food out of the mess-hall.

"I just sailed right into that guy"—the Mess Sergeant is a large and husky specimen—"and I sure did wipe up the floor some with him. And since then the whole gang of 'em has been scared stiff. Those frogs just watch me all the time. There ain't a minute when I'm in the mess-hall that one of 'em takes his eyes off me."

The other day, they tell me, one of the boys in the company, possessed of a practical turn, employed his newly-issued "tin derby" as a kettle in which to boil some eggs. The delicacy proved dear. Betrayed by the blackened helmet, he was tried and fined twenty dollars.

Bourmont, January 20.

I'm off for Paris! My eyes have been in a horrid state for the last week. I have had all the doctors in the neighborhood treating them and they only get worse and worse. The Chief is going up to Paris tomorrow and has decided that the best thing to do is to take me along to see a specialist.

Madame is so much better that I don't feel uneasy at leaving her. But I hate to desert the boys, especially as the hut is in such a state. Yesterday we had a storm and the wind almost wrecked our tent. There was one moment while I was out at dinner, when such a gust hit it, that, as the boys said, "She sure seemed a goner." At that moment there was a stampede for the door, the boys shooting out of the tent "just like seeds from an orange when you squeeze it." But thanks to the Secretary and a crowd of boys who got out and hung for dear life on to the guy ropes, the tent came through damaged but still standing. When I returned after mess I found our hut with two great gaping rents torn in the outer walls and the inner lining all ripped loose and hanging down from the ceiling, so that one felt exactly as if one were inside a punctured zeppelin.

Reports coming in this morning from other points on the division state that two tents actually did collapse during the tempest, and that one man, caught beneath the wreckage, had his collarbone broken. So we can count ourselves lucky.

Tonight I said *au 'voir* to Company A, telling them that if payday should occur during my absence, I hoped they all would be very, very good. Some of the boys lugubriously predicted that I would never return, while others darkly insinuated that they suspected I was "goin' to Paris to git married." To show them what my intentions honestly were, I inquired if there were any errands I could do for them in the city. Corporal G. looked at me, stammered, hesitated. There was something he would like, only he didn't want to bother me. What was it? He paused, grew red, then blurted it out.

"If it ain't too much trouble, could you send me a picture post-card while you're away? I ain't never had a post-card from Paris."

Hôpital Claude-Bernard

Porte D'Aubervilliers

Paris, January 25.

This is a hideous hospital. They wake you up in the middle of the night to wrap you in a mustard poultice. They wake you up in the wee sma' hours and order you to brush your teeth. And nobody in the whole establishment from head-doctor to scrub-lady knows a word of English; except the night-nurse and she knows "mumpsss!" like that she says it, "MUMPSSSSS!" Not that I have them; I have the measles. I don't know where I got them. They were, so far as I am aware, almost the only known malady which we didn't have at Bourmont. Probably some lad who was passing through the town and stopped in at the canteen gave them to me. It was undoubtedly the measles that were affecting my eyes; sometimes it seems they act that way.

They sent me to this hospital because it was the only hospital in Paris admitting women that had room for me: known officially as the city hospital for contagious diseases, among Americans it passes as "the pest-house."

They think I'm a weird one here, because I want my window open. Twenty-nine times a day at least an *infirmière* will come hurrying in and bang it shut and twenty-nine times a day I crawl out of bed and open it again.

The nursing here is all done by *infirmières*, or untrained women under the direction of two real nurses, one in charge of this wing during the day, the other during the night. Some of these *infirmières* go about in curl papers, others wear sabots. They mean well enough, but they are overworked, and frankly peasant types, with little education and almost no notion of cleanliness or of much else that is supposed to pertain to nursing. Last night a fat old soul without many teeth came waddling into my room to have a look at that interesting curiosity, *la pauvre petite Dame Américaine*. When she saw my open window she was so overcome with astonishment that she hurried out and fetched a companion to regard the phenomenon. The two of them stood and stared at it and discussed the matter between themselves for quite a while, then the fat one turned to me and remarked with a toothless but engaging smile; it was very warm in America where I lived, was it not?

When I replied that, instead, it was much colder in winter there than here in Paris, they looked aghast and flatly incredulous. Their only explanation of the matter had been, it seemed, that I was accustomed to living in the tropics and just didn't have sense enough to suit my habits to the atmosphere.

Just outside the hospital there is a munitions factory. At night the light over the front door shines into my room and day and night the machinery keeps up an incessant thudding hum that says as plain as words over and over and over: *Kill the Boches. Kill the Boches. Kill the Boches.* Once in a long while the machines stop for a few moments in order, I suppose, to catch their breath and then I grow dreadfully worried, for I know that if someone doesn't keep on killing the Boches every second, they will be breaking through the lines and pouring in over France in great drowning grey waves.

January 27. I haven't got the measles after all; I have the German measles, only they don't call it that in French I am glad to say. At first I was so very red and speckled that they thought I had the *rougeole*, but now they have decided it is only the *rubeole* after all. A concourse of doctors considered me yesterday morning and pronounced the verdict. "But then," I demanded, "if it's only the *rubeole* can't I be leaving *tout de suite*?" For the French do not consider quarantine necessary for the rubeole. "Eight days," they answered, and when I expostulated they turned on their collective heels and marched callously out the door, each one holding up eight fingers apiece as a parting rejoinder.

Last night I resisted a great temptation. This place is full of doors with little glass panes in them. As I lay awake in bed in the middle of the night, a wild desire grew on me to seize my big green bottle of mineral water by the neck and see how many panes of glass I could account for before they nabbed me. I had a perfect vision of myself, flying down the hall in my little flour-sack chemise of a night-gown, long legs stretching out beneath, going zip, bang, right and left into those window panes. I have seldom wanted to do anything quite so badly. And then just to top off with I was going to wring the interne's neck. He is a little shrimp of a man—that interne, with no chin and a sort of scrawny picked-chicken neck, a neck that gets on one's nerves.

When they sent me to this hospital I comforted myself with the thought that I would at least learn a little French while staying here, but the only thing I have learned so far is that *gargariser* means gargle and any goose might have guessed that.

January 28. The Chief has sent me a rose-pink cyclamen. It is a lovely thing and very elaborately done up with pink crêpe paper and a large bow of shell-pink ribbon. Now I am no longer an object of any interest. Every last doctor, nurse, interne and *infirmière* who comes into my room to take a look at *la petite Mees*, immediately turns his or her back on me and admires the cyclamen instead. I gather such objects are rare in French hospitals, for they examine and discuss it at the greatest length, always winding up with the remark that it must have "cost very dear."

Not having anything else to do I lie with my eyes shut and think. And of course I have been thinking chiefly about Company A. I have thought among other things of a play, or rather a dramatic charade in three acts, which we might give in the hut. It is to be entitled *Slum*. In the first act,—*Bill*— three doughboys hit on a plan to encompass the Kaiser's death and so become rich by gaining the proffered reward:—they will send him a dish of slum! The second act,—*et*—shows a room in the Potsdam palace with Kaiser Bill and His Side Whiskers, the Lord High Chancellor, discussing the food situation. The slum appears; the Kaiser partakes of it and falls writhing to the floor. The last act shows a typical barn-loft billet, with rats squeaking, chickens clucking et cetera, where the Soldiers Three of the first act have their lodging. They receive the tidings of the Kaiser's death; wild rejoicings ensue, as in fancy they spend their fortunes; only to be cut short by the discovery that the cook who made the slum has already claimed the reward. I think we can stage it successfully, though the costumes for the Kaiser and His Side Whiskers present some difficulties. One thing only troubles me; will it hurt the Mess Sergeant's feelings?

January 30. They have relented. They have shortened my stay. I am to be let out tomorrow, but I must *reposer* a few days before going back to work. Bother! I haven't heard anything from Bourmont for ten days and I am full of uneasy apprehensions. Since I have been in the hospital the cyclamen has been the only word I have had from the outside world. I have been cut off as completely as if I were in a tomb. Ah well, some day I'll get back to the hut again I suppose, and when I do, if those boys aren't almost half as glad to see me as I am to see them, why I'll know that some other canteen lady has been surreptitiously stealing their affections, and I shall put poison in her soup.

Hôpital Claude-Bernard

Paris, January 31.

I have been in a big air raid; this is just how it all happened:

It was a white night in the hospital for me. I had lain for hours, it seemed, in the little blue room watching through the glass panes of my door the coiffed head of a young *infirmière* bent over her embroidery. She sat outside my door because there was a light in the hall just there. Suddenly my drowsy ears were pierced by a long weird hoot. In an instant the girl had leaped to her feet and switched off the light, then she turned and ran down the hall. A moment later and the building was in darkness. I jumped from my bed and ran to the window. The light in front of the munitions factory was out, there seemed an uncanny silence, the machinery had been stopped. I hurried to the door. The corridor was full of hastening forms, *infirmières*, their loose white robes showing dimly in the grey light.

"*Qu'est ce qui arrive?*" I demanded.

"*Les Boches!*"

The night nurse was peering from my window.

"It's the first warning," she whispered. "See! the lights of Paris still shine."

But even as we looked, the light across the sky that was Paris flickered, dimmed, flashed out. At the same moment two great golden stars rose over the munitions factory.

"*Les avions!*" cried the night nurse.

And all the time the sirens kept up their ghostly wailing, like nothing one could imagine except a vast host of lost souls. Then the guns began. A moment later a crashing thud told that a bomb had fallen in our neighborhood. The night nurse drew me hurriedly into the hall.

"Lie down against the wall,—close—like this," she ordered.

Up and down the corridor every space by the wall was occupied by the huddled form of an *infirmière* buried beneath a mattress. The night nurse, who had a whole heap of mattresses to herself, pushed one across to me. I lay on the top, finding it more comfortable that way.

The bombs were falling nearer. A child in one of the wards woke up and began to wail fretfully. No one heeded her. There was a flash and then a tearing thud that shook the hospital. I had one ghastly moment, a thrill of panic terror at our utter helplessness as we lay there awaiting what seemed the inevitable coming of destruction. The moment passed. I got up and slipped down the side corridor to the glass door. The sky was full of moving lights; some burned with a steady brilliancy, some flickered and went out like fireflies, a few flashed red. There was no telling which was friend or foe. They seemed to be proceeding in all directions without plan or purpose. The air pulsated with the humming drone of their motors. They were like a swarm of angry hornets I thought. Across the road, standing on the top of a high wall, in sharp silhouette against the sky, three poilus stood to watch. Every now and then an *infirmière*, curiosity outweighing caution, would leave her hiding-place and creep to the door beside me only to burrow like a bug, a moment later, underneath her mattress once more.

"Mees! N'avez-vous pas peur?"

"Mais non!"

"Ah, vous êtes un soldat!"

I went back to my room and climbed out on the window-sill. At first I thought the lights of Paris had been turned on again, but this time they were color of rose. As I looked the pink flush deepened, grew ruddy, flamed across the sky. I called the night nurse.

"C'est une incendie," she wailed staccato. *"Quel malheur!"*

So Paris was on fire.

As we watched two big puffs of white smoke rose over the munitions factory, spread into a cloud, drifted slowly toward us. The night nurse sniffed, then shut the window hurriedly.

"La gaz," she whispered. I questioned it but left the window shut.

An aeroplane swung low over the munitions factory, so near that it looked like a great lazy fish with the rose light from below shining on its belly. Was it friend or enemy?

The bombs were dropping close again. One could see the flashes and feel the jar of the explosions which made the windows rattle.

"Oh les sales Boches!"

"Oh la la!"

The agonized wails sounded half stifled from beneath the mattresses.

"Taisez! Écoutez!" It was the night nurse's voice.

The front door slammed. A fat *infirmière* in a badly shattered state of nerves stumbled down the hall weeping out unintelligible woes. At my mattress she came to a standstill, then ducked and tried to crawl beneath it; failing, she sat down on top of me. I ventured a polite protest,—in vain. The night nurse heard me. She emerged from beneath her heap. Followed a scene dramatic, unforgettable. Mattresses scattered to each side of her, heedless of the falling bombs, with Gallic passion she proceeded to point out to the sobbing *infirmière* the shortcomings of her behaviour. But the fat lady proved unrepentant, her terror at the bombs superseding even her awe of the night nurse. She sat tight, holding her ground. She even ventured to answer back. The scene grew more intense. After I had heard the night nurse discharge the *infirmière* some six times over, feeling a trifle out of place, I managed to crawl from beneath and made my way back to the window. No more bombs were falling but the guns still barked. As I watched, a burning plane looking like a great tinsel ball seared its way through the sky, falling just to the right of Paris.

"Pray God it is a Boche!" I thought.

A round-eyed *infirmière* peered in at the door, staring curiously at me.

"Mees! Vous allez retourner en Amerique?"

"Mais oui! A près la guerre!"

The red glare over Paris was fading out. The machines in the munitions factory began to throb once more. In the grey light at the window I looked at my watch. It was fifteen minutes past one. I turned to crawl into bed feeling cold and very sleepy. Some one touched my sleeve; it was the night nurse. She was staring out the window with eyes that saw nothing.

"And how many little children will be dead in the morning do you think?" she asked.

Bourmont, February 5.

The blow that I somehow dimly apprehended while I was in the hospital has fallen. Last night late I arrived from Paris. The first thing I learned was, that with the addition of some new workers a general shuffle of the women at Headquarters was to take place. This morning the Chief called us together and gave us our new assignments. The Gendarme and I are to leave Bourmont. Since I have been away regimental Headquarters have been moved from Saint Thiebault to Goncourt, a town about two miles to the south, and the whole regiment with the exception of the First Battalion concentrated there. The Y. at Goncourt has had a hard time of it. Originally it occupied a barracks; then the regimental machine-gun company moved in and the Y. must move out. So the Y. settled itself in an old stone mill by the Meuse, only to have the military authorities decide that they needed that mill for a guard-house. So once more the Y. moved, this time to a little old house in the centre of the village; and here according to last reports it still is, for the simple reason that nobody else has any use for the little old house. Meanwhile, however, they are putting up a Big Hut which is to be ready in from one to three weeks, all according to who is making the estimate. It is to Goncourt that the Gendarme and I have been assigned. According to the Chief this is a "promotion."

"It's the largest, the most important place on the division now," he declared; "I'm sending you there because you made good at Saint Thiebault."

But this little piece of taffy doesn't seem to help matters a bit. The only way to look at it is that it's a case of the greatest good for the greatest number, and of course numerically Goncourt is about ten times as important as Saint Thiebault. And anyway it wouldn't do the least good to kick against the pricks because when all is said and done one is under orders like a soldier. After all it isn't as if I were going to Greenland or to Timbuctoo. And yet at even only two miles distance, so tied to the work one must be, one might almost as well be in a different planet.

As for Saint Thiebault, they are going to have to do with just a man secretary there. The place is too small, the Chief says, to be allowed more than one worker.

We won't be moving for several days yet. I'm not going to say a word about it to Company A until the very last moment. I hate partings.

CHAPTER II
GONCOURT—THE DOUGHBOYS

Goncourt, February 11.

The little old house which now harbors the Y. formerly served, it seems, as guard-house. To some it must have a strangely familiar air. Downstairs there are two small rooms; the front one stone-paved, with a dark carved cupboard in one corner which formerly enclosed the family bed, and a huge fireplace; the back one with a dirt floor over which uncertain boards have shakily been laid. The front room we use for the canteen, the back, with four rough tables, serves as a make-shift writing room. The walls are dim with smoke and grime, the windows in both rooms lack half their panes, yet the odd little place has an atmosphere, a charm all its own. Upstairs soldiers are billeted. When the din of business dies down in the canteen, one can hear the crisp rattle of dice as the boys shoot craps on the floor overhead.

In accordance with military regulations here we cannot open the canteen until four in the afternoon. But a large part of the morning is easily spent in cleaning out the hut and arranging the stock for the afternoon and evening onslaught. At Saint Thiebault the detail that "policed up" the camp in the morning swept out our tent for us, but here one wields one's own broom and shovel,—for first of all one must shovel out the mud that's on the floor! Cleaning the canteen, however, I find, though a dirty, is quite a remunerative job, for in the heaps of litter on the floor money lurks. According to the ethics of the game if money is found back of the counter it belongs in the till, but if in front it goes to the finder. Sometimes the find is five centimes, sometimes fifty and once it was five francs! The litter—chocolate wrappers, orange peels and cigarette boxes—is all swept into the fireplace and then touched off with a match; a regular bonfire ensues. This morning we had left the front door open; immediately the fire was started a throng of villagers crowded around to look in. They were scandalized at the conflagration. The house was old, they cried; we would set the chimney on fire, we would burn up the building, we would burn down the whole town! One ancient and portly dame in a frenzy of protest dashed into the room and fairly danced about the hearth, shaking her apron at the flames and calling for ashes to cover them. But before she could get her ashes the fire died down and the excitement with it.

The Gendarme and I are billeted in a tiny house just at the village edge. Our low second story looks down upon the street, so narrow that it seems one could almost reach out and touch hands with the houses opposite. But what a street it is! Underneath our low window the whole world goes by; American officers on horseback, French officers in limousines, American mule teams, French wood teams with three white horses harnessed one in front of the other, and always the troops; going by at dawn in the semi-darkness, their rhythmic incessant tramp weaving itself into one's waking dreams, passing by at noon, swinging back down the hill as it grows dusk, singing snatches of song as they tramp. As I lie a-bed in the morning before getting up to peer out the window into the yellow misty atmosphere I can always calculate the exact state of the weather by the amount of squelch which those marching boots make in the muddy road.

Company H is billeted on this same street with us. The first morning after we arrived the Gendarme and I were startled out of sleep by First Call blown directly underneath our window. Hardly had the last note sounded when a shout fit to wake the dead went up.

"Get to hell up, all of you! Rise and shine!"

Followed a tremendous banging and kicking at all the stable doors along the street accompanied by a torrent of vivid and spicy admonitions. The Gendarme and I gasped and chuckled. This was rich. Were we always to be awakened in so picturesque a fashion? But the next morning we listened in vain. First Call was blown at the far end of the street and followed by a solemn silence; and so it has been ever since. Now that American ladies are known to be living on the street Company H must get up decorously.

Goncourt, February 12.

The fireplace is easily the feature of our funny little hut. Around this at night the lads crowd perched on packing-boxes to smoke, chew gum and gossip. As the first mad rush of business at the canteen dies down a little I edge up towards the fireplace in order to get a wee share in the conversation.

They have caught a spy! One of the cooks in F Company. He was a deserter from the German Army some one said. They caught him putting dope in the slum. The doctors were analyzing it now. It's a wonder the whole company wasn't poisoned. Yes, and they found plans of the camp in his pocket too. He hasn't eaten a thing since they arrested him. All he does is just to walk up and down the guard-house. Seems as if he were kind of crazy.

And so they gossip. A sad-eyed bugler remarks to me that he'd be a rich man if he only had all the hob-nailed shoes that had been thrown at him. Another boy wonders what he'd do if he had "both arms shot off and then the gas alarm sounded." And always they must be rowing about their respective states.

"Neebraska! Where's Neebraska? Is that in the United States or Canada?"

"Noo Hampshire! Huh! There ain't nothin' but mountains there. Why my old man told me that when they let the cows out to grass there they had to put stilts on one side of 'em so they won't fall off'n the pasture."

Then they turn on me.

"Boston! When you get ten miles from Boston you can smell the beans bakin'."

"But I don't come from Boston," I protest.

"Well there ain't nothin' much in Massachusetts outsider Boston. Why the state of Noo Hampshire is goin' to rent the rest o' Massachusetts for a duck-yard."

And so it goes.

"Gee! but it's good to get into one shop where you don't have to talk frog talk!" exclaimed one lad tonight.

"I've just heard the greatest compliment for you," another lad declares solemnly, "the greatest compliment that could possibly be paid any woman."

"Why, what was it?"

"I just heard a feller say; 'My! don't she look different from the French girls!'"

A flushed-faced lad leans over my end of the counter;

"You know to talk to an American girl like this again, it's like, it's like—"

Again and again he tries only to become helplessly inarticulate. Then pulling a large bunch of letters "from lady friends" from his pocket, nothing will do but he must tell me about each one. Finally in a fit of prodigal generosity he bestows a handful on me, "Because I'm an American and you're one too." As he makes the presentation something falls to the floor with a little click. We search among the litter on the floor, the lad on all fours; finally the lost is found,—a broken bit of comb about two inches and a quarter long. This is a happy chance, he explains, for he is company barber and with the company comb gone E Company would be out of luck.

Always our presence here is something that seems so strange to them as to be almost incredible.

"Will you please tell me," asked a serious-looking lad tonight, "what consideration could possibly induce two American girls to come to a place like this?"

Continually I am encountering boys who are sure that they've "seen me somewhere."

"Say, didn't you use to live in Milwaukee?"

"Haven't I seen you in Seattle? Well, if it warn't you, it was somebody that looked just like you!"

I suppose it is simply because I look American that I look familiar to them. But the facts in the case seem to be that I have been observed by some member of the A. E. F. in practically every one of the large cities of the U. S. A. One boy nearly started a fight in camp the other night by declaring that in spite of the evidence of my nose he knew I was of Hebraic origin. He had seen me, he solemnly insisted, "goin' with a Jew feller in Philadelphia."

Undoubtedly it is because they have so little to think about in these drab days that they are so pathetically curious. Every little thing you say or do is repeated, discussed all over camp. Sometimes curiosity gets hold of one of the bolder spirits to such an extent that he ventures the question;

"How much do you get paid for smiling at the soldiers?"

And when they learn that you are a volunteer and are paying for the privilege of being there, their amazement is so blank as to be positively ludicrous.

Goncourt, February 13.

One of the nicest things about Goncourt is our mess. This we have at the House Across the Street, which is next to the House of the Madonna. We mess *en famille* with the family Peirut, the Gendarme, Mr. K. and I, and we eat the family fare which consists chiefly of soup, boiled meat and carrots, supplemented by various additions such as sugar, cocoa, jam and canned corn from the commissary. I can never quite decide which is quainter, the family or the setting.

In America we have the phrase *living-room*, in France they have it. In this one high-ceilinged room the daily life of the family is complete. Here is the kitchen stove and the dinner table, here are the beds of Madame and Monsieur, Madame's in one corner hung with dim flowered chintz, Monsieur's in another brave with a beautiful old red India shawl. Here is the broad stone sink under the window, with the drain running out into the street, where the family makes its morning toilet. Here are the great dark armoires which hold clothing, china-ware and stores of all sorts. Here is the littered desk where the family correspondence is carried on; and here is the larder, a huge slab of pork and a ham hanging from the beams over one's head, while on a stick in front of the fireplace a row of little fishes hang by their tails in dumb expectation of a Friday. And here too is the family shrine, a little wooden Madonna in red and blue, found as Madame tells us in the ancient city of La Mothe, which, destroyed in 1645, now exists as a wonderful ruin crowning a hill some two miles to the west.

If the stove-wood is found lacking at meal-time, Monsieur rises from his chair and saws an armful beside the dinner-table. If Madame decides while we are eating our soup that a piece of ham will improve the menu she stands upon her chair and cuts a slice in the air over our heads. On wash days one picks one's way to the table past the pails which hold the family linen in soak, and later eats one's soupe *à pain* under a brave array of drying garments slung from wall to wall.

The family, which consists of Monsieur, Madame and Mademoielle, the two sons being in service, are the most hospitable souls alive. Continually they urge, *"Mangez, mangez!"* and then, *"Vous êtes timide!"* Their feelings are dreadfully hurt if each one of us refuses to eat enough for two. They seem somehow to have acquired the idea that Americans need a vast deal of sweetening, so they offer you sugar, commissary sugar, with everything, and they are gently but definitely disappointed when you decline to heap it on your mashed potato.

Mile. Jeane, clear-skinned, bright-eyed, capable, energetic yet possessed of a warm charm withal, is forewoman of the little glove factory in town.

"Are there many employees?" I asked.

"But no. Eight only. Since the Americans came to town all the women have deserted the factory in order to wash the Americans' clothes."

Monsieur, it appears, is a wood-cutter by profession. He comes home from a hard day's chopping looking like a genus of the woods himself with his worn brown velour suit, his wrinkled brown skin and his ragged brown beard which resembles exactly those bundles of fine twigs which the French burn in their fireplaces. When Monsieur was ten years old the Germans occupied the town and sixteen of them slept in this very room. They were perfect pigs, he says, and ate everything they could lay their hands on; "But," he adds, "they didn't like our bread!"

Sunday mornings all the men in town, including the Man With One Leg, and all the dogs start off together, the men armed with guns and each carrying a musette bag or knapsack. Papa puts on his shooting coat with the fancy buttons each depicting a different bird or beast of the chase, takes down his old shot-gun from the wall, and joins them. At dusk they come back again, empty-handed, but seemingly well content. Their modus operandi, I gather, is to proceed to a comfortable spot in the woods, then all sit down, drink vin rouge and wait for the game. Indeed one doughboy declares, that passing by one of those open alleys which intersect the forests here, he once saw an old Frenchman standing with his gun in a drizzling rain, patiently waiting for a shot while by his side stood another "old frog" holding an umbrella over him.

Goncourt, February 14.

The woman who lives in the House of the Madonna is an unconscionable old scalawag. Not that you would ever suspect it to look at her, for with her round rosy face, her smooth parted hair and her comfortably rotund figure she resembles nothing so much as somebody's genial and respected grandmother. Yet the facts in the case remain. She sells doped wine to the soldiers at ruinous prices and she sells at forbidden hours. Moreover we have reason to suspect that at odd times she carries on an utterly illicit commerce. According to our hostess, when the time from the last pay day grows too long, certain soldiers are not above smuggling in their extra shoes and shirts to her, and she pays them back in drinks.

This morning while I was at breakfast she came bouncing in and proceeded to fill the house with lamentations. Last night a tipsy soldier had stolen the key to her front door! Then she delved into history for my benefit, recounting how, some weeks before, two soldiers, having sent her out of the room on an errand, had proceeded to rob her till, the sum amounting to almost three hundred francs!

"Oh! Ils sont des monstres, des cochons!" she wailed.

Whereat I, with some asperity, remarked that if the French people wouldn't sell drink to the Americans, the soldiers wouldn't become *zig-zag* and do such things. Immediately she became conciliatory. Of course, everyone knew that there were good people and bad people in every nation, but certainly! Then she changed the subject abruptly, demanding; why, why in the name of common sense did I do anything so contrary to all the dictates of reason as to sleep with my window open?

Last night, as Mr. K. and I were coming home from the canteen, the door of the cafe opposite was suddenly opened and a man's figure appeared, half pushed, half thrown outside. The door slammed shut,—it was long after closing hour for the cafe,—the figure fell like a log to the ground. We watched a minute to see the fellow pick himself up, but he lay motionless. It was a freezing night. Mr. K. went over to investigate. The man was in a drunken stupor.

"You go along," he called to me, "I've got to get this fellow home."

I left reluctantly. Subsequently Mr. K. told me the night's history. After considerable coaxing, he had finally succeeded in extracting the information that the boy belonged to F Company. So to F Company barracks, a good half-mile north of the canteen, they had proceeded, Mr. K. half dragging, half carrying the fellow who was head and shoulders taller than he, and broad to boot.

When they had nearly reached their journey's end, Mr. K. by this time fairly in a state of collapse, his burden suddenly baulked. The barracks evidently didn't look like home to him. Mr. K. began to have a sickening sense of something gone wrong. At last the wretch drowsily recalled the fact that he didn't belong to F Company at all, but to I Company far on the other side of town. So around they turned and back through town they crawled until finally they arrived at I Company's abiding-place; and this time the derelict was satisfied.

Indeed a walk home from the canteen at night with Mr. K. at any time is likely to prove an adventure. For should we meet a boy who has had more than is "good for him" and is in an irritable mood, we must stop and talk with him, in order, as Mr. K's theory puts it, to divert his mind. "Get them thinking about something else," is his slogan. The other night we stood out in the sleety drizzle until my feet fairly froze solid into the freezing mud, carrying on polite conversations with two boys who had just been put out of the House of the Madonna and were in a state of mind to wreck the town. One of them Mr. K. got started on the subject of taking French lessons. He was ambitious to study French he explained and would Mr. K. kindly arrange for a teacher and a course of lessons? I listened with one ear; here was the first man I had found in France who expressed an earnest desire to learn French and he was tipsy! The other one, evidently ashamed, explained to me at length how he hadn't wanted to get drunk, the trouble was that he was just naturally "dishgushted with this country, just dishgushted." And that it seems to me is the whole thing in two words. The boys are "just dishgushted." Considering it all, who can blame them?

Goncourt, February 15.

The M. P.s who live in the second story of the Guard-House are my good friends. They help sweep out the hut often in the mornings and when they make taffy in their mess kits they bring me some. These M. P.s are in reality cavalrymen detached from their regiment for the time being in order to do police duty. As far as I can see, there seems to be no special hard feeling between them and the doughboys.

One slim young M. P. in particular is a crony of mine. He keeps me informed as to the gossip of the town. He tells me how the French women who run cafes, our neighbor of the House of the Madonna among them, seek to curry favor with the law in Goncourt, by bringing him out coffee and sandwiches as he walks his beat in the middle of the night; and how, the other night after closing hour, he put his head inside the door of one of these cafes to be greeted by a frantic shriek of "*Feenish! Feenish!*" from the hostess, only to find, when he insisted on entering, a crowd of doughboys making merry in the back-room; how he took their names and then was inspired to look at their "dog tags" in confirmation and found that not one of the names agreed! He tells me about the cross old Frenchman whose beehives have been stealthily, inexplicably, disappearing one by one, in spite of the fact that the Frenchman had tied his unfortunate and much suffering dog underneath the hives to guard them; until now the old gentleman had taken to sitting up nights with a shot-gun in order to watch the remaining ones. "He's a kind o' snoopy old man and nobody likes him. I reckon the boys are taking his beehives just to spite him." He tells me about the old lady who wants to marry him to her daughter; but chiefly he tells me,— under the strictest oath of secrecy,— the latest development in the case of the old woman whom he suspects of being a spy. I advise him to hand the matter over to the Intelligence Officer, but no, he must have the honor of catching her red-handed himself. It's quite like reading a detective story in installments.

The other night while I was talking to one of the M. P.s in the canteen, we heard a shot up the street. The next moment another M. P. appeared at the door. After the exchange of a few whispered words, the two of them ran out of the hut, and as they went, I saw them both draw their revolvers. Fifteen minutes later the doughboys coming into the canteen brought a ghastly tale. There had been a fight between the M. P.s and the soldiers. The M. P.s had shot and killed two. "Yes, so-help-me-God, it's the truth!" The narrator had himself seen the two slain doughboys lying in the street; one had been shot through the head, the other through the heart. So the story went around. We went to bed that night with a dull sense of horror hanging over us.

The next morning I confronted my friend the M. P. with the story. Then I learned the true version. He had been on his beat not far from the church, when down a dark alley he had heard sounds of a tremendous fracas. In spite of the fact that he didn't have his stick with him he had plunged down the alley to come upon "a bunch of wops beating each other over the head with beer bottles." When they caught sight of the M. P. they had quickly abandoned their family disagreement in order to turn upon the intruder. He had shot his revolver into the air and this had been enough to frighten them into taking to their heels. The two fellows who had been seen lying on the ground were the casualties resulting from the bottle-fight: they had been stunned and gashed so badly as to bleed a good deal, but were later patched up with complete success at the hospital.

Indeed life at Goncourt is seldom unrelieved by incident. Last night I was sitting by our open window reading—the Gendarme was out—after my return from the hut, when I heard an angry voice snarl something abusive directly beneath me; a moment later a fusillade began. I jumped for the candle, blew it out, then stood close against the wall. After a minute the shots ceased; immediately excited people began to pour into the street. I heard the M. P.s pounding on the door of the House Across the Way, demanding information; I leaned from the window and told them what I knew. All the French people in the neighborhood stood out in the street and chattered excitedly for hours afterward it seemed. This morning Madame told us what had happened. In the house next door lives a tall and handsome girl. A sergeant suitor of hers, crazy with jealousy and cognac, had shot wildly at a rival entering her door, emptying his automatic, fortunately without effect.

Goncourt, February 16.

Twice a week each one of us goes to pay a visit at the local hospital. This is a depressing place—two large dingy rooms in what was once, to judge from the inscription over the door, some sort of ecclesiastical school. We take the boys magazines and newspapers, oranges and jam. This week I had a new idea. I would read aloud to them. In the Bourmont warehouse I came across a volume of W. W. Jacobs' short stories. Here was just the thing, I thought, such simple slap-stick humour must appeal to the most unsophisticated understanding.

I hurried to the hospital with my prize. The orderlies, not expecting a lady visitor, were in the midst of a Black Jack game. Red and flustered, one lad tried to hide the little heaps of money on the floor by standing on them; I pretended not to see. Yes, they thought it would be all right if I should read to the patients. They went ahead to the ward to announce me. All the cots were full, making sixteen invalids in all. I selected a story—an old favorite, I was sure it would prove irresistible—and started to read. The story tells of an eccentric skipper with a fad for doctoring. One by one, his crew, realizing his weakness, develop mysterious maladies. They are excused from duty, put to bed, petted and cossetted. Finally the mate becomes desperate. He guarantees that he will cure them all; the skipper is sceptical but allows him a free hand. The mate sets to work to compound some "medicine," a wonderful and fearful brew made of ink, vinegar, kerosene and bilge-water. After a few doses, presto! the crew is hale and hearty once again.

I read with all the animation I could muster, and to me the story had never appeared funnier, but try my hardest, I couldn't seem to "get it over." Not a chuckle, not a grin lightened my solemn audience. They were utterly, blankly, unresponsive. I began to wonder if it were possible that not one of them could understand English. At last I ended. As I closed the book a whoop of delight went up from the orderlies;

"That's you all over, Johnny!"

"Gee, that guy must have wrote that story about you, Slim."

"Say, Miss, can't you let us have the recipe for that medicine? We need it in our business."

The invalids grinned sulkily. In one awful moment I realized what I had done.

"Of course," I stammered, "this wasn't meant to have any personal application!" But the mischief was already done. There was nothing to do but to retire with dignity.

However, I couldn't bear to give up my scheme entirely. Today I went again; this time having carefully selected my story. To my astonishment the ward proved empty, all except for three boys who were crouching on the floor shooting craps; I drew back.

"Perhaps they would rather not be disturbed."

"They ought to be in bed anyway," growled the orderly, and chased the patients back to their cots.

I read to them; there was no way out of it. They listened politely to the end, but all the while I felt they were longing to resume their interrupted game. Tonight I expressed my surprise over the deserted ward to Captain X. He roared at my innocence.

"You didn't expect to find any fellows in hospital *today* did you? Why, this is Saturday, and there isn't any drill tomorrow!"

Goncourt, February 18.

Every day we must go to see how the new hut is progressing. This involves wading through a wilderness of mud. I had thought that Bourmont had taught me everything that one could learn about French mud this side of the trenches, but Goncourt has shown me that it has possibilities hitherto undreamed.

The new hut is on the far edge of the town, on the east bank of the Meuse. Near it are grouped the barracks of the Milk Battalion, so called not because, as I first supposed, it is composed of heavy drinkers, but because it is comprised of Companies I, K, L, and M. These barracks, which were bequeathed to us by the French, are, the boys tell me, infested with vermin. In the mess-hall of Company M we hold our weekly movie-shows and our occasional concerts.

The hut, which is very large, and shipped here in sections, goes up slowly. Army details are proverbial in their ability to consume time. Then we are constantly being held back by shortage of materials; lumber and nails and such things being desperately hard to obtain in France at present. Not long ago the divisional Construction Man, who is a young fellow with poor eyes and considerable initiative, was driven to the desperate resort

of appropriating French Army lumber. For a while all went well, then the thefts grew too bold, and the Construction Man was summoned before the French colonel in command. As the colonel knew English, and so could not be put off by any "no compris" bluff, the Construction Man had a pretty bad quarter hour of it, but in the end was let off with a warning.

The window frames of the hut are to be filled in with *vitex*, a curious glass substitute, which looks like a thin celluloid glaze over very fine meshed wire. It is only slightly transparent, rather fragile and very costly but it does admit the light, in this respect being far better than the oiled cloth in use in most barracks. When the *vitex* is cut to fit the frames, many odd scraps are left over and these I have been distributing among the boys so they can substitute them for the old newspapers or sacking now in vogue for billet windows.

If they only could hurry up that hut!

"You wait and see," say the boys; "just as soon as that hut is finished we'll be moving. That's always the way with this regiment. Sure as you live, when that hut's done, we'll be off for the front."

And it begins to look as if this might come true.

"Do you really think so?" I asked Mr K. today.

"There's no telling," he replied. "Perhaps. But anyway the boys will know we did our best."

Meanwhile the state of the men is worse than ever. An order has been issued in Goncourt that no soldier may enter a civilian house without a special permit. The reason given is that certain of the townspeople have been illegally selling the men strong drink. The soldiers, however, declare bitterly that the real reason is that the officers wish to have a clear field with the village damsels.

Goncourt, February 21.

We have had our first taste of the trenches; these are not real trenches to be sure but simply practice trenches which lie on the hilly uplands west of Goncourt. For two days we have been in a tumult with a dress rehearsal of manœuvers at the front. The whole brigade in battle array has passed under our window. Colonels and soup-kitchens, mules and majors, supply trains, ambulances, machine-guns, everything. Yesterday as Company F was starting on its hike to the trenches, word came that the mules who pulled their field-kitchen were indisposed. Company F had no mind to eat corn-willy and hard bread for dinner. They seized the soup wagon and pulled it by hand, all the way up the hills. Meeting their major on the way, they shouted in unison; "The mules went on sick report and got marked quarters. We went on sick report and they marked us duty." But they got their dinner hot.

Tonight I heard the sad tale of Mr. B. the new secretary at Saint Thiebault. Company A had marched off to spend the day in the trenches. Mr. B. had an inspiration; he filled a large suit-case full of chocolate and cigarettes: hailed a passing ambulance and set out to carry first aid to Company A in its ordeal in the trenches. Unluckily neither Mr. B. nor the driver knew just where the field of operations lay. Two miles north of Goncourt Mr. B. got out and started to "cut across lots." It was raining; he waded through swamps, he scratched through thickets, he wallowed in ploughed fields, with that suit case which must have weighed a good eighty pounds growing heavier at every step. There being no sun to guide him, he got lost and wandered about in circles. Finally, after several hours, he arrived in a state of collapse at the field of manœuveurs. Then instead of A Company he encountered another company, a perfectly strange company; they demanded chocolate and he didn't have the heart to deny them. After the last cake of chocolate and the last package of cigarettes had disappeared an officer came up, an officer from still another company, and proceeded to tell Mr. B. in very plain language what he thought of him for leaving his men out. And when that officer had done with Mr. B. an officer from the company which had been fed came up in an awful temper and "bawled out" Mr. B. because forsooth his men had made such a mess, throwing away the chocolate wrappers that when the others left, his company would have to stay behind to "police up" the trenches!

Poor Mr. B! My heart goes out to him.

This evening as we were about to close the canteen, my friend, the mule-skinner from Texas appeared in the hut. He had a sort of a weak-in-the-knees expression on his face.

"What's the matter?"

"Met the Old Man," he answered ruefully,—the "Old Man" is the general in command of the division—"Gee! but he sure did give me some bawlin' out!"

"But why?"

He explained that his sergeant had misunderstood orders and told him to go out in his usual rig. The general, encountering the mule-skinner without his proper war-paint, had expressed his mind to him on the matter.

"Jumpin' Jupiter! but the langwidge that that old bird used! I sure will hand it to him! Why, my ears ain't done burnin' yet!" And he shook his head like a man half dazed.

"What did he say?"

The mule-skinner grew red as a beet, stared at me horrified.

"I couldn't repeat it, ma'am! I couldn't repeat nary word of it!"

That a general should so scandalize a mule-skinner, and a Texas mule-skinner at that, by his address, was so intriguing to my fancy that I laughed all the way home.

We have a new colonel; he has declared that the regiment is not fit for the front, and so has laid out a two weeks' programme of gruelling hikes and intensive training, in order at the eleventh hour to try to jack us up to standard.

The Gendarme leaves tomorrow to go *en permission*.

Goncourt, February 25.

If I were God I would lay a blight on every grape-vine in France; then I would sink every still, wine press, distillery and brewery to the bottom of the sea.

We have had payday. It happened Friday. The total results didn't make themselves evident immediately; it was instead a cumulative effect, a crescendo, beginning Friday and reaching its climax yesterday. On these three days, out of the twenty-five hundred men stationed here, twenty-four hundred and ninety-three, I could take my oath, have come into the canteen and leaned over the counter, drunk;—that is to say, visibly and undeniably under the influence of liquor. When a lad, as some half dozen did,—those composing the regular attendance in the group about the fire,—came into the canteen entirely and unmistakably sober, one welcomed him as a drowning man does a spar. For a moment one had come in touch with something stable in a reeling world.

Out of a company of two hundred and fifty last night ninety were capable of standing Retreat.

I have learned to gauge the stages. When a man looks you squarely in the eye and declares vociferously, "Never took a drink in all my life!" he is very drunk indeed. And there is always someone nearby to wink and comment; "He must have joined the gang that pours it down with a funnel."

Saturday night a very red-faced lad came up to the counter and insisted on conversing; from each pocket in his raincoat protruded a long-necked bottle. I stood it for a few minutes, then:

"Please," I said, "won't you take those bottles out of here? I just hate to see them."

"Bottles!" he expostulated. "What do you mean, *bottles*!"

"I mean just those." I pointed.

"Why I ain't got a bottle on me!" he burst out indignantly, fairly glaring at me. Seeing it was hopeless, I edged away toward the other end of the counter, leaving him standing there, a perfect picture of outraged and insulted virtue, with those bottles bristling all over him.

The whole town is pervaded by a warm glow of geniality. Boys that used to nod shyly in answer to your "Good morning" now lean from their loft windows as you pass to call a greeting. Last night, my friend the M. P. tells me, he heard a racket in one of the sheepfolds up on our street. Going to investigate he met a "bunch o' drunken wops" coming out of the door, every man of them carrying a struggling sheep under each arm. He shouted at them; they dropped the sheep and fled.

The French find it all vastly amusing. *"Beaucoup zig zag,"* they cry. It means, I suppose, riches for them.

And yet in all this orgy I have not yet encountered a single word of disrespect, nor heard one objectionable expression uttered. Last night I caught an angry splutter from the crowd in front of the counter. One boy, evidently a shade less tipsy, had admonished another boy apparently a shade more so, to be careful of his language out of respect for me. "Whu'd 'you think? D'you think I ain't got sense enough to know how to talk when there's an American lady present?" For a moment it looked as if there might be a fight.

Meanwhile the guard-house, the real guard-house, is so crowded that they have had to put duck-boards across the rafters for the prisoners to sleep on.

From a nearby town where part of another regiment is stationed come even more startling stories. Certain officers there went so wild that they started to blow up the town with hand grenades. And one of them coming into the Y. held up the secretary at the point of his pistol until he sold him—instead of the ordinary allowance of one or two packages—several cartons of his favorite brand of cigarettes.

The new colonel is said to be horrified. But what could he expect? Take an odd lot of twenty-five hundred boys, remove them from every decent restraining influence, hike them all day through the interminable mud and rain until they drop by the roadside, bring them back at night to dark, cold, damp, filthy, vermin-ridden lofts and stables, add the nerve strain of the imminent prospect of their first time at the front, close every door to them except the door of the café, give them money;—what could anyone expect?

Goncourt, February 27.

My friend Pat is in the hospital; not the local hospital, but Base 18 situated at Bazoilles, some six miles to the north of Goncourt. This afternoon, having our time free between one and four, Mr. K. and I decided to go to call on him.

"Are we going to walk?" I asked.

"Oh we'll get a lift; one always does."

But the lift didn't heave in sight until we were half way there; then it was an ambulance that slowed down in answer to our signals.

"Give us a ride?"

"Sure, if you aren't afraid of the mumps."

I was, dreadfully afraid. But Mr. K. wasn't, he had already had them, on both sides. I hesitated, then decided to take a chance. We rode into Bazoilles in an ambulance full of mumps.

As for Pat, we hadn't an idea in what sort of shape we might find him. Once, Mr. K. told me, he had come upon Pat in one of his visits to the Saint Thiebault infirmary. Pat was lying on a cot with his eyes closed and a sanctified look of patient suffering upon his face.

"Why what's wrong with you, Pat?"

"Ssh!" Pat squinted about to see that neither doctor nor orderly was within ear-shot, then an Irish grin spread over his impudent features. "Nothin' at all," he whispered joyously, "just nothin' at all!"

But this time we found Pat's ailment real enough. He was in the "bone ward" with a badly broken wrist.

"How did it happen?" we inquired.

"Sure an' it happened this way," and he told us both the official and the confidential versions. Confidentially, Pat's wrist had been broken by a blow from an M. P.'s billy in an after-payday argument at Saint Thiebault. Officially it had been broken two days later in the barracks by an accidental knock from a gun-barrel. *Pat had hiked and drilled with a broken wrist for two solid days in order to be able to claim that he had been disabled in the line of duty!* After the second day, convinced that the encounter with the M. P. was sufficiently a matter of past history to be discredited, Pat had reported at Sick Call with his trumped-up tale and had as usual gotten by. Now as he lay on his cot he was occupying himself by conjuring up visions of the party to which he and his buddy were going to treat that M. P. just as soon as he (Pat) should get his hospital discharge.

As we talked I noticed a lad who was walking about the ward with his right hand done up in bloody bandages. He looked self-conscious and embarrassed as if he half hoped, half feared to be recognized. I caught Pat's eye, his voice dropped to a whisper.

"That's Philip R. Don't you remember him?"

Of course! I smiled at Philip, but he turned away and wouldn't come to speak to me. Mr. K. went over to him; they talked for a long while in undertones. Later I heard the whole pitiful story. He had been drinking, the terror that was haunting him had suddenly gripped. He had taken his rifle and shot himself through his right hand, mutilating it, in order that he might not be sent to the front. Placed under arrest on suspicion, his nerve had utterly given way. He had made a full confession. It was likely to go hard with him.

While Mr. K. was listening to Philip, Pat was telling me about the regiment of southern negro engineers who had come to Bazoilles to help build the new hospital. Every time there was an air-raid alarm, Pat declared, they knelt down and prayed by companies.

I emptied out my *musette* bag onto Pat's cot. Pat looked at the oranges, dates, chocolates and cigarettes that we had brought, then took a squint along the hungry-looking ward.

"Well, I guess I'll get a taste," he said.

He was "in soft" he told us. The nurses let him help serve the meals. He had free run of the kitchen and all the milk that he wanted to drink. Yet he was already chafing at the restraint and in his wicked head he was scheming schemes. Some day in the not-too-distant future he was going to give the hospital guards the slip, make a night of it, and paint "Bazooie" red.

Tonight word reached us that a Y. M. C. A. woman worker has been killed in Paris in an air-raid. She was sick and they had sent her to the Hôpital Claude-Bernard. This time the bombs found it.

Goncourt, March 2.

The new hut is opened. Finished or unfinished, we made up our minds that we would open that hut Saturday night, and open it we did. The last two days have been fairly frantic. Yesterday we washed up; today we dried out and decorated. The cleaning was the worst of it. The hut, as I have hinted, is a sort of island in a sea of mud. Consequently as the building went up, the floor, walls, counter, ceiling, everything was splotched, streaked and plastered with dirt. Thursday night as I looked around the hut my heart sank. The place was a sight.

"You can't do anything about it," they told me.

"But something has got to be done!"

Friday morning arrived a detail of eight prisoners from the guard-house. They had come to scrub. The guard in charge took his stand, leaning against one of the pillars, his loaded rifle in his hands; to see that no one escaped was his only responsibility, the rest was up to me. My detail proved a sullen, stubborn lot, slouching, cursing under their breath, all their self-respect turned to a smouldering rebellion; after the first few minutes I saw just how much work left to themselves they would be likely to accomplish. So I told them in a matter-of-fact way just how things stood: that we had promised to open the hut the next day, that it was, as they could see, in a frightful mess, that I realized they were up against a stiff job, but I did *so* hope that we could put it through. Then I got a pail and a scrubbing-brush and went out and scrubbed side by side with them. It is of course strictly against the rules to talk to prisoners, but all the while I worked I "jollied" my "jail-birds" for all my wits were worth. I admired ecstatically the spots which they had scrubbed, I moaned in despair over the unscrubbed places. Inside of an hour the prisoners were all grinning cheerfully as they worked like beavers. When the guard was looking the other way I sneaked them cigarettes. By night the hut was very damp and somewhat streaky, but it would pass, at least by candle-light. I didn't care though my arms were so lame I could hardly lift them, and my hands in ruins.

"I congratulate you," said the new Secretary, "I never thought it could be done."

"If only nobody looks at the ceiling!"

For the ceiling was beyond our reach, and back and forth over every one of its boards had tramped the hob-nailed boots of the A. E. F. and every step had left its muddy print. As I looked I thought; if we only had the signatures to put beside each footprint, what a fascinating autograph collection it would make!

Today we spent in a mad tear, making the hut beautiful and moving our effects over from the "Guard-House." The moving was accomplished by the aid of the Wall-Eyed Boy and his donkey. These are two of Goncourt's leading citizens, the donkey, an ancient moth-eaten beast, being particularly intimately known to a certain group of doughboys who would joyfully murder him. His stable is directly beneath the loft in which they are billeted and every morning, prompt as an alarm clock, at 4 A. M. that donkey brays, and brays until the soundest sleeper is awakened. The Wall-Eyed Boy's name is Martin, and as a donkey in France is slangily called *un Martin*, as we call a mule "Maud," the two go under the title of *Les Deux Martins*. When *les Deux Martins* and I went trudging along the muddy streets of Goncourt, side by side, with the little tippy cart loaded with canteen truck bumping along behind, the M. P.s thought it a rare joke. "I wish Sister Susy could see you now," called one.

The last few hours were spent frantically decorating. Our color scheme is red and blue. This came about through accident rather than intention. We had a bolt of turkey-red cotton bunting for curtains, only to discover that this did not darken the lighted windows sufficiently to comply with the now strictly enforced aeroplane regulations. So I asked a secretary starting for Paris to bring me a bolt of black cambric in order to make a set of inner supplementary curtains. The secretary returning, brought bright blue; black, on account of the demand for mourning, had proved too expensive. At first I was non-plussed, but then discovered that the bright red and blue made rather a jolly combination. So each one of our many windows is now giddy with red and blue draperies and the seat that runs all around our writing room is brave with blue and red cushions (stuffed, if the truth must be told, with shavings!) Between each two windows is tacked one of my stunning big French war posters, the long counter is covered with red-checked oil-cloth, a bouquet of flags flies from the proscenium arch over the stage which, for the occasion, is banked beautifully with evergreens. Altogether we present rather the appearance of a perpetual Fourth of July celebration, but then who cares? If one can't be aesthetic one can at least be gay, and it's anything to take one's mind off the mud!

The Gendarme came back from her leave tonight just in time for the Grand Opening. This took place at seven o'clock. The hall was packed to the last inch. As one boy said; "There's plenty of room for me, but there ain't none for the buttons on my coat." There was a reason for this. The new colonel was to make a speech and he had advised all the officers and non-coms, in the whole regiment to be present. I caught a glimpse of Company A wedged in among the suffocating mass. Everything, I understand, went off very nicely; there was much music by the band and somebody sang Danny Deever very thrillingly, but I was too busy in the kitchen to pay much attention. The new Secretary had wanted me to sit on the platform, but after a three days' debate, he had finally agreed to let me off, and luckily, for the minute the last note of the S. S. B. had sounded we were ready to start handing out the hot chocolate and cookies over the counter to the mob. When everyone else had been fed the colonel himself appeared back of the counter, to graciously accept a cup of chocolate, and make himself generally charming.

When the last guest had gone and we were getting ready to shut up the hut for the night, the Chief who had come over from Bourmont for the occasion drew me aside, looking solemn.

"I have a question to put to you."

"What is it?"

"The division leaves for the front within a short while. Do you wish to go with them?"

"Of course!" said I.

Goncourt, March 8.

This week has gone by in a whirl. Because it was our first and presumably our last week in the big hut we wanted to make it just as nice as was humanly possible. And this hasn't been an easy task because with the regiment putting on the last touches before they go to the front, there hasn't been a bit of spare man-power available to help us; and the mere problem of keeping that huge place anything like clean has almost swamped us. After mess at night, to be sure, we have no lack of assistance. The boys swarm into the little kitchen in droves, eager to help stir the chocolate, or cut the bread for the sandwiches. If only ten out of every dozen would be content to stay the other side of the counter, it would simplify matters, but much as they may be underfoot one hasn't the heart to turn them out. Those who can't get into the kitchen hang about the doors, looking in, teasing for a "hand-out" of bread and jam. "I'm just so hungry," sighed a lad plaintively today, looking at me out of the corner of his eyes, "I could eat the jamb off the door!"

We have a Frenchwoman to help us in the kitchen. She is a treasure, shy and bright-eyed as a brown bird, and so tiny that we have to set a packing-box by the stove for her to stand on when she stirs the chocolate. She is deaf and speaks *patois,* so between her strange French and mine still stranger we have droll times making each other understand. Yet, none the less, she and the boys manage to keep up a running fire of badinage and when they become too rowdy, the tiny thing turns ridiculously bellicose and threatens to whip them all with her chocolate paddle. At night we all go home together and one tall lad must always come along in order to help Madame over the road of a thousand mud holes that leads from the hut to the highway, lest she be drowned in transit. She carries a funny little gasolene lamp that gives about as much light as an ambitious fire-fly and all the way to the main road one can hear her moaning; *"Mon Dieu, quel chemin! Mon Dieu, quel chemin!"*

This has been our week's programme:

Sunday.	Hot chocolate and cookies Religious Service with special music Song Service. More chocolate
Monday.	French Classes Hot chocolate and jam sandwiches
Tuesday.	Boxing and Wrestling Matches Hot chocolate and sardine sandwiches
Wednesday.	Band Concert Hot chocolate and jam sandwiches
Thursday.	Movies Hot chocolate and cookies

Friday.	Sing Fest with Solos Hot chocolate and jam sandwiches
Saturday.	Stunt Programme Canned fruit and cookies

The hut has been filled every night, hundreds and hundreds of soldiers, the auditorium packed and the writing-room holding at least a hundred more, while the chocolate line, coiling and curling about like a monster snake, has for hours seemed absolutely endless. We have worked out a system for the chocolate serving—the Gendarme is cashier, taking the money and making change, fifty centimes or nine cents for a cup of chocolate and a sandwich, or six spice cookies, or four fig ones. One boy ladles out the chocolate. I push the cups over the counter, another boy hands out the cookies, a third gathers up the dirty cups and carries them to the kitchen, where three or four others are busy washing and wiping them, while Heaven only knows how many more are around the stove, helping Madame stir the next kettleful, opening milk cans, or dipping water into a third container. Thus we keep the line merrily wagging along.

Last night, quite unknown to the men, Pershing himself came to town, whirled in after dark in his big limousine and whirled away again as suddenly and secretly as he had arrived. He came to give the officers final instructions as to their conduct at the front.

The first faint wistful scents of Spring are in the air. This morning Madame brought to our room a tiny bouquet of snow-drops. And one hears from Saint Thiebault a rumour of early violets.

Goncourt, March 10.

This morning shortly after I reached the hut, one of the men from the Bourmont office came in with a note for me, it read:

> My dear Miss —
>
> I am glad to be able to tell you more or less confidentially that you will probably go to the front very shortly. You had better have everything ready so you could leave on short notice any time after tomorrow noon.
>
> Very sincerely yours, —

Enclosed in the envelope was a little slip headed *Suggestions for Men going to the Front*. It began "Go light, take no trunk," and ended "We provide helmets, gas masks, etc." The note was dated yesterday.

I left the canteen and hurried back here to my billet to pack, while the Gendarme, who does not wish to go with the division but prefers to stay back and be reassigned, remained at the hut. What with sorting and mending things, the packing took all afternoon. What to leave behind in storage and what to take is no end of a question. Unfortunately the *Suggestions* were compiled with a view strictly to masculine necessities.

It has been a grey dismal afternoon. A melancholy donkey in somebody's back-yard has kept up an incessant braying. "He does not please himself at Goncourt," explained Madame. "He is a Saint Thiebault donkey." Meanwhile half the regiment, it seems, has strayed by under my open window. I never knew before how consistently and persistently profane the A. E. F. could be when left to its own devices. The amazing part of it is;—since this seems to be their natural style of expression, how do they manage to slough it all and talk with such perfect prunes and prisms propriety in the canteens?

At supper time we were surprised by a Concert Party which had arrived today unexpectedly in this area. We were particularly glad to have them as the nervous tension among the boys is marked enough to make us welcome anything to divert their attention. We could have the regular Sunday evening service first, we decided, and then the concert to finish off with. The Concert Party came to supper at our mess. There was an ornamental Russian violinist, male, an American accompanist, also male, and a little French actress-singer. The minute we laid eyes on her we knew that the concert would be a success. She was all frills and frippery; lace, pink-rose buds and pale blue silk, with yellow curls and great blue eyes peering from beneath a quaint little rose-wreathed poke bonnet; an amazing vision of femininity to appear suddenly in the mud and dingy squalor of Goncourt!

The family Peirut was in a great state of mind over such distinguished visitors. They brought out food enough to feed the company a week, and kept hovering about the table, urging the dishes on our guests and emitting little wails of dismay when any one of the artists refused to eat enough for all three.

I stayed at our billet to finish up my packing, and went over to the hut late in the evening. The concert was half finished. As we anticipated, the little singer had made a hit. She gave some French songs, accompanying them with clever pantomine. Then she sang *Huckleberry Finn* and *Oh Johnny!* As the phrase has it, she "got them going." She proved a past-mistress in the art of using her eyes. They winked at her and she winked back. Every last man in the first six rows was flirting with her, and every one was convinced that he was making a hit all his own. Several, it was confided to me afterwards, developed matrimonial aspirations on the spot. Then a tragic thing occurred. For the closing number they must give the Star Spangled Banner. Everybody rose, and everybody in duty bound removed their hats. The little singer took one wild survey of the audience, gasped, choked, then retreated precipitately in order to conceal her giggles. A week ago an order was published that the regiment should have their hair shaved off before going to the front;—every head in the whole auditorium, thus suddenly laid bare, was bald as an egg!

From latest advices it appears that the troops will start entraining the middle of the week. We are going on ahead in order to be there to serve them hot chocolate when they detrain after the journey. Every one has a different idea where that will be, but the best guess seems to be the Lunéville sector. What sort of conditions we will find at the front I haven't the least idea. I missed the special conference held at Bourmont the other day, in which instructions and information to the personnel bound for the front were given. The driver who was to call for us, failed to do so; I set out to walk, only to find on arriving at Bourmont that the conference had been cut short, and was already over. Nobody has told me a word except to tease me by telling me that I will have to have my hair cut off in order to wear a gas-mask. Mr. K. amuses himself by predicting cellars and cooties. The Peiruts shake their heads and talk about my *courage,* but I can see that they mean folly. As for the Gendarme's friends, Lieutenant Z. warns: "Take my advice, stay out of it. It's a man's game out there." While Captain X. splutters; "Sending you to the front without any gas-drill, it's nothing short of cold-blooded murder." Thus do our friends encourage us.

CHAPTER III
RATTENTOUT—THE FRONT

Bar-le-Duc, March 12.

It's not to be the Lunéville sector after all, it's to be the sector just south of Verdun!

We arrived here at Bar-le-Duc last night after a six-hour trip by motor car. Mr. K. came by motor-cycle; most of the other men travelled by truck, sitting perched on top of a load of luggage, canvas cots, and chocolate boilers. The truck broke down somewhere *en route* and never reached Bar-le-Duc until this morning, when it rolled in carrying a rather weary-looking lot of passengers.

Tomorrow we go on to our station behind the lines. Today we have spent shopping for supplies. We have bought writing paper; materials to make hot chocolate, paying two francs and a half apiece or almost fifty cents for a small-sized can of condensed milk; and dozens of gross of little jars of confiture. Ever since I was a child *Bar-le-Duc* has meant just the one thing to me,—those little glasses of delectable currant preserve which bear its label. We went around to the wholesale houses which handle the famous *Confitures Fins de Bar-le-Duc*. The sight of all those gleaming rows of glass jars filled with deep crimson or amber-colored currants was one that I shan't easily forget.

Bar-le-Duc is a city which shows the wounds of war. Time and again, unfortified, defenceless as she is, she has known *the terror that flieth by night*. Last summer several blocks in the very heart of the city were completely demolished by bombs and the wilderness of ruins lies there untouched. All over the city great black signs are painted on the houses; *Cave, Cave voutée,*—vaulted cellar,—*Place Pour 40 Personnes*. At the end of the afternoon we climbed, Mr. K and I, to the top of the ancient clock-tower which stands on the edge of the fortress-citadel of the Dukes of Bar, overlooking the city. Just above the clock we came upon a tiny platform transformed for the time being into light-housekeeping apartments for two poilus who night and day keep watch there for enemy aircraft. As we stood on the little balcony outside and looked down on the house-tops of the city spread beneath us, with the little children playing in the streets, a telephone bell in the tower tingled. A moment later one of the poilus announced; "A squadrille of Gothas has just crossed the lines, headed for Paris."

Alas, poor Paris! Yet the news brought a feeling of relief with it. The little children of Bar-le-Duc are safe for the night, it seems. The avions are out after bigger game.

Rattentout, March 14.

Out from Bar-le-Duc one swings into a separate world, the World-Behind-the-Lines. Here one is at the back door of the war, as it were. Passing through the half-abandoned villages one sees war in its *déshabille;* you get no sense of the thrill of it, nor even of its horrors; only the weary disgust, the stultifying stupidity, the unutterable ennui.

Here everything that moves or lives, it seems, is blue; faded blue, dingy blue, purplish or greenish blue perhaps, but blue nevertheless. Everywhere the color insists. It streaks along the roads in long, broken lines, the meagre trodden villages are blotched and patched with it. Indeed the whole horizon, at this season of the year, might be expressed in just two tones; the almost uniform grey-yellow tint that washes over the fields, the rolling hills, the dusty roads, the squalid villages, and the ever-insistent poilu-blue.

You pass by tilled fields labeled *Culture Militaire;* great grey-green aerodromes with flocks of little planes resting in rows beside them, in their gay paint resembling nothing in the world so much as dicky birds fresh from the toy shop; and always dotted here and there over the open fields, the little lonely graves, sometimes hedged in by fences made of sticks and always marked by a grey wooden cross on which hangs, in painted tin, the tricolor. Farther on you come to the world where men live underground, burrowing in the earth like hunted animals. Scattered along the roadside, or in rows under the shelter of a hill-slope, everywhere you look, are dugouts, some with the entrances covered with pine-boughs, others thatched with sticks, still others hidden beneath earth-colored camouflages.

We arrived here last night about dusk. The poilus as we passed stared at us as if we were so many lunatics. Rattentout is on the right bank of the Meuse, about six miles from the trenches. This means for one thing that you must carry a gas-mask with you wherever you go. One even sees the little children, what few of them are left, trudging about with small-sized masks slung over their shoulders. The Y. here is short of masks and as yet M.—the only canteen worker besides myself to come with the advance guard—and I have none. This morning when the Chief went out he hung his mask on a peg in the hall. "If anything happens," he said to M. and me, "you two can settle it between you, which shall have it."

Our home here is in a lordly mansion, evidently the Big House of the village. French officers were living here before we came. The regiment to which they belonged moving out just as we arrived, they graciously made over the house to us. The officers had started a vegetable garden in the back-yard and this they relinquished with deep regret, one young lieutenant fairly having tears in his eyes as he took a last survey of his rows of tiny lettuce and young cabbages.

Today is to be given over to house-cleaning, and getting settled. Tomorrow the troops are due to begin detraining at the two points Landrecourt and Dugny and we are to be there to serve them hot chocolate.

Last night we took our supper at the dingy little house next door, a surprisingly delicious meal, bread and butter, omelette, salad and cocoa. The house next door is one of the half-dozen or so in town still inhabited by civilians. The family consists of grandmother, mother and little girl of five; the husband is in the trenches. The child Pauline is half sick with a feverish cold. They could get no medicine, the mother fretted; we promised some from Bar-le-Duc. The house itself is painfully unkempt and dirty, yet Pauline is always fresh in a spotless white pinafore, her glossy hair immaculately brushed. This morning we went to the house next door again for bread and coffee.

"Did you sleep last night?" asked Madame.

"But yes,—and you?"

She shook her head. "I was afraid of the Boche aeroplanes. I could hear them overhead."

"But I should think you would be used to them by now."

"Ah! But that makes no difference!"

What consideration keeps her here, clinging to the very door-step of the war, as it were, hounded as she is, by terrors? Just the one reason, I suppose,—that she has nowhere else to go.

Rattentout, March 15.

Lafayette, nous voilà! The first battalions of the division have arrived.

The car called for us early this morning to take us to Dugny-Est where half the men are to detrain. We followed along the east bank of the Meuse running parallel to the *Canal de L'Est*. The canal was a dismal sight, filled with an endless line of empty abandoned barges, many of them settling slowly down as if water-logged, a few, already sunk, leaving nothing but a bit of prow protruding above the water's surface. We ran along the bank for about three miles, then swung across the Meuse to Dugny. Dugny-Est is a half mile north of Dugny proper,—the terminus of a strip of railway taken over and run by American engineers. Viewed from the detraining tracks the landscape was bleak enough; the morasses of the Meuse, strung with barbed-wire beyond, an austere deserted-looking church in the foreground, and, dreariest of all, right under the boys' feet as they detrained, almost, a large military grave-yard.

Arriving at the little stone station-house made over to us for the occasion, we found the chocolate already made. Four of the Y. men had spent the night there and by dint of stoking the fires all night long, as they declared, they had gotten the five huge containers hot. The equipment assembled in haste at Bar-le-Duc was evidently proving none too satisfactory.

I had just time to suspend a small American flag from the front of the station-house before the first train puffed up the track. Nothing I think has ever looked quite so good to me as that old American locomotive. It was the first one I had seen in France. I wanted to throw my arms around it and hug it. As one of the boys said afterwards: "Why, you'd be happy just to lie down on the track and let the darned thing run over you."

I stood under the flag and waved frantically, first to the American train crew and then, oh joy! to my Company A! There they all were, crowded in the open doors of their box cars, "Side-door Pullmans" as they call them, Magulligan the prize fighter, comically conspicuous with his head done up in a sort of night-cap made from a large white handkerchief. The train pulled by, slowed down, came to a standstill up the track. We hustled the chocolate cans out by the roadside. Company A, the first off the train, came marching down the road; each man held out his mess-cup and got a dipperful of cocoa.

"Where are we?" they demanded.

"Four miles south of Verdun. How do you like the scenery?"

"All right except the grave-yard. That's too handy."

"Say," spoke up one of the boys, "I heard the mud out here in the trenches was pretty deep."

"Is that so?"

"Yes they said a feller went in over his ankles there the other day."

"I wouldn't call that very deep!" I bit.

"Mm, but he went in head-first!"

I asked one of the corporals how things were going.

"We were feelin' kind o' lost," he confessed. "Then we looked out and saw the old flag and you. After that it seemed just like home somehow."

They marched off down the road looking very business-like and military. Next came the other companies belonging to the first battalion, and the regimental machine-gun company. These were not permitted to stop by the station-house on account of the danger of being observed by enemy aircraft, but were halted at a distance down the road. We picked up the chocolate cans and chased after them.

When every man in the First Battalion had had a drink, we hurried back to the stone-house to get ready for the next trainload. As I stirred the chocolate on one of the little stoves set up outside, several of the train crew came to talk to me. I was the first "real honest-to-God American girl" they had seen in months they told me; and they were just as excited over me as I had been over their engine.

If the history of America in the Great War should ever be written down in detail, surely one chapter should be given over to a Little Iliad of the "Six Bit Railway" that runs from Sommeil to Dugny-Est, five kilometers south of Verdun; how, as I had it from the lips of one of those engineers, the English took it over from the French and tried to run it and failed, how the Canadians took it after them and failed too, how then the — Engineers fell heir to it. How they lived with the French, eating French rations which were gall and wormwood to them. How they struggled with an alien tongue and finally reduced it to a weird unholy gibberish which was yet somehow intelligible both to the French and to themselves. How they came through shell-fire and gas and bombing raids, seemingly bearing charmed lives. And how they worked forty-eight hours at a stretch whenever the big drives and shifts were on.

Tonight one of the secretaries told us that, as he was standing by the roadside watching while we ladled out the chocolate, one of the boys said to him:

"I'm thinking of a toast."

"And what might that be?"

"God bless American women," the boy answered him.

Rattentout, March 16.

When we reached the station-house this morning we found everyone agog over the night's events. The detraining had gone on all night; at first without incident. All precautions had been taken, no one was allowed to so much as light a match. About midnight one of the marine soup-kitchens had been unloaded and rolled down the road puffing sparks and scattering coals. Some enterprising mess sergeant had evidently planned that his men should have a hot meal. The French spectators in consternation had followed the soup-kitchen down the road, extinguishing the trailing embers, but the mischief was already done. There were German planes scouting overhead, they noted, evidently, the sparks, and signaled the range to the German gunners. Fifteen minutes later a six inch shell exploded a few hundred yards from the little stone-house, then another and another. One shell had fallen in the very center of the grass-plot where Company D had lined up to eat their luncheon of cold corn-willy sandwiches and hot chocolate. The gas-alarm had been sounded. A mule team had become frantic and bolted, encountering the marine band's big base drum, had made toothpicks of it. Meanwhile confusion, it seemed, had reigned in the little stone-house. One secretary, seizing an article of underwear and putting it on his head in mistake for a helmet, had dashed madly up and down the road as the shells fell, and ended by bursting, in his *déshabille,* into the private dugout of a French colonel.

No Americans were hurt, but one poilu had been injured and another killed.

"They have our range now," said everybody. "And look at those Boche balloons, will you?"

We looked to the northeast; three German observation balloons were hanging just above the hills.

We stirred the chocolate and served it to whatever boys happened to be about, boys on detail, drivers of mule-teams. One can, having been kept warm all night, had turned. Some bright soul suggested that it was the concussion of the shelling that had soured the milk, just as thunderstorms sometimes do. Two poilus leaned in at the window.

"What are you doing?" they asked curiously. We explained; they shook their heads. "You spoil your soldiers." Then, "Was anyone killed last night?"

"Yes, one Frenchman."

"Oh that's nothing!" (*Ça ne fait rien.*) They strolled away.

The friendly interpreter came in and told us that they were about to hold the poilu's funeral.

A troop-train pulled in. It was loaded with soldiers from my own regiment, the Second Battalion. The chocolate was ready, smelt delicious.

"You can't serve it," they told us. "On account of last night's shelling, the troops won't be allowed to stop until they're well beyond the town."

"Isn't there *some* way we can manage?" we teased.

"No, they've got our range."

"Well at least we can say hello to them!"

We went down to the tracks where the men were spilling out of the box cars. They were gathering up their equipment and forming in companies in double time. One red-in-the-face sergeant was furiously demanding who in blazes had stolen his revolver on him; it was evident that he found the presence of ladies sadly hampering to his flow of language. Three companies marched off. The last to go was H Company, the company that had been billeted on the same street with us at Goncourt. We waved and they smiled back at us. They marched down the road, disappeared over the brow of the hill.

We stood chatting with two boys who were on a billeting detail.

There was a dull heavy detonation beyond the hills. A moment later a strange whistling screech shrilled over our heads. I stared into the air, trying to see—I knew of course it was a shell, but I had never thought one would travel so slowly or be quite so noisy about it. The whistling shriek passed over us, changed to a dropping whine. Down the street there was a thunderous explosion followed instantly by a shattering crash. Timbers, tiles, stones, a mass of debris splashed for a moment up against the sky. The shell had fallen at the cross-roads. I stared at M. I was cold all over.

"It must have got them," I heard myself whispering. "My God! it must have got them!"

We stared down the road. Everywhere figures in poilu blue and some in khaki, were running like rabbits towards the dugouts. It seemed to me the uncertainty was more than I could bear.

"I'm going to go and see."

"I'll go with you," said M.

We stopped at the station-house and put on our helmets; then we started down the road. Just beyond the station-house we passed a little cortege of poilus carrying the body of their comrade on a stretcher-bier. They were on their way to the church. When the first shell came over I had seen the funeral procession waver, hesitate, seem uncertain for a few moments whether to proceed or to seek shelter, now, their indecision conquered, they were continuing their march with what seemed an added dignity. A limousine drew up behind us, stopped. In the back seat sat an American major.

"Give you a lift?"

We climbed in. Half way down the hill another shell shrieked over our heads, burst in front of us. We reached the cross-roads.

"Let us out, please."

The major stared, then stopped the car. We scrambled out. The car whirled off. Two houses lay, crushed heaps of stone. In the road were three dead horses and an automobile with a crumpled radiator. That was all. Another shell struck, sending us cowering against the nearest house-wall. As far as we could see the place was utterly deserted. There was nothing to do but go back. Half-way up the hill we met a poilu, he was carrying an

O. D. blouse. He asked us where the wounded American was; he had been carried into some house nearby; this was his coat. We could of course tell him nothing. The wind which had been strong all morning, was filling the air with blinding clouds of yellow dust. The shells were coming over at regular intervals, so many minutes between them; they were all falling, it seemed, in the vicinity of the cross-roads. A little further up the hill and we began to meet mule teams from the supply train driving down. The mule-skinners on their high seats looked calm enough, but a number of the mules were becoming quite unmanageable. I recognized the slim lad of seventeen with whom I had driven into Bourmont from Goncourt once after a load of canteen supplies. As each team passed, we waved our hands and wished them luck; but all the time I kept repeating to myself:

"They're going right down into it. God help them! Why does it have to be?"

A French officer encountered us, asked us politely if we wouldn't like to step down into a dugout. I was amused at his manner which was as casual as if he were offering us an umbrella in a shower. There were some excellent dugouts up on the hill-side he assured us. "But I don't want to go into a dugout!" *"Mademoiselle a beaucoup d'esprit,"* he observed, *"mais ce n'est pas prudent."* Obediently we climbed the hill, to come upon a little group of Americans gathered about the entrance to a dugout, watching the shells as they came over. Taking a peep into the dugout I found it had already been patronized by several poilus. We sat on the ground and watched the shelling. On the other side of the town we could see Company H flung out in skirmish line, marching over the open fields.

Presently a boy in olive drab came panting and laughing up the hill. The group welcomed him with a shout. He was one of the billeting detail. They had been staying in a house at the cross-roads. When the others had gone out this morning he had been left to clean up and get dinner. He had washed all the dishes, he told us, and had just gone out and bought a basketful of eggs to make an omelette for dinner, when crash! the first shell had fallen demolishing the house next to theirs. He had stepped out to look at the ruins and returned, when bang! went the house on the other side of him! He began to think it might be time for him to move, when, oh boy! zowie! a shell had wrecked the upper story of the billet over him. Then he had left. But he was feeling very badly about those eggs. Corporal G. also of the billeting detail looked at him with widened eyes. "And I was half a mind to stay upstairs in bed and not get up this morning!" he remarked. The boys found solace for the loss of the omelette in the thought that all the effects of the very unpopular captain billeted next door must surely have been annihilated.

After an hour or so the shelling stopped. One by one blue forms emerged from the dugouts. The Chief had ordered the flivver to report at eleven. It was noon and it hadn't appeared.

"We must walk to Rattentout," said the Chief. "No use our staying here."

It was hot and dusty and my helmet weighed like a mountain on my head, but at last we made it. Some two miles or so from Dugny we passed two marines sitting in discouraged postures by the roadside.

"What's the matter?"

"He's had a fit," growled one of the warriors, jerking his thumb in the direction of his comrade's back.

"He has 'em. They never ought ter let him come."

There was nothing we could offer them but sympathy.

Rattentout, March 17.

Here I am sitting on a bench in the little garden back of our billet, soaked in spring sunshine. Over my head the lilacs are leafing out against a sky of Italian blue, at my feet are golden crocuses and the first pale primroses. But the sky, as one gazes at it, has an odd trick of breaking out in little puffy dots of white like nothing so much as kernels of corn in a corn-popper. These are of course the bursting shells fired by French anti-aircraft batteries at the enemy aviators overhead; sometimes you can see the plane itself, skimming like a gnat among the smoke puffs. "They don't seem to get 'em often," as a boy remarked to me. "But golly they do make 'em move!"

Ever since the Americans began to arrive the German planes have been constantly overhead. They are taking photographs; they say. Where, oh where are our American aviators?

In my ears as I sit here is a curious sound, a sound like the pounding of tremendous breakers on a stormy shore: it is the guns of Verdun, Les Eparges and St. Mihiel. At rhythmic intervals this sound is punctuated by heavy crashing thuds nearer at hand. They are shelling Dugny again. All the civilians fled yesterday. A driver, coming in last night, told us how they went, empty-handed, creeping along the edges of the roads under the cover of trees or brush, fearing to step out in the open lest they be spied and bombed by the German aeroplanes overhead. The church where they held the poilu's funeral has already been struck by a shell and the steeple demolished.

In front of the house the street is quiet. All through the day the town seems a sleepy deserted place, but at night it is a different matter; then the real business of the day begins. Carts and camions may straggle past at odd intervals during the daylight hours, but with darkness, the traffic starts to pour by in a perfectly unbroken stream. One lies awake and listens, it seems for hours, to the absolutely incessant rattle of carts, trucks, caissons and gun carriages passing along the road, until it seems as if the whole French Army must be on the move.

Little Pauline is better today. She has just come running into the garden through the back gate, in company with a big curly dog. Rattentout they tell us is the "Dog Town" for this sector; every dog picked up near the front, lost mascots, faithful beasts looking for their masters, strays of every sort, are sent back here for keeping.

Presently I must go in and help M. get the supper. Our food, over and beyond what we brought from Bar-le-Duc in tins and sacks, is furnished us by the French Army. Every morning a dapper little corporal calls to take our orders. When the official interpreter is out it falls to me to do the parleying. The corporal is patient and very military and oh so polite! He brings us fresh butter, fresh eggs, even so much as a quart of fresh milk, and the most delicious fresh French bread I have ever tasted. The first day he came he was dreadfully distressed; he had no fresh meat to offer us. This morning he shone with smiles. There was plenty of fresh beef now, plenty! We ordered some and ate it stewed for dinner. It was dark and tough and stringy. I could dare swear that I saw that "beef" freshly slaughtered yesterday at Dugny cross-roads.

A French *liaison* officer called here this afternoon. He told me that it was quite true that a certain regiment of French infantry had gone into battle, each man carrying with him the wooden cross which was to mark his grave if he fell. To earn *le croix de bois* is the current slang phrase among the French to designate dying a soldier's death.

Yesterday noon a detachment of marines arrived in Rattentout. During the day they must keep under cover, but last night after sundown they came out and played baseball in the street. When I looked out my window and saw those lads in olive drab nonchalantly throwing and catching a baseball under my window, I felt as if something safe and sane had somehow appeared in the midst of a strange nightmare world.

Rattentout, March 18.

I have said; "Good-bye, Good luck!" to my boys.

Today we received word that the first battalion of my regiment was to take its place in the trenches by Les Eparges at twelve o'clock tonight, leaving Genicourt where they have been billeted, at eight. I breathed a piteous appeal to the Chief. At five o'clock the car called for us.

Earlier in the afternoon there had been an air battle over Genicourt. I heard the soft *whut, whut* of the anti-aircraft guns, and later the staccato rattle of machine-guns in the air. Looking out I could see the planes, one German and two French darting among the shrapnel puffs, the German escaping, sad to say, unharmed. Now a French observation balloon was floating over Genicourt, a curious-looking thing shaped like a huge ram's head, and a dull green in color. As we neared the town they started to haul the balloon in: it came down with astonishing rapidity.

We rolled into Genicourt, a sodden desolate village clinging under the lea of a low hill, just now alive with suppressed vitality. The boys had been ordered to keep their billets until the last moment, as any unusual number of men about might be observed by an enemy aeroplane. Nevertheless there were plenty of stragglers in the streets, while out of the windows were leaning several hundred more, craning their necks in order to get a glimpse of the descending balloon.

We went to the *Foyer du Soldat*, a bright clean barracks, the walls covered with posters in vivid hues. It was full of our boys. They laughed, joked, played checkers and pounded the piano, some were dancing together. Yet through all the gaiety one had a sense of tension, of nervous strain. Some of the boys asked us to sing, one lad evidently in a more solemn mood repeatedly requested "My Country 'Tis of Thee." We sang the "Long, Long Trail" and "Keep the Home Fires Burning." Then we went out in the street again. The French, we gathered, were quite astonished at the high spirits of the Americans. "Ah, but it's their first time," they said. "After four years it will be different."

In the public square they had been holding some sort of ceremony, an interchange of formal greetings between the French and American officers. A French military band had just finished its programme. As we passed they played the Marseillaise and the Star Spangled Banner; we all stood at attention.

We came to the street where Company A was billeted. The boys leaned out of the windows and waved and called to me. Everywhere it was the same question:

"What shall I bring you from the trenches?"

"Do you want a live Boche for a souvenir? I'll get you one!" They thought my gas-mask was a lovely joke. "What's that strap across your shoulder for?" they teased.

"That? Oh that's my new Sam Browne belt!"

"Say! Bet you don't know how to put it on!" Then they would yell "Gas!" just to frighten me.

In the street a little crowd of boys were tossing coppers. Everybody was anxious to get rid of his "clackers," in order not to have to carry all that useless weight into the trenches with him. They invited me to join. I tried one penny while the boys all cheered, only to miss by a good yard. Lieut. B. came by: "Will you take tea with me in my dugout?" he asked.

The order was given for the companies to form. The streets filled up; dusk was gathering. The Chief said that it was time to go. We found the car in the public square. Slowly we moved out of town. I shall never forget those long brown files drawn up against the dim grey houses. Five hours hence and those very boys would be in the front line trenches, face to face with the enemy. We passed Company A. I called out to them to be sure not to stick their heads up over the top, and not to dare to take off their gas-masks before they were ordered to. Never before did I realize how much those boys meant to me. Each face I saw flashed some vivid unforgettable association to my mind. "When you come back," I called, "I'll be waiting for you with the hot chocolate ready." They smiled and waved Good-bye to me. Some of them held up their fingers to show how many Germans they were going to account for. A turn in the road shut it all from sight. On the way back to Rattentout we passed the Third Battalion, who were marching in on their very heels to take over their billets.

It's eleven o'clock now. They must be almost in. They are marching, I know, in darkness and silence; not a cigarette is to be lighted, not a word spoken above a whisper. One hour more and the relief will be completed.

Rattentout, March 19.

I am to be sent to Paris for reassignment. I have, it seems, been guilty of conduct unbecoming a lady under shell-fire. This sentence has been hanging over me ever since that day at Dugny. I knew of course that I was in disgrace but never dreamed that it would come to this.

It seems, what no one had troubled to hint to me, that we have been allowed to go farther front than any women of any of the Allied Nations in France have been permitted to go to work before. Moreover that the French, whose guests we are in this sector, were very much opposed to the presence of women here, and only finally, after much persuasion, allowed us to come here on trial. Now the Chief says that he is afraid that my indiscreet action at Dugny in going down to the cross-roads instead of into a dugout may have shocked the French. In order to forestall any possible protest by our Allies I am to be made an example of the discipline of the organization.

Etretat, Normandy. March 28.

I have been here a week on leave. Tomorrow I start back for Paris once more. Where I am to go after that is uncertain.

It seems strange to be in France and not be wading through seas of mud, but to have firm turf and dry roads beneath one's feet. The hamlets here, while picturesque, are quite spruce and tidy, amazingly different from the quaint but indescribably dirty little mudpie muck-heap villages to which I have been used.

This pretty little coast town, once a fishing village, then a summer resort, is now chiefly a hospital. All the large hotels have been taken over for wards and nurses' quarters, the big casino filled with row on row of iron cots. It is an American hospital with American doctors, nurses and orderlies, but attached to the B. E. F. and filled of course with British patients. As in all the English hospitals, as soon as a patient is able to get out of bed he is dressed in a "suit of blues;" trousers and jumper blouse of bright blue cotton, white shirt, scarlet tie and handkerchief to match, making him look exactly like a grown-up Greenaway boy. The men hate them, they tell me, but I for one am grateful to the designer as the bright blue and scarlet makes wonderful splotches of color in the landscape.

There may be a more disgusted set of boys in France than these here in the hospital corps at Base No. 2, but if so I have yet to meet them. One of the first units to come across, landing in May of 1917, every man enlisted, so they tell me, because he thought it was the quickest means of getting to the front in field hospital service and most of them enlisted to do some form of specialized work; but, medical students, college professors, and motor experts, they each and all were given the job of hospital orderly which means scrubbing floors, washing windows, shovelling coal, doing the hard and dirty work of a hospital, and, most galling I fancy of all,—taking orders from girls with whom you are not allowed to associate or even speak except in the line of business. The X-ray expert has been delegated to the job of keeping the hospital pigs. I saw him in a pair of grimy overalls trundling a well-worn wheelbarrow down the street. The man who speaks eight languages, and enlisted as interpreter, spends his days checking up clothes in the laundry. And here as hospital orderlies in spite of their frantic efforts to get transferred, it seems likely that they will stay.

But these are dark days for us all just now, with the news that comes in every day of the German drive. "What do the officers in the hospital think? What do they say about it?" I tease the nurses.

"They think that we will hold them," they reply, but none too hopefully.

At the hotel where I am staying there is a French officer *en permission*, with his wife and apparently unlimited offspring. With them is an English governess. She is a little nervous thing all a-twitter these days with excitement and apprehension. Will the Germans get through to Paris? Monsieur's aged mother is there. He is thinking of going back to get her, together with a few essential household treasures. She herself had fled with the family from

Paris in 1914. It was a dreadful experience; fourteen people crowded in a coach for six, and nothing to eat. Oh dear! wasn't it all just too terrible!

There is also an old French lady here who frankly fled from Paris to escape the air-raids; now someone has taken all the joy out of life for her by suggesting that Etretat might be shelled from the sea by a German submarine.

The Tommies in the hospitals, they say, flatly refuse to believe that Paris is being shelled. It isn't possible, they declare, for a gun to shoot as far as that, and to them that is the end of it. But tonight a little crowd of the hospital boys who had gone on pass to Paris came back as eye-witnesses. One of the first shells had fallen very close to them, killing a number of people who were sitting drinking in a sidewalk café. The boys had gone up to the Church of Sacré Cœur on Montmartre and from the tower there had watched the shelling of the city. It had been a beautiful clear day: they could see where each shell struck. One of the boys brought back with him for a souvenir a piece of a French lieutenant's skull, picked up, after the shell had wrecked the café, from the sidewalk.

Tonight there was a concert at the Y hut here. The hall was crowded; the concert party, a group of pretty girls, had just completed, to much applause, the first number, when a horn sounded in the distance. Everybody started up. The Y man stepped forward and announced the programme over. In a few minutes the hut was deserted. "The convoy is in," they said, which meant that a train load of wounded had arrived at the station.

Paris, Easter Sunday.

On the way here from Etretat I saw a sight which brought the war closer to me somehow than anything before; at the junction station connecting the line to Le Havre with the line to Amiens, a string of box cars full of women, little children and decrepit old men, packed in like cattle, fleeing before the German drive, many of them empty-handed, others with a few pathetic futile treasures, a hen or two, a copper cooking-pot, snatched up evidently in a moment of half-witless panic haste.

Nor is Paris itself without its refugees. The German advance, the air-raids, the shelling, culminating in the Good Friday horror, have combined to render the city half deserted.

"Paris? We call Paris 'the front' now-a-days," one Frenchman on the journey had remarked to me.

Yesterday I went shopping. Everywhere it was the same reply. Nothing could be made to order for an indefinite period, the workrooms were all deserted, the workers fled. As for those who remain, they seem to take life calmly enough; what else can they do? When, as yesterday, every sixteen minutes a tremendous jarring crash tells you that a shell has fallen somewhere in the city,—and the concussion is so great that it always sounds as if it had fallen in the next block!—you see people turn their heads as they walk, staring in the direction of the explosion; others come out on the balconies to see what they can see and that is all.

Of course the danger of all this lies in its effect on the civilian morale. In connection with this I learned an interesting thing today. While the hospitals outside are overcrowded, the hospitals in Paris with their splendid equipment and staffs are left half empty, because they dare not show the people of Paris too many wounded. And when convoys are brought into the city, they are often detained outside, sometimes for hours, in order that the wounded may be transferred to the hospitals at night.

Yesterday at Brentano's I got talking with a boy who belonged to the American Ambulance Section which is attached to the French. He told me an incident which struck my fancy:

One night, at the front, after a hard day's work, he had just dropped off to sleep when he was awakened. There was a *blessé* to be taken back to the hospital, he was in bad shape, they had placed him in an ambulance. The boy rolled out of his blankets, started up the car. It was a bitter night. Once he was on his way everything went wrong; the water had frozen in the radiator, he had to get out and crawl along the ditches on his hands and knees, trying, in the dark to find a pool that was still unfrozen. And all the while he was tortured by the thought that the life of the wounded man in the car depended probably on his speed in reaching the hospital, and this urged him to an agony of haste. Finally, as the dawn was breaking, he reached his goal. They came to carry the blesse in. The wounded man was dead; he had been dead, it was evident, some while before the boy started. At the front, he explained, they hate to take the time and trouble to bury bodies. So whenever it is possible they work this method of passing on the task to someone else. You have to be constantly on the look-out for such tricks. This time they had fooled him.

Last night there was an air-raid. It was a mild affair. I was awakened by the sirens. They make what is to me quite the most fascinatingly horrible sound I have ever heard. That long agonized wail, now sinking to a shuddering whimper, now rising to a banshee screech, flashes vividly to my mind's eye a myriad little demons sitting on the roofs of Paris, cowering, shivering, crying out their abject terror. I went to the window and looked out, but although my room is on the top floor of the hotel, I could see nothing and so went back to bed again. The anti-aircraft guns put up a tremendous barrage; they have them mounted on trucks now so they can quickly be shifted from point to point about the city. I am sure there was a whole battery just in front of the hotel. Today the papers inform us that the Gothas were driven back after reaching the suburbs.

This morning I went to service at Notre Dame, entering through piles of sand bags heaped so as to hide the carvings about the doorways. In that vast cathedral only a few were present, a fair share of the congregation being comprised of Americans.

Tonight an ambulance driver attached to one of the Paris hospitals came to the hotel for dinner. He spread a startling tale. Every ambulance in the city has been ordered to be in readiness; for tomorrow, it has been learned, twenty-seven long-range guns are to be turned at once on Paris!

Aix-les-Bains, April 6.

When they said "Leave Area" to me my heart sank. The Lady in the Office explained to me how very important she considered the work, and the assignment, she added, need not be permanent. "Very well" I said, "I'm willing to go there temporarily."

I left Paris Tuesday, taking the night train. Getting off was something of an ordeal. The lighting at the stations, as on the streets, has been reduced almost to the vanishing point. The great Gare de Lyon was filled with a mass of distraught humanity over whom the few violet-blue bulbs cast a ghostly glimmer. There were no porters to take one's luggage; a number of women had possessed themselves of the baggage trucks and were pushing them, heaped high with bags and household stuff, recklessly through the crowds. I could find no officials anywhere about. All the French orderliness and red tape seemed to have been swept clean away and the result was chaos. Somehow, I don't know quite how, I found my train and reached my seat.

Three very fat old gentlemen and one old lady occupied the compartment with me. The fat gentlemen had one little spoiled dog between them which they kept passing from one to the other, in order that each in turn might kiss him. The old lady had a bird in a cage; presently she opened her hand-bag and brought out her supper, a loaf of bread, unwrapped, together with a good-sized turtle. For a moment; such were her raptures over her pet, I thought that she was going to kiss the turtle. The first minute that one of my companions entered the compartment, each informed all the rest that he or she was *not* running away from the air-raids or the long range guns. "I? I am not afraid of the Kaiser's Gothas! I laugh at them!" A few minutes later however they began: Ah, what a fearful night, last night had been! Five hours in the *Caves*! No sleep at all! One might as well be a mole and take up one's dwelling underground. What a life! Oh it was terrible, terrible! Then one old gentleman turned proudly to the little fat canine. "But of a verity, my little Toto is possessed of a sagacity extraordinary. The moment that he hears the sirens, he will run down into the cellar, and nothing can induce him to come up again until the 'all clear' has sounded!"

We pulled into Aix soon after dawn as the rising sun was touching the tops of the mountains and the morning mists were hovering over the lake. Whatever the work may prove to be like here, the place is surpassingly lovely. It is too early for the summer resort pleasure seekers. The French don't care for it here until it grows really hot, they tell us. But to me the season is at its most appealing moment. One glimpses pink peach blossoms against the blue lake over which stand purple mountains with snow still lying on their summits. Several of the large hotels and casinos have been requisitioned for French convalescent hospitals, but the largest of all has been taken over by the Y. From this canteen excursions are constantly setting out, motor-boats on the lake, motor cars to Chambery, the cog-wheel railway up Mt. Revard, picnics, hikes and fishing parties, yet many of the boys seem to find it pleasantest to do nothing,—just to sit around in lazy comfort all day long, watching the others playing billiards, listening to the orchestra in the afternoon Beneath the gold mosaic casino dome, sitting luxuriously in a box at the vaudeville in the evening, gaining a maximum of pleasure with a minimum of exertion. Many of the boys came here with their heads full of pessimistic expectations.

"They told us it would be Reveille and Retreat and one day's K. P. for each of us," confided one lad to me.

Some brought their mess-kits and some even their blankets. When they find themselves guests in hotels that are among the finest in Europe, lodged in comfortable rooms, eating real food off tables furnished with china-ware and linen, at first they are fairly dazed.

"I'm feared somebody'll pinch me an' I'll wake up," declared one lad today.

More than one has told me, that the first night he got here, he could not go to sleep in bed at all and only finally achieved slumber by rolling himself in blankets on the floor.

There are no troops from the line here at present; only boys from forestry regiments, motor mechanics and a few lads from medical detachments. They are holding up the leaves of all combatant troops on account of the drive. It may be that presently they will hold up all leaves altogether. Then we will have to shut up shop here temporarily.

It is the pleasant custom here for the Y ladies to go down to the train every night to see the boys off.

"It's a shame you can't stay longer," we say to them.

"I'll say it is!"

"I'm awfully sorry you have to go."

"You ain't half so sorry as I am, Lady."

"Maybe some day you'll be coming back again."

"I'll tell the world one thing; I'm going to be good as gold when I get back to camp, so they'll let me."

One of the Y women tonight repeated what one boy on leaving had confided to her:

"If I said to you that this had been my happiest week since I joined the army it wouldn't mean much," he told her, "but that's not what I'm going to say. What I'm going to say is that this has been the happiest week of all my life."

So far I have found just one man who wasn't enjoying himself here. He had been stationed for six months at Paris. Aix, he declared, "Weren't no town at all, nothin' but a one-horse place." He evidently had no soul for the beauties of nature.

Paris, April 22.

They held the leaves up. The boys kept leaving; fewer and fewer came, then finally none. Last week they disbanded the force of workers at Aix; a few stayed to look after things until such time as the crowds should start to pour in again; the rest were sent back to Paris to be reassigned.

If I thought the trip down was a chore, it wasn't a patch on the trip back. We waited half the night for the train at the Aix railway station. When it finally pulled in, I found my seat was in a compartment which was full, and had evidently been so for hours, of French people. Now life in France tends to cure you of belief in several popular superstitions; one is the idea that it is dangerous to have wet feet, and another that there is anything in the germ theory; but there is one notion to which I still cling, an obstinate belief in the desirability of fresh air. I put my head in the compartment, then withdrew, shutting the door. For the twelve hours it took to reach Paris I stood up outside in the corridor.

Arrived in Paris, they assigned me temporarily to the Avenue Montaigne Club House. This is a beautiful building, the home of one of Napoleon's generals; but the best thing about it is the tea-room restaurant, for here they serve apple-pie, chocolate cake and ice-cream. Since the latest food restrictions were issued, forbidding the French to make desserts employing milk, cream, sugar, eggs or flour, such dainties have been unobtainable anywhere else in Paris; but the Americans drawing supplies from their own commissary, are of course untouched by such regulations. Indeed the saddest sign in France these days I often think is that over the deserted shops which reads *Patisserie*. To be sure some of these stores still make a show at doing business, filling their windows with raisins, dried prunes and other prosaic edibles, together with heaps of pseudo-chocolates wrapped gayly in tin-foil, but which when purchased proved to be nothing but what one boy termed "the same old camouflage,"—an unappetizing paste of dried fruits and ground nuts. Yesterday a curly-headed lad, who looked about sixteen, came into the canteen carrying a big bunch of pink carnations. These were for the waitresses, he said, because they were the first American ladies that he had seen in France. We each pinned a spray to the front of our pink aprons, and then, since he pretended famine, let him have "seconds",—quite against the rules—on everything, with all the ice-cream and cake that he could swallow.

Yesterday I saw Mr. T. who was with us for a while at Goncourt. He told me that French troops *en repos* were occupying that area at present. They had asked for the use of our hut and of course it had been granted them. A Y man, happening by the other day, had stopped in. They had converted our beautiful hut into a regular French *Cantine* with three men to hand the bottles over the counter "and a smell enough to knock you down." Who shall say that this is the least of life's little ironies?

This morning I met N. who had reached Rattentout the day I left. She tells me that all the villages occupied by our troops in the sector have, one by one, been shelled. Rattentout was shelled and two Frenchwomen killed. Because of the constant shelling all the Y women workers had been withdrawn from the canteens and sent back to safety at Souilly where they have nothing to do but sit and possess their souls in patience.

Tonight they gave me my new assignment. It is at Gondrecourt. I leave tomorrow. I am glad, so glad over the prospect of being back on a real job once more! Here at the Avenue Montaigne as in the gilded casino at Aix I have been desperately homesick, to be back in a real hut again!

CHAPTER IV
GONDRECOURT—THE ARTILLERY

Gondrecourt, April 28.

Gondrecourt is quite a place. It boasts a brewery, a hotel, a mediœval tower and a number of little stores. Each one of these stores contains at least one pretty girl on its selling force and the ratio between the sales of goods and the charms of the ladies is, I fancy, quite exact. From the military point of view Gondrecourt is important as being the site of the First Army Corps Training Schools. But to me the really distinguishing feature of Gondrecourt is the fact that it boasts a bath-tub. If anybody had said bath-tub to me the day before I arrived here, I would have said with the doughboy that,—short of Paris—"there ain't no such animal." But now I have beheld it with my own eyes, a white-enamelled bath-tub, a Y. M. C. A. bath-tub, in the basement at Headquarters. The tub is supposed to be a strictly family affair,—on the door are posted hours for the Lady Secretaries and hours for the Men Secretaries,—but in spite of the plain English before their eyes, it seems that army officers occasionally slip in and steal a bath off us, yes, even impinging on the sacred bath hours of the ladies!

My first day here they sent me to "The Café." This was once a very wild place indeed. When the Y. first came to Gondrecourt it tried to buy the proprietor out, but the proprietor refused; he was doing too profitable a business. Then one night Providence sent some Boche planes wandering in this direction. There was a panic among the populace; the proprietor, with visions of his place wrecked by a bomb, sold out in a hurry and left town. Since then the Cafe has led a reformed and decorous existence but the old name still clings. My second day I spent at the "Double Hut," the big hut built up on the hill close by the Infantry School. The third day I was introduced to my own canteen.

According to directions, I climbed the hill by my billet, went past the athletic field, past the warehouse and out along the edge of the rolling open upland. About half a mile out of town I came to a group of seven French barracks, covered with black tar paper, built at the edge of the railway cut. This was the Artillery School. I crossed the field, entered the nearest barracks which bore a Y. sign at one end, and found myself in a Greenwich Village Tea House. I stood and stared. Some modern-school interior decorator had been at work. The place was a riot of red, yellow, salmon-color and black, worked out from a nasturtium motif. In the wall panels were paintings, some conventionalized fruits and flowers, evidently done by the decorator; others, landscapes, Japanese scenes and some rather awful Indians just as evidently executed by the boys. The whole effect to be sure was a bit sketchy and in spots frankly unfinished, and yet to one used to such simplicity in the huts as I, the *ensemble* was startling. Back of the black and orange partition which screens the canteen and the kitchen from the hut proper, I found the staff, secretary and canteen worker. The lady whom I am to replace, it appears, belongs in reality to the Motor Transport Section. She turned canteen worker to help out in a pinch, and now is anxious to return again.

When dinnertime came the Motor Transport girl told me that we had been invited to dine at the camp. We went over to the mess-hall. "Let's help feed the chow-line for a lark!" said the M. T. girl. So we stood behind the serving-bench and ladled out big spoonfuls of mashed potato and gravy. This amused the boys immensely; and as they passed they would sing out:

"When did they put *you* on K. P?"

"What have *you* done to deserve this?"

The kitchen was white-washed and specklessly clean, the earth floor was covered with cinders. These cinders which are in use for floors and walks in all the camps about, come, I am told, from a great heap down by the river which marks the site of one of Napoleon's cannon foundries.

"Why are the boxers in a company always found on the kitchen force?" I asked one of the cooks.

"That's so they can handle the boys when they come back for seconds."

As soon as the chow-line had been fed, the M. T. girl and I had ours with the Top Sergeant. After dinner the Top Sergeant, who had formerly been mess sergeant, was moved to unburden his soul as to the sorrows of a mess sergeant.

"When I was mess sergeant," he reminisced, "I sure got to know the way to a man's heart all right. Why, the days when I gave them a good dinner there wasn't a man in camp who wouldn't positively beam at me; but if something had gone wrong and the chow wasn't up to scratch, half the fellers in the company wouldn't speak to me the rest of the day."

Then he grinned. "I wouldn't want Mother to know the way I used to get stuff for the boys last winter."

He went on to tell us. French freight trains have no brakemen and the conductor rides in a caboose directly behind the coal car. Trains pulling into town from the north hit a grade curve close to the camp, up which they must pull very slowly. The camp guard kept a lookout; when a freight train with flat cars was sighted, word was immediately passed to the mess sergeant who with a number of K. P.s hurried to the tracks and boarded the slow-moving train; if the cars proved to hold anything of value for the mess,—be it coal or cabbages,—all the way up the grade the sergeant and his assistants were busy, hastily throwing or shoveling what they could over the sides of the cars. At the top of the grade they would jump off and returning along the tracks, gather up the spoils.

Tomorrow the Motor Transport girl departs and I "take over" the canteen.

Gondrecourt, May 4.

The Artillery School consists of some few hundred officers and non-coms enrolled for each four-weeks' course, in addition to the two batteries who are here for demonstration work; Battery D from a regiment of "75s" and Battery A from a regiment of the big "155s." Selected for this exhibition work on account of their exceptional ability, they are, I suppose, the equal of any batteries in the world. When the boys enlisted these batteries were declared to be about to be "motorized," but at present the motor power is being supplied by a particularly unresponsive set of French cart horses, whose daily care is the greatest trial of the boys' lives. Last night we had a movie-show; one reel gave the story of a discontented boy on the farm—showing him at one moment disgustedly grooming Dobbin. For a full minute it seemed as if the roof of the hut was going to be lifted right off.

The officers' quarters and the class-rooms lie across the railroad track from the camp, in the grounds of the Château. Here they have a canteen of their own, a cool little place in cream color and blue presided over by a most refreshing and delightful English lady. The Château itself was partially destroyed by fire a few years ago and though the lower story is available for offices, the upper story stands roofless, with empty windows staring against the sky. Every now and then a rumour goes the rounds:—Pershing is going to move his headquarters to Gondrecourt,—the Château is to be repaired for his use! The Château and the school buildings stand on high ground. To the south the ground falls away suddenly; below is "off limits" and is Fairyland. Here are meadows warm with the color of spring flowers, here are groves such as one sees in the pictures of Eighteenth Century shepherds and shepherdesses, and here is the river flowing so placidly that its waters seem to form still lagoons, white-flecked with swans and arched with rustic bridges. Here while the boys are at their mess, I have been stealing to eat my picnic supper; an orange, a sandwich and a piece of chocolate. The guard walking post at the foot of the embankment shuts one eye as I go past,—and usually gets half of my supper! For that matter I gather he is there largely for the sake of appearance, for there's not a boy in camp I'm sure who hasn't explored those groves, fed the swans, and angled for fish in the river. And the only reason, I'm certain, that they don't surreptitiously go in swimming there is that the water, fed by springs, is cold as ice! Nor is the touch of romance that should go with such a setting absent. One of the cooks in the officers' mess kitchen is deep in an affair with Lucile, the caretaker's daughter, a girl like a wild rose, shy, slender, freshly-tinted. Every other night when he is off duty he carries her chocolate from the canteen and she "gives him a French lesson."

"Serious?" I asked inquisitively.

"Fat chance!" he glowered at me frankly. "She tells me that she's engaged to twelve fellows now already and that twelve's enough."

The proprietor of the Château, Monsieur S., has the distinction of being the father of ten girls. I like to fancy that the spirits of the ten lovely daughters,—for lovely they must be, as no Frenchman, I am sure, would have the courage to father ten homely ones!—haunt the Château gardens.

The boys, however, don't have to rely on phantoms for thrills of this sort. Yesterday, they tell me, that during the progress of an exciting ball-game on the Y. athletic field a beautiful lady dressed *à la Parisienne* strolled by. The batter dropped his bat, the pitcher forgot his ball; the game came to a dead halt until the beautiful lady had passed out of sight.

Gondrecourt, May 13.

The Secretary is sick. He lies in his little bed-room office and reads the latest magazines and gossips with his visitors while I attempt to run the hut single-handed. At times during this last week I have been strongly tempted to get sick myself. Indeed I think I probably would have done so if it hadn't been for Snow. Snow, Snowball or Ivory as he is variously called, is Battery D's albino cook. "Say, ain't I the whitest-haired beggar you ever did see?" he asked me the other day in a sort of naive wonder at himself. "Anyway, nobody ever had a cleaner-looking cook," remarked the Top Sergeant, ex-Mess Sergeant. Snow has the sweetest disposition in the world. "If Snow was starving to death," declared one of the boys to me today, "and somebody gave him a sandwich, and he thought you were the least bit hungry, he'd give you that sandwich." Ever since the Secretary has been sick, Snow has been bringing him toast and eggs and things while he has brought me lemon pies, the most wonderful lemon pies that ever I tasted. Already Snow has come to be looked upon by the boys as an authority on all things pertaining to the canteen and has to stand a battery of searching questions, such as, whether he thinks that my hair is really all my own?

Just to add to all our other troubles this week we have run amuck of the Major. This I suspect was all my fault. I was furious because when he came into the hut he made the boys stand at attention. This was something I had never seen done before and is, I am sure, contrary to all the rules. I was so angry that when the Major came up to the counter I stood and glared at him.

"You will find the Secretary in his office," I said and turned and walked out the back door. It was the Major's turn to be angry then. He stalked out behind the counter, looking for trouble, and began to hold an inspection in the kitchen. The Secretary appeared, the Major let loose. That kitchen, he declared, was not up to army standards in cleanliness. This was a matter of utmost importance. Hereafter the medical officer would inspect the kitchen daily. Then he proceeded to prescribe a schedule of canteen hours outside of which nothing at all must be sold.

Now I admit that kitchen hasn't been quite all it might be. It is a small, overcrowded place, built of rough dirty boards and there are no shelves, nor of course running water, nor conveniences of any kind. Moreover, the Major, I learn, has the reputation of being a tartar in this respect; "Major Mess Kit" they call him because of the rigour of his inspections.

The next morning the medical officer arrived at the crack of dawn. He found the chocolate cups from the night before unwashed. He was shocked. He too read the Secretary a lecture. Then he departed to do the sensible, the saving thing, which was to recommend to the Major that we be allowed a detail. So it all worked out for the best in the end. "Neddy" as we have christened the detail is now a part of the family. A shy, dreamy lad, he is at hand to help from early morning until closing time at nine at night, and I actually have to shoo him out to his meals. The only trouble with Neddy is that he is so good I am sure that he is going to die young. And besides Neddy I now have a pet bugaboo. This has proved so useful these last few days that I don't know how I ever kept a canteen without one. Now any time that officers come to my kitchen door to tease for cigarettes out of selling hours I can gleefully tell them:

"Oh, but I wouldn't dare! The Major, you know! He's expressly forbidden it! If I did and he learned about it, he would surely have me court-martialed!"

Of course when the boys come out of hours that is quite a different matter.

Then, too, as the Major is detested by the men, this furnishes a common bond of sympathy. This morning a boy came to my back door to borrow our axe in order to chop up the Major's wood.

"You can have it on one condition," I told him.

"What's that?"

"That you chop off the Major's head with it too."

Gondrecourt, May 24.

I have always cherished a secret longing to have pets in my canteen: I have heard of huts that kept kittens and canaries, and once I visited in one where an ant-eater, if not an *habitué*, was at least a frequent and honoured guest and sat in the ladies' laps at the movie-shows. At various times I have considered and regretfully abandoned the project of rabbits, a puppy, goldfish and a goat. But till recently the nearest I have come to realizing my dreams was when I found two large snails with black and yellow shells by the roadside. I carried them into the canteen and set them on a flowering branch in a vase. For two days the boys took a casual interest. They nicknamed them Bill and Daisy.

"The French eat snails you know," I told them.

"You don't say!"

"Yes and I had some myself the other day."

"Aw shucks! You didn't *really*, did you? Why, before I'd eat them things! Say, what did they taste like anyway?"

"They would have tasted pretty good," I answered, "if only while you were eating them you could have stopped thinking what they were!"

One boy staring at my pets asked innocently;

"Will butterflies come but of those?"

After the snails our only livestock for a while was the canteen rat, whom I have never met myself, but of whom I have heard large rumours. The other day however I received a present of two real pets. One of the Y. drivers had been out to a wood-cutting camp in the forest. There an Italian lad had given him two young birds in a beautiful cage he had made himself with nothing but a pen-knife and a hot wire, and the driver brought the birds to me. I don't know what sort they were but they were tame and most amusing. To feed them was the immediate question. I asked the boys to dig me some earth worms, but this they seemed to consider beneath their dignity. Finally Neddy went out with a can, only to return wormless. He couldn't find any, he declared. I considered the advisability of asking the Top Sergeant for a worm-digging detail, but decided against it. Then I confided my troubles to my friend, the Warehouse Man.

"I know," he said, "I'll ask Pierre."

Now Pierre is a little orphan refugee from the devastated district. He lives with one of the families on the edge of the town and I am afraid is none too well treated. When he isn't herding the cows over the meadows, he is usually hanging about the warehouse. A handsome, rather wild looking lad, dressed in a brown cap and an old brown suit, I always think of him as Peter Pan. The next morning Pierre appeared at my kitchen door with a can full of long fat wriggly angleworms and had his pockets filled with chocolate by way of recompense. Later I learned that the Warehouse Man, not being able to pronounce the French word for birds, had told Pierre that I wanted the worms for fishing, and Pierre after taking one look at the bird-cage had gone straight back and told the Warehouse Man that he was a liar. But cunning as my pets were, I couldn't quite reconcile myself to the idea of keeping wild birds in a cage. This morning I looked at Neddy:

"Let's let them out."

"Let's," he answered.

Now the only pet I have in prospect is the baby wild boar which a boy from one of the aviation camps nearby has promised me.

Gondrecourt, June 2.

Night before last, at half-past ten, as I was sitting here in my billet trying to write a letter, I heard a voice calling me from the street below.

"What is it?"

"It's Sergeant B—. I've brought you a gas-mask."

"What!"

"There's a bunch of German planes headed in this direction. They're afraid of gas bombs. We got the alarm out at the school."

I went down to the door. The sergeant gave me two gas-masks. I gave one to the English lady who has the room across the hall from me. Then I sat up waiting for the fun to begin. Nothing happened. I went to sleep with the gas-mask lying on the pillow beside me.

The next morning the Chief declared that all the Y. personnel here must go to gas drill and have masks issued to them. Last night they rounded us up for a lesson. We stood in a big circle at the Gas School over on the hill while the gas instructors instructed us and the boys looked on and grinned. Gas drill consists of learning how to put on and take off your mask in the prescribed and formal manner. It is all done by count. If you can't do it in six seconds you are a casualty. As we popped our masks on and pulled them off again the hair of all the ladies present proceeded to slowly but relentlessly fall down their backs. The English Lady stood next to me. "It's all stuff and nonsense," I could hear her muttering; "stuff and nonsense!"

The noncom instructors walked around and informed each and all of us that if we didn't change the style of our coiffures we certainly would get gassed.

"And now," said the instructor cheerfully, "I am going to send you through the gas-house."

I looked desperately for a chance to sneak away, but there wasn't any; besides, several boys from my batteries were watching.

"Oh this is nothing, nothing at all," declared the instructor. "We've only got the tear gas on tonight. You will go through once with your masks on, and then a second time without them." We put our masks on and marched in a long line into the gas-house. There was a table in the middle with candles burning on it, which gleamed golden through the thick yellowish clouds of gas. We marched around the table and out again. There was nothing to it; the masks were a perfect protection.

"Now," said the instructor," you will go through without your masks. This is to give you confidence in them." The idea being that discovering how very nasty it was without one, you would be taught to appreciate the blessing of a mask. I had an inspiration. I would shut my eyes and hang on to the man in front of me! But alas, for my pretty plan, the line was too long; as I was about to enter: "Break the line here!" shouted the instructor. I had to lead the second line into the gas house. I made double-quick time around that table. Just as I was about to dart out the door an English noncom instructor seized my arm and, halting me, started to explain something.

"Yes, yes," I choked. "It's all very interesting, but I don't feel like stopping now!" I pulled away and made a break out the door. I was weeping horribly. My eyes felt as if someone had rubbed onion juice on them. They stung and burned for hours afterward.

"The next time," said the instructor genially, "we'll put you through the mustard gas."

Now in the mustard gas lesson a fellow must walk into the gas-house without his mask, and put it on after he has entered. If he fails to hold his breath long enough, or is nervous and clumsy and so doesn't get his mask on quickly enough, why it means a trip to the hospital for him. The mustard gas test is an ordeal which causes the boys considerable apprehension.

"Oh thank you! You're very kind," I said.

As we took our departure down the hill I noticed a darky doughboy in a group who were drilling. He was in an awful fix; every time he tried to fasten the nose-clip on his nostrils, it would slip right off again!

When the next lesson is held I have decided to be among the missing.

Gondrecourt June 9.

We have a new detail. His name is Jones. About six weeks ago he was kicked by a mule and had three of his ribs broken. He was sent to the hospital at Neufchateau. Learning that there was a chance that his battery might be sent to the front shortly, he pestered the docters until they let him go, his besetting fear being that he might become separated from his outfit. He returned three days ago. The next day he went out on the range as one of a gun crew. Yesterday he came into the hut and collapsed. The Secretary put him on his bed where he spent the rest of the day. Moved by purely altruistic motives, the Secretary then went to his captain and asked that Jones be assigned to the Y. as a supplementary detail. Now this is very nice for Jones, but I am not so sure whether it is nice for the Y. Jones, it seems, goes by the nickname of "Mildred." At one period of his past life he was engaged in selling soap, a fact which inspires the boys to shout at frequent intervals: "Three cheers for Jones! Soap! Soap! Soap!" He brings echoes of his commercial training to the canteen counter. No east-side shopkeeper was ever more anxious to make sales than he. If a boy asks for tooth-paste when we happen to be out of it, he is sure to answer:

"No, but we have some very fine shoe polish."

Or if somebody wants talcum powder when talcum there is none:

"I'm sorry we're out of it today, but can't I interest you in some tomato ketchup?"

Some day I think I shall write on essay on the psychology of suggestion as demonstrated in canteen sales. Nothing, it seems, ever really wins the boys' approval unless it bears the label; "Made in the U. S. A."—nothing that is, with the possible exception of eggs. Anything originating in Europe, from mustard to matches, is looked upon with a certain amount of suspicion, while goods coming from America are hailed with an enthusiasm often quite inconsistent with their quality. The other day we put a case of "Fig Newtons" on sale. The news flashed all over town. As one of the boys said; "Why it was just as if General Pershing or somebody's mother had come to camp."

Lately we have had for sale quantities of fat French cookies. Some of the boys are mean enough to suggest that these were baked before the war.

"Those cookies ought to wear service stripes," one boy declared.

So "Service Stripe Cookies" they have been ever since.

"They're all right for eating," observed another customer solemnly, "but the Lord help you if you drop one on your toe!" This morning when I reached the hut I found Jones languidly washing dishes.

"Where's Neddy?"

"Neddy? Why he's in the guard-house."

For a moment I was goose enough to believe it, then I learned that Neddy, with a lieutenant and some twenty other boys, had all gone off, the day being Sunday, on single mounts to Domremy to visit the birthplace of Jeanne D'Arc. Late in the afternoon the little cavalcade returned.

"Neddy," I teased, "I hear you've been in the guard-house."

To my astonishment Neddy's mouth twitched, his eyes filled. "I wish I'd never gone!" he blurted out.

"Why, what's the matter?"

Then the whole pitiful tale was unfolded. Neddy hadn't any money, not a clacker, and being too shy to ask for a loan, he had gone on the trip with empty pockets. He hadn't been able to buy himself a bite of dinner. But that wasn't what hurt. What hurt was that he couldn't purchase any souvenirs for his girl, and there had been so many enticing ones!

"Gee," he moaned, "but that's an awful place for a feller to go who hasn't any money."

Then, just as the last straw of misery, his horse had been taken sick on the way home!

We are going through one of those painful periods of pecuniary depletion which are periodic in the army, the inevitable prelude to payday. In Battery A there are two lads whom I have privately dubbed Tweedledum and Tweedledee. They are both short, roly-poly and always smiling and they are absolutely inseparable. When either of them buys anything at the canteen he always buys double; two packets of cigarettes, two "bunches" of gum, two cups of hot chocolate "one for me and one for my friend" as the stock phrase goes. This morning I received a shock. Tweedledum asked for *one* bar of chocolate and *one* package of cigarettes.

"What's the matter?" I asked, thinking alarmedly of how in the immortal poem "Tweedledum and Tweedledee agreed to have a battle,"—"You and your buddy haven't quarrelled, have you?"

"No ma'am, oh no indeed ma'am! It's just that it's an awful long ways from payday!"

Later I saw them carefully dividing the purchases between them. I leaned over the counter, beckoned to Tweedledee.

"You boys go around to the back door, but don't let anybody see you!"

At the back door I gave them each a slice of Snow's latest lemon pie.

Tonight the Major suddenly made his appearance in the kitchen to find Snow, Neddy and myself all sitting on the floor sorting out rotten oranges. Snow and Neddy faded away out the back door, but I stood my ground. For once his Majorship was pleased to be gracious. He complimented me on the improvement in the appearance of my kitchen. Indeed we did look pretty fine, Neddy having just covered the shelves with newspapers whose edges he had cut into beautiful fancy scalloping.

"What do you do with those over-ripe oranges?"

"Put them in a box outside the back door."

"Well? What then?"

"The French children do the rest, sir."

But the boys are more incensed than ever against the Powers That Be. They have been writing too many letters of late for the censor's comfort. So yesterday at Retreat the order was read out that no boy might write more than two letters and one postal card per week!

Gondrecourt, June 13.

The School has closed. It is common knowledge that the two batteries will soon join their respective regiments at the front. Curiously enough, here with the artillery I have never had that same feeling of closeness to the war which I had when I was with the doughboys. The attitude of the men here is so much more detached, impersonal. I fancy this is because, however dangerous their work may be, they do not look forward to any actual physical conflict. It is the imaginative image of "Heinie" with a bayonet thrusting at his breast which makes the front so vivid in anticipation to the doughboy.

But now with the news from Château Thierry there is a certain tenseness everywhere. One feels that the hour is close at hand when every man that Uncle Sam has in France may be needed. The barking of the guns at practice has taken on a new significance. Yesterday indeed it just missed implying tragedy. Shortly after the jarring thunder of the "75s" had started our dishes in the kitchen to rattling, came a frantic message by telephone. A party of engineers were surveying for the narrow-gauge railway just beyond the hill over which the battery was shooting. One shell had narrowly missed them.

Today an aviator in a little Spad machine came down at our back door. He had lost his way, exhausted his gas, and was forced to descend. He had thought he was over Germany so his relief on finding himself among friendly faces may be imagined. But aviation doesn't mean what it used to any more to us. We have lost our aviator. Shortly after I came to Gondrecourt we began to have an aerial visitor. Every few days about sundown he would appear; flashing up over the eastern hill horizon, to circle the big open drill ground, dipping, soaring, playing all manner of madcap tricks just for the sheer joy of it, now he would sweep so low as almost to touch the ridgepole of the hut, then up, up again with a rush, waving his hand to us below as we waved and shouted with all our might up at him. The whole camp would turn out to see; it was one of the events of the day. "It's Lufberry," some one told me. Not long ago we read in the paper that Major Lufberry had been killed. We waited in suspense. Had it really been he? Would our aviator never come again? Night after night we watched for him; he never came.

The fields about, which have been golden with buttercups and primroses, white with daisies, and purple with flowers whose names I do not know, are now crimsoning with poppies. "Artillery flowers," the boys call them. They pick them and stick them jauntily in their overseas caps, or in great bunches, bring them to me to brighten the canteen.

Since the boys are going soon I have been trying desperately to make them extra special goodies; candy, stuffed dates, frosted cookies, and—what pleases them as much as anything—hard-boiled eggs. It has been a revelation to me here in France, the American appetite for eggs. The boys will walk miles to get them; they will cheerfully pay as high as two dollars a dozen for them. I buy twelve dozen at a time, carry them out to the canteen and boil them in the dishpan. Placed on sale they disappear in the winking of an eye, and then the cry is always, "Ain't you got no more?" Sometimes I take Neddy with me on my shopping expeditions; Neddy carries my market basket, smokes his pipe and looks as pleased as Punch. Today in our quest we stopped in at a store kept by two extremely pretty *Mademoiselles*. As we entered we were greeted by peals of girlish laughter. In a chair in the corner sat a tired M. P. fast asleep, his mouth wide-open; between his lips one of the pretty girls had just at that moment popped a round ripe strawberry.

Gondrecourt, June 18.

Besides the American Camp Hospital there is a French Hospital at Gondrecourt, a place with a hint of old-world flavour to it, the nursing being done by Sisters of Charity. Here through some freak of chance a week ago arrived sixteen Tommies from the English front, after having travelled half over the map of France. They were none too pleased to find themselves in a French Hospital and several, being walking cases, straightway deserted and sneaked over to the American Hospital only to be regretfully returned again. They have a little Algerian in a red fez with them whom they have nicknamed "Charlie Chaplin." Although intercourse between them is restricted entirely to sign language, the Tommies have adopted Charlie as their mascot and Charlie follows them about just like a dog.

My friend the English Lady, having little to do in her canteen since the School closed, has appointed herself as a sort of foster-mother to the whole cockney brood. She acts as interpreter and sometimes as intercessor, for the Tommies are impatient of the hospital discipline and cause the authorities frequent anxiety, helps the Sisters out in nursing them and, best of all, makes them tea at four o'clock or thereabouts, accompanying it with bread and butter sandwiches. Frankly, the Tommies think that they are little short of starved on the French Hospital rations, and the tea helps. When they can they sneak over to the American Hospital and beg a meal there, but such excursions are frowned upon by those in authority.

Yesterday the English Lady gave a tea party for the Tommies in her canteen. She arranged to have a truck go fetch them. To her astonishment, instead of one, two trucks appeared and instead of just the Englishmen, the whole hospital that was able to stand on two legs or one arrived with them; big black Algerians and Moroccans in every shade of duskiness and poilus by the half score. The hut was crowded, there weren't enough chairs to go around. The English Lady sent out a hurry call to bring up the reserves in refreshments. Neddy and I came over from our hut with our arms full of cups; more water was put on to boil for the tea, new packages of biscuits opened. Then while the water heated the English Lady took all the liveliest ones out for a walk through the Château grounds, while "Skipper", her detail, who is a clever pianist, entertained the rest with music. During the playing one enormous Algerian, as black as night, stared fascinated at the piano, then edged slowly nearer and nearer to finally lay one incredulous finger, with infinite caution on one of the end keys. He had evidently never seen such a thing before, and more than half suspected it was all magic.

Then the water boiled and we made the tea and carried cups and bowls of it around with canned milk and commissary sugar. The Frenchmen, true to type, with the scarcity of sugar in mind would only take one lump, until you invited them to have another, when each, with evident pleasure, took a second. As we could only muster six teaspoons between our two canteens to supply the whole company, we had to pass the spoons from guest to guest allowing each man just long enough for a good stir and then on to the next. The men with wounded arms got their neighbors to stir for them. With the tea we served sandwiches; these were a special treat to the poilus because they were made with American army bread. Now to my mind our white army bread is very poor and tasteless stuff in comparison with the grey well-flavored French war-bread, but the French, probably on account of the novelty, prize highly any scraps of the *pain Américaine* that they can obtain. "Why, they eat it just like cake!" one boy said to me. Besides the sandwiches, there were little cookies and candies and cigarettes and finally, the gift of an American officer who happened in, an orange for each man to take home with him.

When the tea was finished it was time for the guests to go. Crowded into the trucks they rolled out through the Château gates, the poilus smiling and waving their good hands, while the Tommies raised a ragged cheer.

As Neddy and I returned to our canteen we paused at the door of one of the barracks to listen to the band producing pandemonium within. This band is the pet project of Battery D, the dearest hope of Corporal R. who is theatrical producer, impresario, librettist, base soloist, and band leader for the battery. The instruments were finally assembled some ten days ago. The one thing required of a member seemed to be that he had never played that particular sort of an instrument before. For the last ten days the band has been practicing, mostly in the Y. They have always played the same tune, yet I have never been able to decide what that tune was. Now that the battery is going to the front, the instruments must be put in store and our budding band disbanded almost before it had begun. The instruments are to be interned at Abainville, the town next door. When the day comes to relinquish them the band is going to march all the way from Gondrecourt to Abainville in state, playing their one tune over and over.

Tonight Corporal R. sat on a barrel in the kitchen polishing his French horn with the Secretary's pink tooth-paste. It made excellent brass-polish he had discovered.

"It's too bad you can't take that band of yours up front," remarked Snow.

"What for?"

"'Cause it sure would make the boys feel like fighting."

Gondrecourt June 22.

The boys have gone! We saw the last battery off on the train tonight. The guns were loaded on flat cars, horses and men lodged together in the box cars, the boys sleeping under the horses' very noses and in danger of being nipped, it seemed to me, by an ill-tempered beast. The boys who were to sleep with the guns on the flat cars would be much better off I thought; they had made themselves cozy little nests of straw underneath the gun-carriages. Some of the boys in the box cars, I was pained to observe, had smuggled in bottles with them.

The English Lady and I had arrived at the station none too soon. We had no more than walked the length of the train, inspecting each car and wishing every boy Good-bye and Good-luck when the engine whistled and was off. We stood on the platform and waved to the boys who leaned from their cars and waved back until a curve in the track cut off our sight.

These last few days have been hectic. Wednesday was my birthday. Neddy found it out and told the boys. They had observed that I didn't have any raincoat; indeed rainy nights I was always embarrassed by the offer of half a dozen different rubber coats and ponchos to go home in; so they decided,—bless them!—to supply this lack. A crowd of non-coms went downtown; they took along one boy with them as a cloak model because he was about my height and "looked like a girl"; and they made him try on every raincoat in Gondrecourt. Finally they selected one, brought it back and made a ceremonious presentation. The raincoat is a beauty, and ever since I have worn it every day, rain or shine, just to show them how much I thought of it.

It was hard to part with little Neddy. The Secretary presented him with a farewell pipe. I clasped around his neck a chain bearing a little silver cross; it was to keep him safe, body and soul from harm. He was almost moved to tears. The Secretary and I, he told me, had been "like a little papa and a daddy to him," and then, flushing, joined in my laughter.

At the last moment one of the D Battery cooks came stealthily to the back door.

"Me an the other fellers in the kitchen," he confided *sotto voce,* "we wanted to do something to show you folks how much we thought of you. So we just made up our minds to send yer this."

This was a ten pound can of issue bacon.

The Secretary leaves tomorrow for Paris. He is going in order to buy himself some new clothes. It seems that all his belongings entrusted to the local laundresses disappeared one by one until he found himself reduced to a single set. Last night he washed these out himself and put them in the oven to dry. When he remembered them this morning it was to find nothing left but a little cinder heap.

The camp, for the present at least, is to be abandoned; the hut, for the army wishes to use the barracks elsewhere, torn down. In a few days the little Artillery School Canteen will be nothing but a memory.

CHAPTER V
ABAINVILLE—THE ENGINEERS

Abainville July 1.

"Abainville is going to be bombed off the face of the map." Every time anyone has mentioned Abainville in my hearing during the last six weeks they have wound up with some such prophecy as this. Abainville is an engineering camp, Abainville is the starting-point for the narrow-gauge system that is to supply a certain sector of the American front. Already the great car shops have been built and stand gaunt and staring with more glass in their glittering sides than I have seen on this side of the Atlantic. It is these shops in particular that are held to be such shining marks for enemy aircraft. Anyway we have this comfort that if the Boche gets us we will all go together, for the town is so tiny that if a bomb hit it anywhere, it would wreck the major part of the village and there isn't a single cellar in the whole vicinity!

Just at present Abainville is in a state of suspense. There is some question among those in high places as to whether after all the site, for such extensive operations as have been planned, is well selected. Work on the narrow-gauge goes on, but the work on the shops has been suspended. Everyone is anxiously awaiting the decision.

The hut, which is on the far edge of the camp, is a huge empty shell, for work on this too has been stopped pending developments. Up till the day I arrived the Y. was doing business in a tent near the highway, but being notified that the engineers were going to run a railway through that spot the next day, they had moved out and over to the unfinished hut in a hurry.

My billet has a fine central location,—at the corner of La Grande Rue and the national highway that runs through the town. My window overlooks what approximates the town square, an open dusty space, bounded on the south by the principal café, on the east by the butcher's shop, on the west by manure-heaps and on the north by my billet. In this square, it appears, all the village pig-killings take place. It is incredible and painful how many pigs of a marketable maturity a town no larger than Abainville can produce. Arguing from the frequency of the pig-killings I am convinced that if a census were taken Abainville would be found to contain more pigs than people.

Further down la Grande Rue one comes to the church and the town-hall. Upstairs in the Mairie my co-worker, Miss S., has her billet. Downstairs is the village school and the living apartments of the schoolmaster's family, refugees from the invaded territory. I peeped in at the empty schoolroom yesterday: on the wall was a large pictorial chart designed to impress upon the infant mind the advantages of drinking beer, cider and wine, rather than the more potent alcohols; a lesson vividly demonstrated by a series of cuts portraying a pair of guinea pigs. The guinea pig who indulged in cognac and kindred beverages was depicted in successive stages of inebriation until at the end he is shown expiring in all the horrors of delirium, while the prudent guinea pig who took nothing stronger than *vin, biére et cidre* is pictured first in a state of mild and genial intoxication, and then the "morning after" with all the zest of a good digestion and a clear conscience, breakfasting on a sober cabbage leaf.

The church next door to the Mairie is remarkable for nothing except the peculiar sound like a wheezing snore which may be heard every evening issuing from the belfry. At first this sound was a mystery to us. I inquired of Madame; she was blank.

"Perhaps," I suggested remembering how in medieval lore evil spirits were reputed to haunt church towers, "perhaps it is the devil in the belfry."

"But no!" cried Madame scandalized. "The devil doesn't live in Abainville!"

"To be sure," I amended hastily, "the devil is a Boche! He lives at Berlin."

"Mais, oui, oui, oui!"

But now the riddle has been read. The devil in the belfry is in reality an ancient owl, *une chouette*, who has inhabited the church tower time out of mind.

There is a Salvation Army hut here, the first one I have seen. It is down by the main road; the canteen occupies one end of a barracks, which is used as a store-house, then there is an ell containing the kitchen. The staff comprises one man and two women; they are pleasant people, "real home folks." Two or three times a week, for supplies are hard to obtain, they make pie or cake or doughnuts. On these nights, passing the hut on our way back from mess, one sees a long line stretching down the road, waiting patiently for the chance to get a piece of pie "like Mother used to make." Our relationships are cordial. We help each other out in the matter of change. They come to our hut for sweet chocolate and movies; we go to them, when our consciences will permit, for doughnuts. I only wish that one of their huts could be in every camp in France.

Abainville, July 8.

By courtesy of a group of officers we are messing at a house with a particularly noisome front-door gutter and the Most Beautiful Girl in France to wait on us. La Belle Marguerite, as I always think of her, is tall and stately with a lovely gracious bearing and a sensitive, responsive face; what's more, she only paints a little. She affects to speak no English but I suspect she understands a good deal. At meal times when we are present the officers never look twice at her, but any evening that one happens past the house one can see two cigarette ends gleaming from the darkness just inside the mess-room window: the officers are making up for lost time. Yesterday La Belle looked so pale and *distraite* at dinnertime that I was quite distressed, fancying heart-break. "Mademoiselle Marguerite is sad," I told Madame my hostess. Madame immediately went forth on a Visit of investigation. "Mademoiselle has the tooth-ache!" she announced on her return. Today at dinner, having finished our salade, we waited in vain for dessert. La Belle Marguerite, usually so prompt and so efficient, simply did not appear. After waiting until I grew tired I gave it up and left. Passing by the kitchen door I glanced inside. In front of the hearth stood Marguerite and a handsome Russian officer, and oh! the coquetry of her eyes, the seduction of her smiling, scarlet lips! It was evident that the mess in the next room was wiped as clean from her mind as if it never had been! Whether my messmates ever got their dessert or not I haven't heard.

Besides La Belle Marguerite, the one unique feature of our mess is a certain set of plates. These are French picture plates with jokes on them. The jokes are all of a gustatory nature and pertain to things which most people would prefer not to think about while they are eating. One rather striking design represents the proprietor of a Swiss resort hotel delicately sniffing a platter of fish as he says to the waitress:

"These trout are passe. Keep them for the customers who have colds in their heads."

On another an irate diner is exclaiming over an item on his bill:

"Three francs for a chicken! What's that?"

"Why that was the little chicken that Monsieur found in his egg!"

There is always an anxious moment of suspense whenever a guest comes to dinner, a moment in which one peeps furtively out of the corners of one's eyes to see whether the newcomer has noticed the picture on his plate, and if so, whether he has got the point. Sometimes the guest will ask to have the text translated for him and then there is an awkward pause.

The question of what to serve at the canteen is a vexed one these days as it is quite too hot for chocolate. By scouring the country we managed to procure several cases of lemons, and then found our work for the day laid out,—just squeezing them. A few days ago, however, a shipment of bottled fruit juices arrived at the warehouse; by mixing this syrup with water and a small amount of lemon a delicious drink can be obtained. The boys have dubbed it a dozen different names, "*Camouflage vin rouge*" being one of them, but "*pink lemonade*" is the title it commonly passes under. Already it has become famous and every drunk in camp if questioned as to how he came to be in that condition will unblushingly assert that it was through drinking "that Y. M. C. A. pink lemonade."

If we could only get ice! Yesterday I investigated the possibilities, to find that if one were very ill and in desperate need of it, could produce a certificate to that effect signed by half a dozen doctors, approved by the Sanitary Inspector, passed upon by the local Board of Health and sealed by the Mayor with the sanction of the Town Council, one could, by means of this document, procure at the brewery at Gondrecourt a piece of ice about as large as a small-sized egg. Somehow it doesn't seem quite worth the trouble.

Lacking ice, we do our best with freshly-drawn water which comes pleasantly cool from the deep wells drilled by American engineers to supply the camp,—when it does come. But often just when the thirsty ones are crowding thickest you make a frantic dash to the faucet only to find that the supply has been cut off: there is not enough water in the wells, it seems, to supply all the engines and pink lemonade besides for the whole camp. Then there is nothing to do but to take a pail and set out. After climbing over a couple of freight trains and ploughing through a dozen cinder heaps one comes at last to the pump-house, where one may, by assuming an ingratiating manner, beg a pailful,—strictly against the regulations,—from the man at the pump. And then, after all, what use is a mere pailful of lemonade in a thirsty camp?

Abainville, July 10.

We have stopped fighting the war and have gone into the movie business. For two days all work has been suspended while the camp has posed before the camera. They are making a big propaganda film for use in the States, entitled "America's Answer to the Hun" and Abainville and the Abainville-Sorcy narrow-gauge is to be part of that answer. "Camouflage pictures" sneer the boys, and camouflage pictures I blush to say they frankly are. For on the screen the peaceful valley through which the narrow-gauge is being built is to masquerade as a field of battle. Camouflaged engineers, armed and equipped as infantry will march valiantly across the landscape, while other engineers in helmets, with their gas-masks at the alert, are plying their picks and shovels amid the smoke of camouflage shrapnel; the climax being attained when the helmeted engineers effect a lightning repair feat by bridging over a carefully dug camouflage shell-hole.

Yesterday I saw a photograph cut from the Sunday Supplement of one of America's best known and most respected newspapers. Underneath the picture ran the text, "American boys playing baseball on a field in France where shells fall daily." To my certain knowledge the only shells that have ever fallen on that field or within many miles of it are peanut shells. For the field in the picture is most plainly and indisputably the Y. athletic field at Gondrecourt. Will I ever, I wonder, recover my pre-war faith in newspapers and photographs and movies and such things?

But now we have done our turn before the camera, it's back to work again and very hard work at that, for the officers are determined to set a record for all the world in laying track. Already the little railway has shot ahead at an amazing rate; though whether track laid in such a hurry is really going to make for speed in the long run is a question on which the trainmen, sipping their pink lemonade at the canteen counter, have their own opinions. For no train, it seems, can make the run at present without leaving the track at least once during the journey. "Sun-trouble" say the officers, which means, being interpreted, that the heat of the sun's rays has warped the rails. "Sun trouble nothin,'" grunt the men. "It's just not takin' the time to do the job decent." When the "sun trouble" doesn't serve to throw a train off the track, the French children see to it that the same effect is produced by the simple expedient of dropping spikes in between the ends of adjoining rails.

Yesterday I was talking with an engineer from Tours. He and his fireman had just brought a Belgian engine up from that city for use in the Abainville yards. The attitude of the train crew who received it was plainly "thank-you-for-nothing-sirs!", Belgian engines being none too popular with A. E. F. railroad men. The two crews sat in the hut for a long while holding a symposium over the Belgian engine's oddities; at last the home crew departed, looking very glum. In the course of my subsequent conversation with the visiting engineer I happened to ask:

"Would you vote for Pershing for president?"

"No sir!" he answered emphatically. "All the railroad men over here have got it in for him." He went on to explain.

French railroad engineers are allowed a certain amount of coal and oil with which to make their runs; for anything that they can save out of this, they are reimbursed. This idea appealed to the American train crews who were attached to the French. They set to work and saved,—far more than the French were able to! The French proceeded to depreciate the quality of coal allowed them, instead of giving them half dust and half briquets, they gave them three-quarters dust and finally all dust yet still the Americans were able to beat the French at saving. And each man in fancy was rolling up a tidy little sum for himself.

"And then," continued my informant, "Pershing came out and said that we weren't here to make money off the French, but to help them, so we weren't to get the money for all the coal and oil we had saved after all. And that's why there isn't a railroad man in France who has any use for him."

How much of politics could be reduced, I wonder, to a mere question of pocketbook?

He went on to tell me among other things that although a French conductor would be furious if you stopped a train in the middle of a run for any other reason, if you just said; "Come on, ol' top, and have a bottle of *vin rouge* on me," he was all beaming acquiescence. "Just imagine," he concluded disgustedly, "stopping a main-line train in America so the crew could go into a saloon and get a drink!"

Abainville, July 14.

The Bastille has fallen! We celebrated its fall today with much enthusiasm. Ostensibly in order to signalize the Franco-American Alliance, the festivities in reality were planned as propaganda of a different sort. Surreptitiously but quite definitely the end and aim of them was to flatter the Major.

Now the Major in command of the camp at Abainville is what—if he weren't a major—one would be tempted to term a "hard-boiled guy." Being of the bid school he looks with a jaundiced eye at all welfare organizations, particularly, I gather, at the feminine element in them. He calls the college men in the regiment "sissy boys" and believes in treating them to an extra dose of pick and shovel. What's more, it is an open secret that he would like to swap the whole outfit of them for a regiment of Mexican desperadoes, with whom he has had considerable experience. As the boys say, he speaks three languages, English, Mexican and Profane, and of the three he is the most proficient in the last.

So in view of all this, the Fourteenth of July celebration was gotten up chiefly in order to give the Major a chance to appear in all his glory and make a speech, this being, it is claimed, one of the surest ways to tickle the vanity and so win the heart of a man.

We decorated the half-finished hut with flags and bunting, screening the yawning cavern back of the stage with broad strips of red, white and blue cheesecloth. Then we officially invited the whole town to attend. The whole town, from grandmother to baby, came dressed in their Sunday best. The programme started with an informal concert by an impromptu jazz orchestra varied by some Harry Lauder impersonations delivered by an unexpected youth who somehow strayed on to the stage. For a few moments we were painfully uncertain as to whether the effect produced was due just to Harry Lauder or to *vin rouge*, finally deciding that a share at least of the credit should be allowed the latter. Fortunately Harry's appearance on the stage was short; he left us fondly hoping that the French hadn't realized anything was amiss.

The Major of course opened the formal programme. He read his speech. It wasn't a bad speech, representing, as it did, the combined efforts of one captain, two lieutenants and the clerk in the Headquarters office, and was sufficiently fiery in its reference to the Germans to be quite in keeping with the Major's character. The Major sat down amid thunderous applause. The Secretary had vainly tried to arrange to have a little girl present him with a bouquet at the end of his speech: perhaps it was just as well the way it was,—a bouquet might have proved embarrassing to the Major. When the applause had died down the Major's interpreter stepped out and gave a brief summary of the address in French for the benefit of the villagers. Then we had the Mayor of Abainville and after him the Cure, looking very handsome in his beautiful French officer's uniform. They both delivered flowery speeches, enlarging upon the mutual affections of the two nations, which were translated briefly into English by the interpreter for the benefit of the Americans.

After the speeches the school children, who had been fidgeting about like so many little crickets in their front-row seats, swarmed up on the stage and, standing in a long line with flag-bearers at each end, sang the Marseillaise in their funny shrill little voices. Then we all sang the Star Spangled Banner, and after that there was a movie. As luck would have it, instead of an adventure of the western plains, fate had sent us a romance of high finance. We had asked the interpreter to announce the titles of the pictures in French for the benefit of the villagers but when he discovered that this meant making clear the intricacies of the New York Stock Exchange to the mind of the French peasant, he baulked and bolted. It must have been just about as intelligible to them as Coptic, yet they sat tight and at least looked interested.

Everybody considers the affair a success. The Secretary was in high spirits over the evening.

"The Major was pleased, I'm sure," he declared. "As for the French, it was an occasion which they will always remember. Why it was just like transplanting the whole village there. The grandmother and the babies, the mayor, the priest, the school-teacher and his scholars; every village institution was represented!"

"Everything," I said—I was tired, "but the pig-killings."

Abainville, July 20.

I have just established what I think must be the smallest "hut" in France, and such fun as it was doing it!

There is a detachment of about a hundred engineers stationed, while they build the narrow-gauge railway, at a little village about ten miles to the north, called Sauvoy. The other day I went with the Athletic Director in a side-car to take them some baseball equipment. The boys I found were billeted in dark dingy lofts and had to eat their meals, rain or shine, sitting just anywhere in the streets of the village. The thought came to me; why shouldn't they too have a Y? I approached the French Town Major, taking the barber-interpreter with me to lend me both moral and lingual support. After some uncertainty he admitted that there was a room which might be made to serve, a room over a stable to be sure, but a good room for all that; the rent would be thirteen sous a day,—I snapped it up.

Yesterday with all my materials assembled I started out for Sauvoy again. We began work a little before noon, myself and four engineers. Before the afternoon was over we had changed a filthy loft, its grimy walls covered with obscene scrawls, into as cunning a little pocket-edition Y. as one could find I think in France. Sweeping the dust and cobwebs from the rafters, we calcimined the ceiling and walls a pretty creamy yellow; filled in the missing panes with vitex; hung curtains of beautiful blue and green chintz at the windows; laid runners of the same across the tables lent with the benches by the *Major du Cantonment*; decorated the walls, half-dry as they were, with stunning French posters; built shelves in the alcove corner where the built-in bed had been, filled them with books, games and writing materials; hung two big green Japanese lanterns from the beam in the center; and last of all put bowls of the loveliest flowers, larkspurs and snapdragons, begged by the boys from the village gardens, on the shelves and tables, together with heaps of fresh magazines and the company victrola. In the midst of all the scurry and hurry a red-faced frowsy Frenchwoman marched in upon us. She stalked across the room and tried the door which led into the hay-loft: we had nailed it fast. We must open that door immediately, she declared, otherwise she could not get the hay to feed the horse downstairs. I saw my pretty room used as a passage-way by a beery old termagant and my heart sank. After some discussion, however, our visitor proposed an alternative. If we would supply her with a ladder, she could climb up into the loft from below. But how, I asked helplessly, was I to get a ladder? One of the boys winked at me and disappeared; ten minutes later he was back dragging a ladder after him. Our French friend was satisfied.

"But how did you get it?" I asked wonderingly.

He looked at me reprovingly. "In this Man's Army," he remarked, "you should learn not to ask such questions."

When the last touch had been bestowed there was still an hour before the truck which was to take me home was slated for departure. Someone suggested a visit to the Château. So the Top Sergeant, the barber-interpreter, the Town Major and I all set out together.

The Château at Sauvoy is a fifteenth century Château, cut out of an old picture-book, surrounded by a high wall and just about big enough for two. One enters, oddly enough, through the kitchen which is enormous and like a Dutch *genre* painter's "Interior," with a cobble-stone floor, an eight-foot fireplace, dried herbs and vegetables hanging from the rafters and everywhere on the long shelves, the soft gleam of pewter and the mellow tones of old china-ware. From the kitchen one steps into a tiny dining-room paneled in dark carved wood with a bird-cage, empty now, built into the wall. Beyond this is the *salon* with a wonderful old tapestry stretched across one of its walls and some exquisite Louis Quinze chairs in which kings and queens might have sat.

But the best thing about the Château is the Chatelain, an old French gentleman, eighty-nine years of age, the last of his family, who lives all alone, except for one antique serving-woman, in this beautiful dim old mansion, wears *sabots*, keeps bees for a living, and every day of his life cuts from the *journal* the little daily English lesson, pastes it in a tiny note-book, and then his poor old eyes an inch from the paper, cons the words over and over, reading them aloud with *such* a pronunciation!

"In three months," he told us proudly, "I am going to be an American."

He related to us how in 1870 the town was invaded by the Germans and he taken prisoner. But the Germans were gentlemen then and treated him humanely; he couldn't understand what had changed them to such savage beasts. He took us out and showed us his precious bees. We went through the garden, a charming place with little box hedges and rose bushes and currant bushes and gooseberries all growing together in the true French style. Beyond we came to an open oblong of greensward edged by trees with fifty hives ranged around it, the hives,—of all quaint conceits—being made like little Chinese houses, each one different from the rest, each painted red and blue, a bit shabby and worn by time, but still gay and jaunty nevertheless. Monsieur guaranteed us that the bees wouldn't sting, they weren't bad bees he said, so we consented to be led about to each hive in turn and peered in through the little glass windows at the bees making honey. Sad to say, this is a bad year for sweets and instead of hundreds of pounds of honey, there will be scarcely one to sell.

We went back through the garden and here Monsieur must gather a bouquet for me. Around and about the garden he hurried, going to every bush in turn, putting his poor dim eyes down into the very leaves of each, searching for just what he wanted; and finally it was done, pink and white roses, red geraniums, camomile and white pinks, made up in a little stiff bunch and tied with a bit of scarlet string. Then he must present it with a deep bow and a gallant speech "from an old Frenchman to *une jolie Américaine*", while all the rest, including the ancient maid-servant who had just returned from the fields with an apron full of clover for the rabbits, stood about and applauded and cried "Vive la France!" and then "Vive l' Amérique!" in a quite truly stage manner.

We left the little Y. in charge of a boy from the Medical Corps. He has little to do except dispense pills to the French people, so he was willing to look after it.

This morning word came in from Sauvoy that the Germans bombed it last night. Luckily the bombs, evidently aimed at the railroad, fell just outside the village and did no harm; but poor old Monsieur must have gotten a bad fright.

Abainville, August 1.

Abainville's future is at last assured. Work upon the hut has been resumed. The buzz of barracks-building fills all the place, the railroad yards gradually but relentlessly encroach; little by little they are ruining the most beautiful poppy field in all the world.

Meanwhile our family too has grown. A few days ago three new companies of engineers arrived in town. These are draft troops from Texas and Oklahoma, in camp for only a few weeks in the States, shipped here directly from the base port, and so green to France that they don't even know what *oui oui* means. On the trip here one of these boys, they tell, after gazing out the door of his "side-door pullman" in silence half the morning, remarked disgustedly;

"This is a hell of a country!"

"What's the matter?"

"Why all the stations have got the same name!"

"The hell they have! What's the name?"

"Sortie!"

The Major in command of the new arrivals proves to be an old and none too amicable acquaintance of our Major's, their mutual esteem having been obscured by a law-suit some time in the past which resulted in our Major's being forced to part with a considerable sum of money. To make himself more welcome the new Major has introduced innovations. Up till now, in accordance with our Major's theories, we have been a strictly business community, our energies concentrated chiefly upon what the boys call P. and S.—pick and shovel. But now with the coming of the new detachment we have blossomed out with all sorts of military frills. Armed sentinels marching their beats in a military manner fairly encumber the camp. One is halted and challenged a half-dozen times on one's way home from the canteen at ten o'clock in the evening. I am startled out of my dreams in the middle of the night by shouts of, "Corporal of the Guard, Post Number Four!" under my very window. And the best part of it is that these "Long Boys," never having had so much as the A-B-C of military training, make the drollest imitations of real soldiers that ever were. The atmosphere at Headquarters has of late, I gather, been slightly tinged with electricity. But the boys belonging to the older organizations in camp have been enjoying themselves to an unholy degree "stuffing" the new arrivals with ghastly tales of air-raids, gas bombs, and Serial machine-gun barrages.

As in all huts, we have a big map of France tacked to the wall where the boys can have easy access to it. After one of these maps has been up a short while, it is always a simple matter when glancing at it, to locate one's self—one has only to look for a dirty spot; a little later, countless more grimy fingers having in the meantime been applied, one looks for the hole. Yesterday one of our new friends came to me and asked:

"Please, Ma'am, could you tell me where that there place, 'No Man's Land' that they talk about in the papers is? I've been a-lookin' an' a-lookin' an' I can't find it on the map nowhere."

Along with the new engineers Nanny arrived in town. Nanny is an Alabama goat, smuggled on board the transport wrapped up in one of the boys' overcoats. Her fleece is pure white and she is fat as a little butter-ball. Already she is one of our most distinguished citizens. Possessed of an adventurous spirit, she makes herself free of every house in town, being particularly fond of climbing stairs and appearing at unsuspected moments in odd corners of one's billet. Madame explains the attraction here: "She smells an American, you see!" which is a quaint thought. Nanny is the pet detestation of the Adjutant, for she has a *penchant* for straying into his office and nibbling at every paper within reach. Already several valuable documents have disappeared down her greedy little throat. Last night, in revenge, one of the boys in the Adjutant's office, armed with a pot of bright red paint, painted Nanny in "dazzle" designs. Today she is a sight.

This morning I was puzzled to observe that a considerable number of the newcomers were wearing pink tickets in their hats.

"What's that?" I asked.

"Them? Them's meal tickets!" They explained; the report had gone around that the chow of one of the companies was of superior quality; immediately the chow line of that same company had assumed an inordinate length. The mess sergeant, unable, since the company was so new, to distinguish his own men from the self-invited guests, had found it necessary to attach tags to the company.

With the coming of the new engineers, the sale of one article in stock has swelled to unprecedented quantities. One member of the force is fairly kept busy from morning until night cutting off chunks of chewing tobacco. Texas and Oklahoma, it seems, have unlimited capacities for this commodity. Now with all due respect to the honourable American tribe of chewers, this indulgence raises a very delicate question for the canteen lady in whose charge rests the appearance of the hut. The scrap-boxes are already in a bad way, I frankly advocate spittoons, but our detail, who is a very superior lad, known among his cronies as "The Infant" because of his pink cheeks and innocently solemn air, flatly refuses. There are some things, he declares, to which he will not stoop, and he grows very stiff and red in the face if I hint at it.

"I have discussed the matter," he told me yesterday, "with several very eminent chewers, and they all agree that there isn't the slightest necessity for their behaviour!"

There may not be any necessity,—how am I to judge? But there is a very actual and urgent state of affairs. And what is one to do about it?

Abainville, August 13.

The hut is finished. Now if at any time Marshal Foch or General Pershing or President Poincaré should happen this way, we could say: Come in, gentlemen, and behold us; don't we look nice?

The main part of the hut, the big auditorium, is done in creamy yellow and brown with rafters of bright blue, the windows hung with curtains of sumptuous orange chintz. The writing-room is blue and yellow too, with green and yellow curtains on which, in a bower of branches, black-birds perch; runners of the same material lie across the writing tables, the practical advantage of this pattern being that whenever anyone spills a bottle of ink on a runner, it merely gives the effect of one more black-bird. In each window of the writing-room is a little pot with a scarlet geranium, while the walls of both writing-room and auditorium are bright with beautiful French posters.

But the best of all the hut, to my mind at least, is the Tea Room,—so-called until we think of something better to name it,—for the Tea Room was my own particular pet scheme. According to the plans, the ell behind the canteen counter was cut up into half a dozen little rooms. By eliminating part of the central hall, the "mess-room" and the "ladies' room" and moving the office out to an unused corner by the movie machine booth, we got space for a fair-sized room connected by a serving-window with the kitchen. Our matched lumber having run short we used rough lumber and covered it with burlap; each strip was a different weave and texture, to be sure, but all the same it was burlap! The woodwork and little tables we painted a bright green, hung vivid green curtains at the windows, then, taking the covers of chewing tobacco boxes, stained these green too, pasted in the centre of each a bright little water-color reproduction cut from an English art magazine, tacked them up on the walls, and *voilà!* as pretty a little room as could be found short of Paris!

In the Tea Room we serve pink lemonade, hot chocolate, jam sandwiches, cookies and canned fruit. The boys are living on a diet of what they call "goat's meat" at present;—whenever it is time for a chow line to form you can hear a chorus of bleats and baas half across the camp,—and so sick of this have they become that many will sup off chocolate and sandwiches in the Tea Room by preference. Yesterday I took a chance and tried making a ten gallon boiler full of raspberry tapioca pudding, using the bottled fruit juice. At first the boys were inclined to be cautious.

"What do you call that?"

"How would raspberry slum do?"

"Well, I'll try anything once!"

But after the first taste it went all too fast.

"Say, are there any seconds on this?"

"Lady," said one lad solemnly to me, "with pudding like that I could stay four years more in the army."

One of the divisions from the lines arrived in this area, a few days ago, for a short period of rest. A number of the men are encamped up on the hill near the old Artillery School and they come straying down to our hut. Poor lads, it is pitiful to see how wonderful it seems to them to be in a place that is clean and pretty.

"This looks like a bit of heaven to me," declared one boy.

Another, sitting in the Tea Room stirring his chocolate, commented, "Gee, this is a swell place in here. You ought ter get some fancy name for it."

"What would you suggest?"

"Well I should think," he looked around, "you might call it Canary Cottage."

Yet occasionally I wonder if it really all pays, as when I pick out the cigar butts which, in spite of the trash boxes beneath the tables, the boys will persist in sticking in the vases of flowers and planting in the geranium pots, or when, as last night, I catch a fellow using one of the beautiful chintz runners from the tables with which to wipe the mud off his boots.

Abainville, August 21.

Talk kills men.

Don't talk. The walls have ears.

Keep mum, let the guns talk for you.

Thus are we placarded. Every hut, every café, every garage, every place of any sort where the A. E. F. may meet together and indulge in conversation, now bears a board with some such legend printed on it and after each terse warning is the terser admonition; Read G. O. 39. A campaign of silence is on foot. These catchy phrases, American variations on the classic French line: *Taisez vous, méfiez vous, les oreilles ennemies vous ecoutent!*—Be still, beware, the ears of the enemy are listening!—are to be perpetual reminders to us that we are all too prone to gossip indiscreetly.

As to just what one may say and mustn't say, I for one confess, not having read G. O. 39, that I am in a quandary. I find myself hesitating before mentioning the fact that we had baked beans for dinner. As for talking about the weather, why that leads naturally to the subject of moonlight nights, and moonlight nights, as every one knows, now imply not romance but air-raids and air-raids are of course a tabooed topic. Indeed I am beginning to have a sneaking conviction that perhaps it would be better to discard speech entirely and take to conversing in dumb show.

Sometimes some small thing that comes to one's attention will crystallize a difference between two races so sharply as to be startling. This was impressed on me the other day by two posters. Both the French and American authorities have recently issued warnings to their soldiers concerning the practice of riding on the tops of railroad cars, since this habit has led to a number of casualties. The French poster reads something like this:

Whereas it has been brought to the attention of the Commissioner of Railroads, that various accidents have occurred resulting from the practice indulged in by soldiers of obtruding a portion or the whole of their bodies beyond the limits of the car; it is urgently requested that the soldiers in transit upon the railroad should henceforth restrict themselves to the interior of the cars.

The American sign runs thus:

"If you want to see the next block, keep yours inside! Your head may be hard but it's not as hard as concrete!" Pithily it states the number of casualties resulting from this trick, explains that the French bridges and tunnels only allow six inches clearance above the top of the cars, and ends;

"Your life may not be worth anything to you, but it may cost your country $10,000."

But the triumph of American sign art, a specimen of which hangs in the Adjutant's office, is the gas-defense poster. It starts off with the Gas School slogan:

"There are two classes of men in a gas attack, the quick and the dead," proceeds to poetry:

"The hard-boiled guy said gas was bunk,
It couldn't hurt you, only stunk....
The hard-boiled guy went up the line,
Fritz spilled the mustard good and fine;
And now some people wonder why
It's flowers for the hard-boiled guy,"

and ends with the admonition that seems a little ironical to one who must struggle to make green wood burn in a broken-down French range; "Cook with it, don't croak with it."

Today we put up a sign fill of our own over the counter. For some reason, transportation probably, there has been a most distressing lack of supplies in this area recently. Not only are we suffering, but the Salvation Army and even the sales commissaries have all been stricken with the same famine. Indeed I was told of one commissary which bore the warning; "We have salt, mustard and baking powder. That's all." Tired of replying several hundred times a day; "I'm awfully sorry but we haven't any so-and-so," I made a sign which was a list of all the "haven't gots" and tacked it up over the counter. Thinking to be funny I included strawberry ice-cream among the rest, to be promptly punished by an innocent-eyed youth who inquired hopefully; "What kind of ice-cream *have* you got?"

Another boy read through the list once, twice, then looked up at the Infant disgustedly.

"Why don't you put 'Hell!' at the bottom of it?" he queried.

"'Pears to me it would be easier to make a list of the things you *have* got," suggested another.

A little while longer and if no help comes, we shall be doing this. I can see that sign in my mind's eye now. It will read something like this:

We have
chewing tobacco
indelible pencils
and
shaving brushes

Abainville, September 2.

Once a month, according to schedule, the whole personnel of the division is summoned to Y. Headquarters at Gondrecourt for a conference. Formerly these conferences were largely religious in significance, consisting of much righteousness with a slight leaven of business. Each one in turn was looked forward to as a pious but unprofitable duty and evaded when possible,—which wasn't often. Now with a change in the directorship the conferences have taken on an almost entirely practical tone. Incidentally they have gained amazingly in popularity. For now one can attend a conference with confidence that during its progress one will surely glean more than one quaint bit of human comedy.

Today it was the Aviation Camp Secretary who supplied most of the spice. This is an odd but very earnest little man whom I shall always remember as I saw him at the Gondrecourt railway station last May, starting for Paris dressed up in a "tin hat" and a gas mask. Whether this was in order to bluff Paris into thinking that he had come straight from the front, or whether this was to protect himself against the assaults of Big Bertha while in the city, I could not determine, but never since have I been able to take the gentleman quite seriously.

The Aviation Secretary created the first sensation by rising suddenly to his feet and reading a motion to the effect that the Gondrecourt Division of the Y. M. C. A. should go on record as registering a protest against "the wicked state of the Paris streets," citing Mr. Edward Bok and his action in the case of the streets of Liverpool. For a moment no one said a word, then a secretary arose and requested that the motion be amended to read more clearly, as in its present form it might be taken to refer to the condition of the paving, or the criminal recklessness of the taxi drivers. The Warehouse Man then solemnly proposed that in view of Mr. Bok a ruling should be passed that while in Paris all secretaries should be required to travel by the subway or in a cab. I wanted to ask if it wouldn't do just as well if special prayers should be offered for each secretary on his departure for the wicked city, but refrained.

No sooner had the excitement over the Paris streets subsided, than the Aviation Secretary was on his feet again with a second resolution. This was in effect a petition to the Paris office that they send us proportionately less tobacco and more sweets for sale in the canteens. This precipitated a fiery argument, the smokers lined up against the non-smokers. Listening to the non-smokers you became convinced that the manhood of America was on its way to ruin through excessive cigarettes; listening to the smokers you became equally certain that the war would be won by tobacco smoke. The situation became so tense one could almost see the sparks in the air. In the end the smokers had it.

The next thrill was caused by one of the women workers who in the course of a speech took occasion to deprecate the housekeeping abilities of the men secretaries. On Fourth of July, she declared, when the chocolate cups from all over the area had been sent into Gondrecourt for the celebration there, some of them had been discovered to be in a shocking state. These had later been traced to a hut where there was no woman worker. Instantly the Aviation Secretary was up again. This charge was a personal matter, he declared, as the cups in question had been his. However he denied the implication. The cups had been perfectly clean when they left the hut, they must have become soiled en route. And so the conference comedy is played out.

At the town of X. there is a secretary who declares he is devoting his life to the service of the Lord. Some years ago he found himself becoming deaf. So he told the Lord that if He would restore his hearing he would spend the rest of his days in performing good works. He was cured. Last week he created a corner on eggs in this vicinity by buying one hundred and twenty-five dozen at five francs per. Now he is reselling them for six. Wanting eggs badly to make custard for some sick boys here, and not being able to obtain them any other way, I walked over to X. and bought two dozen. When I got home I counted them, there were just twenty-three. Surely the Lord got the worst of that bargain!

Abainville, September 9.

Something is going to happen.

We have been used to seeing the French Army go by; interminable lines of camions, so many feet apart, rolling through the town for hours on end. Sometimes we have seen a section pass through on its way to the front, only to return again some ten days later. Once seen, a French camion train is never forgotten, for each automobile section bears painted on its sides the distinctive insignia of the unit. These are sometimes droll, sometimes sentimental, but always cleverly designed and usually striking,—a poilu drinking *pinard* from his canteen, a pelican, a polar bear, a dancing monkey, a soldier embracing a peasant girl, a grinning Algerian's head in ear rings and a red fez, a gendarme holding up a threatening club.

But now by day, by night, it is the Americans who are passing through, their faces set toward the front, on troop-trains, in camions, on foot. Coming home from the canteen in the evening one hears the heavy rattle that means artillery on the move, and standing by the roadside peering through the darkness one can just discern horses and caissons, slat-wagons, supply-wagons and, looming ominously in the dim light, the formidable bulk of the great guns.

Night before last I was awakened by the sound of troops passing, a regiment of infantry on the march. I lay and listened; the tramp, tramp, tramp of the rhythmic feet was unvarying, incessant, then came a break. The order had been given to halt for a rest. The boys were evidently sitting down by the edge of the road. But though they rested they were by no means still.

"Oh Mademoiselle!" they entreated the dark and unresponsive houses, *"Oh, Mademoiselle! Deux vin rouge toot sweet s'il vous plaît, Mademoiselle!"*

They swore genially. They sang snatches of *Hail, hail the gang's all here* and *Tipperary*. One boy had a mouth organ which he played with vim. Someone introduced a barnyard motif and they were off, crowing and cackling, mooing and bleating, imitating every animal known to domestic life. They sounded like schoolboys off for a holiday and my God! they were soldiers on the march to the front, their faces set to the battle!

Tonight as we came home from the hut, we were startled by a strange sight. The sky was clear, except for one dark mass shaped like a cloud of smoke which hung above the horizon to the north. As we looked, suddenly the under side of the cloud turned an angry crimson, then in a moment grew dark again. A minute later the red glow showed again only to fade but and be repeated. We knew that the angry light must be the glare reflected from the flashes of the guns which were belching red death across the lines. All at once the battle-field seemed very near.

Abainville, September 14.

We have taken the Saint Mihiel salient! The news came in yesterday over the wires. At first we couldn't believe it. We have heard so many wonderful but alas! too hopeful things over those wires! But now the newspapers have proved it, with their maps showing the salient cut off as clean as by a knife. And if we wanted concrete proof, why we have that too. They have sent for a detail of engineers from Abainville to build hurry-up prison pens. They simply haven't any place to put the thousands of captive Germans. The detail set out in high spirits looking forward to doing a brisk business in souvenirs; already reports have come in to the effect that buttons and shoulder-straps may be had in exchange for a cigarette, and a ring for a sack of five-cent "smoking."

The inhabitants of Saint Mihiel, they say, were terror-stricken at the sight of the Americans. When our troops first entered the town they believed the city had been retaken. The Americans, they thought, were Austrians. No one in Saint Mihiel had ever seen an American; they hadn't even known America was in the war!

But even in Saint Mihiel I don't believe that there was any greater joy than the joy that was here in our own kitchen. Madame who helps us with the dishes at the hut is the daughter of the refugee schoolmaster, a shy, sensitive, appealing little woman, girl-like in spite of her half-grown daughter. When we told her that the salient had been taken she went white and trembled. And what of Vieville? she begged; Vieville, her own little village? We got the map and showed it to her. Sure enough, there was Vieville and the new line stretching the other side of it! It was true past doubting. Madame shivered. "I don't know whether to laugh or to cry," she told us and there were sobs in her voice while she smiled at us. She tried to go on with scrubbing the floor, but she couldn't. Would we mind if she ran home for a minute? She must tell the news to Papa and Maman. But certainly, stay as long as you like! we told her. In an hour she was back again, to go about her work in a dazed uncertain fashion, smiling tremulously while the tears stood in her eyes. We must get someone to take her place at the canteen, she told us,— they would be going back to Vieville right away. It was plain to see that she would have liked to start that very moment. We said nothing. Of course it was impossible. Vieville though liberated was close to the lines. When I looked at Madame so happy, so confidently eager to return to her home, I sickened to think of the ruin that probably awaited her. How do they have the courage to face it, these French people? I thought of the words of the old schoolmaster: "We are living under tension now, it is the strain that keeps us up. When the war is over there will be a terrible reaction." They have been brave, so brave, these peasant villagers, but how will they bear the future? Where will they be swept when they are caught in the fearful ebb of that reaction?

Already odd-looking little German narrow-gauge engines and freight cars have begun to appear in the yards, part of the Saint Mihiel booty. It does the eyes good to look at them.

One doesn't want to hope too greatly, but is it possible that this may be the beginning of the end?

Abainville, September 18.

Last night they bombed Gondrecourt. We were startled out of our sleep by the explosions. Lying in bed I could hear the angry growling gr-gr-gr which distinguishes the German plane, as it flew over Abainville headed back towards the lines. Would it drop another bomb? It seemed to take an interminable time to pass over us. Finally the growling hum grew faint, died away. Then the real excitement of the night began. Swarming into the streets, men, women and children, they proceeded to turn the occasion into a social event. Standing in the square in the moonlight, all talking at once and all talking at the top of their voices, they discussed, narrated, compared, commented, sympathized, while high above all the din I could hear Madame's voice in semi-hysterical outbursts of emotion. How they could find so much to say about it I can't imagine. If Hindenburg's whole army had suddenly appeared in Gondrecourt they couldn't have been more excited. I went to sleep and left them still busy analyzing, as I took it, their psychological reactions.

This morning we learned that the bombs, falling at the edge of the town, had injured nothing except a few trees.

"What would you do if they should start to bomb Abainville?" I asked Madame when she brought me my morning toast and chocolate.

"I? I would go to the church."

"What you, the infidel! You who never go to mass!"

"I know." Madame smiled a little sheepishly. "And yet all the same, one would feel safer there."

At the canteen a lieutenant who was just finishing his course at Gondrecourt came in.

"Nobody can imagine who should have wanted to bomb the school," he declared, "unless it was some former pupil."

"Why I was told that the Gondrecourt School was the ranking school of France!" I exclaimed.

"Made a mistake in the last syllable," he responded sourly, "it should have been spelled e-s-t."

But if the inhabitants of Abainville have experienced no losses through air-raids yet, they have nevertheless, suffered a minor casualty. Victor, the town simpleton, the genial, harmless Victor, was knocked down by a passing automobile yesterday and became separated from his left ear in the ensuing confusion. Poor wretch! I saw him this morning hobbling down the street with a cane, his head swathed in bandages, but the same old cheerful smile on his half-wit face, as he cocked one eye warily on the look-out for approaching autos. Meanwhile a heated controversy is being waged between the medical officers of Abainville as to whether or not that ear might after all have been saved.

Saint Malo, Brittany, September 23.

Today I took tea with a Baroness, not only I, but about eighty odd members of the A. E. F. here *en permission* like myself. Our hostess was an American lady, the widow of a French Baron; the tea a weekly party held at her Château out in the country, to which all boys on leave in this Brittany area are invited.

We took the funny little narrow-gauge train from Saint Malo, a "mixed" train and so crowded by the tea party that the boys must ride in the baggage car and on the flat freight cars, and started our journey out to Châteauneuf. The feature of the train trip was the blackberries. Here in Brittany these grow all along the roadsides, the bushes topping the narrow earth-covered walls like dykes that serve for fences. Strangely enough in this land of thrift, the blackberries go untouched, untasted. A Frenchman who lectured to us last spring declared that as a child he was warned not to eat them: they would give him lice, he was told. This, he explained, was the method which French parents took to dissuade their children from eating berries which, growing along the roadsides, would be full of dust—a quaint scruple to find among people ordinarily so superior to sanitary considerations! But the Americans had no such superstitions; at every cross-roads stop we made, the boys swarmed off the cars and fell upon the wayside bushes. I tasted some that one of the boys brought back for me. Compared to our blackberries at home they were flat and flavorless, but anyway they were fruit and they were free and that was all the A. E. F. demanded.

Arrived at Châteauneuf, we must first file through the reception room where each and all of us shook hands with the Baroness, a gracious, stately old lady dressed in black, and then out upon the lawn beyond the long ivy-covered, many-gabled house, to sit upon the grass and drink our tea. But tea was a misnomer unless it might have been the sort which the English call "high tea," it was a supper; salad, sandwiches, buttermilk and fruit punch served on real china plates and in dainty goblets. Many a covetous eye I saw fixed on the silver forks with the coronets engraved on them, while the whispered word "souvenir" caught my ear, but to the boys' credit I am glad to say that, as far as I know, they one and all resisted this temptation.

After supper the boys sang and then we were invited to go through the house and wander about the grounds and garden. Coming back to the house after having made the rounds, the boy who was with me suddenly stopped stock-still.

"Well I'll be darned!"

Before us wound a tiny stream and perched on its bank an old, old peasant woman was busy scrubbing what was evidently the Château wash. The boy turned and looked at me despairingly, "And for all that's such a fine house," he groaned, "I suppose there ain't so much as a speck of plumbing in the whole blamed building!"

On the lawn we found games were in progress. All the youngsters from the neighborhood had assembled to watch the Americans at the tea party. At first they had hung shyly on the outskirts, but now a lad from the air service had started them to romping. Taking hold of hands a long line of these little gamin would pursue a soldier victim, encircle him, bring him to earth, then pile on him, holding him a helpless prisoner until he bought his liberty with a ransom of cigarettes, gum or coppers. It was a wonderful game for the children but I could not help but watch with apprehension, every time there was a pig-pile, to see where all those wooden shoes would land.

Coming home, we walked to the little fishing village next door and took the train there. As this visit to the village is also a weekly affair, all the inhabitants were on their door-steps to greet us, the women with their red cheeks, dressed invariably in black dresses and little stiffly starched net caps. We went into the church with its array of votive offerings in the shape of tiny models of fishing boats and then, on our way to the station, stopped to view, over the hedge, the picture-book garden of one old fisherman in which the trees and shrubs were all clipped and trained into the quaintest shapes—peacocks and animals and little ships. As the crowd moved on I lingered. An old man leaning on a cane, who had been watching from the roadside, stepped forward and spoke to me. He was the owner of the garden. He wanted to express to me his gratitude to America, America who had saved France! *"Ah! Vive l'Amérique!"* The old fellow's tribute, unsolicited and unpremeditated evidently, touched me deeply.

Abainville, October 4.

While I was away it seems several things occurred. For one, we lost Nanny. Whether some enterprising mess sergeant thought the day's menu would be improved by the addition of kid pie, whether some French family lured her away to be interned in their back yard, or whether, as one might more darkly suspect, the Adjutant had something to do with the matter; nobody knows. The bare fact confronts us: Nanny has disappeared.

We have also lost one of our most picturesque customers. This was a handsome young Greek with a beautiful curled mustache, named Niccolo. He used to hold up the chocolate line, while, his eyes fairly shooting fire, he rolled up his sleeves and showed me the scars of the bayonet wounds which he received fighting the Turks. "The German, he just the same the Turk! I tella the Captain he letta me go front, killa ten, twenty, hundred Germans!" Why such a bloodthirsty soul as his should be cribbed, cabined and confined in an engineer regiment, he never explained. Just before I went away on leave a detail of prisoners from the guard-house arrived at the hut one morning to scrub the floor. To my regret I noticed Noccolo was among them. Niccolo, however, did not seem to mind, he was quite happily occupied with telling the others how the work should be done.

"That feller's nuts," complained a fellow-prisoner to me, "he spends all his time when he's in the brig, tryin' to read the Bible to us."

While I was away they sent him to the Gondrecourt hospital on suspicion of insanity. The other night he escaped and made his way back to Abainville clad in his hospital pajamas, only to be caught and taken back again. Poor Niccolo with his beautiful mustache and his fiery spirit! I am sorry he never had the chance to get those Germans.

Worst of all, the Y. is in disgrace with the officers. It came about through the matter of seats at the movies. The officers wanted to come to the shows and they also wanted seats reserved for them; naturally they wanted the best seats. Now this is always a vexed and delicate problem in a hut, for if the officers ask for reserved seats one can't very well refuse them, and yet to grant them is to raise resentment among the men. When I left the matter was hanging at loose ends. Shortly afterwards our Secretary, who is more distinguished for sentimentality than tact, had an inspiration; he would put it up to the men. Undoubtedly when the case was laid before them, their nobler natures would be touched and they would discern that it was their patriotic duty to voluntarily relinquish the best seats in the house to their military superiors. So one night just as the show was due to start the Secretary walked out onto the stage and made his little speech, ending with the appeal:

"And now boys, where shall we put the officers?"

A perfect roar answered him. "Put 'em on the roof! Put 'em on the roof!"

It was frightfully embarrassing. The officers were furious. They withdrew and called a mass-meeting to consider the matter. What the exact statute that covered the case was I don't know. I suppose the crime was one of a sort of military *lèse Majesté*. Anyway the Secretary had indisputably laid himself liable to a court-martial. In the end, however, the officers decided that as long as the case was one of stupidity rather than malice, they would let the Secretary go with a warning.

And now they have stationed spotters among us! The hut, it seems, has proved to possess an all too potent charm for boys who should by rights be engaged at "pick and shovel" and other uninviting but necessary occupations. In view of this the authorities have taken drastic action; passes must now be issued to the boys to allow them to enter the hut during work hours, and alas for the unhappy lad who ventures in without a permit, the lynx-like eye of the amateur detective detail is sure to light upon him!

Abainville, October 11.

Nanny has returned! She was found tethered in a back-yard in a nearby village. Since the French household which claimed her as their lawful property refused to relinquish her peacefully, she was taken by storm. There was a scrimmage, the neighbors rallied to their friends' assistance. But the two lads who had been the discoverers managed to break away bearing the struggling Nanny with them and, followed by the whole village shouting "Stop thief!" gained their truck and rolled triumphantly away. No longer, however, does Nanny wander at large, innocently trimming the villagers' cabbage rows, or slipping slyly into the Adjutant's office to sample his latest orders. Nanny is under guard. The engineers are taking no chances.

Yesterday we acquired a kitten,—a wild-eyed yellow scrap brought in last night by a lad as an offering. The boys immediately christened her "The O. D. Cat." Every time I give her a caress some one of the boys leaning over the counter is sure to remark: "Gee, wish I was a cat!"

"But what shall I feed her?" I questioned, thinking of the difficulty of fresh milk.

"Corn willy and cognac! What else would you give an O. D. cat?" they chorused.

"And where shall she spend the night?"

"I'll keep her for you ma'am," volunteered a brawny Texan. "She'll sleep right in the bunk longside o' me."

This morning the canteen was full of tales of the night. "Yes sir! he tied her up to a post with a rope as big around as your arm! An' the pore cat nearly hanged herself. She hollered all night long!"

This the Texan emphatically denied; he had a tale all of his own to tell however.

"There was a mouse last night in the barracks. It was the littlest mouse you ever seen, but it chased that cat all around them barracks. Yes ma'am, it sure did run that cat ragged!"

"Did you give her any breakfast?" I asked, disdaining any comment on his story.

"Sure ma'am! I gave her a saucerful of cognac."

"You never did!"

"Yes, an' it did that cat good, it did. Soon's she'd lapped up that saucer; 'Bring on your mouse!' she says." He shook his head reflectively. "My, but that cat sure was feelin' its strength this mornin'!"

"Waste cognac on a cat! That's a likely story for that guy to be telling!" was the single comment of the bystanders.

Right here I wish to record a formal apology to the Secretary at X who sold me the six-franc eggs a month ago. Today I was talking to the Top Sergeant whom I encountered on my way home and who carried my basket for me. From something he let fall I now more than suspect it was he who accounted for that twenty-fourth egg!

Abainville, October 16.

His real name, of course, is Horace but since Madame refers to him as 'Oreece, as 'Oreece he must go,—'Oreece is our new detail. He is cautious, conscientious and slow. If 'Oreece ever showed signs of having spunk enough to do something that was really bad, I would feel that there was

hope for him. Madame, who adores the Infant, is very cold to 'Oreece. The other day she requested him to save her all the cigar stubs he found while sweeping. She wanted them for an old derelict of a Frenchman who is a sort of scavenger around camp. Poor old papa could smoke the butts nicely in his pipe she declared. But 'Oreece was so disobliging as to turn his nose up at their proposal. Anyway 'Oreece cuts the bread for the jam-sandwiches very, very nicely.

Three nights ago we had an air-raid alarm. The evening's programme was over but the hut was still full of boys. Suddenly without any warning, all the lights went out. We looked out the door, the camp was in total darkness. In the machine-gun pit nearby we could hear quick excited orders interspersed with curses,—the gunners were getting ready to stand off the aeroplanes. The boys left the hut. We waited for a while and then, getting tired of the dark, went home. The planes didn't show up; I went to bed feeling that it had been a case of Hamlet without Hamlet.

Last night we were in the middle of a movie show when a shattering explosion sounded outside. Back in the kitchen where I was serving hot chocolate to the Tea Room line, everyone started and stared. Was it a raid? Surely that was a bomb! There was another explosion. Then the lights went out. So it was the real thing! I seized the Cash-box and stood pat. Another crash; instantly outside there was a stampede. In the dark it was impossible to see just what was happening, but from the sounds it appeared that about seven hundred pairs of hob-nailed shoes were doing double-quick time out the doors. In less time than one could believe the auditorium was empty. I heard Madame's voice behind me in staccato exclamations. Somebody scratched a match and lit a candle, a little group of boys were still standing at the window waiting for their chocolate, their faces looked a bit white I thought. Then the Infant put his head out the kitchen door:

"Why, the lights in camp are all on!" he exclaimed.

A boy came up to the window. "They're practising at the school," he told us. "I heard the other day that they were going to pull some stunts in the trenches tonight."

"So that was it!"

The lights flashed on.

"But why did they go out?" I asked confused. Nobody could explain it.

At that moment 'Oreece drifted into the kitchen, he wore a very pale and apologetic grin.

"'Oreece!" I gasped, "Did you—"

"I turned the lights off," he admitted. "I knew where the switch was. I thought it was a raid."

I glared disgusted: "And a nice night's work you've done!"

My friend the Texan strolled up to the deserted counter.

"I met 'em all coming down the road," he remarked. "Gee, but it was like the retreat of a whole division!"

Today the boys have been asking to tease me: "Where were *you* in the Great Air-Raid?"

"I? Oh, I was under the kitchen-table," I reply.

Abainville, October 23.

The Chief has just brought me great news. I am to have a hut all of my own. I am to be head cook, bottle-washer, and grand high secretary all in one. And I am to go out into the wilds of France and start a new hut alone.

It seems there is an ordnance depot at a village called Mauvages about six miles north of here. The camp itself is small, some two hundred men, but the town has a large billeting capacity and additional bodies of troops will be stationed there from time to time. The C. O. of the Ammunition Reclamation Camp,—that is its official title,—has requested that a hut be established there. With the personnel in its present state no man secretary, says the Chief, can be spared, but if I care to undertake the job on my own I am welcome to it. And if after two months or so of solitary confinement "out in the sticks," as the boys say, I get to hankering too badly for the flesh-pots of civilization, why they will arrange to have me relieved. Need I say that I snapped up the offer on the spot? I had asked to be transferred from Abainville some while ago, as the conditions here have been none too congenial, but to have a hut all of my own is beyond any luck that I had dared dream.

I would like to sling my old kit bag over my shoulder, tuck a chocolate container under one arm and a case of cigarettes under the other, and catch the first truck that passes bound northward for Mauvages. But it seems they won't let me go until a New Lady comes here to take my place. They have telegraphed to the office at Nancy. If the New Lady doesn't come quick, I have a good mind to go A. W. O. L. and start my canteen willy-nilly.

Meanwhile I am planning plans. Because of the grey chill days of winter I am going to paint my hut inside the brightest sunshiny yellow I can find, hang it with orange curtains, and then in honor of the ordnance, christen it the Pumpkin Shell!

CHAPTER VI
MAUVAGES—THE ORDNANCE

Abainville, October 26.

I have been to Mauvages; a reconnoitering expedition. As regards the town the most striking feature about it is the Egyptian Fountain. A somewhat startling structure to come upon in a little French mudpie village, it stands in the centre of the town and consists of the façade of a temple in front of which towers an ancient God of the Nile—or so I take him—in dull green bronze, pouring from pitchers held in either hand clear streams of water into a broad semi-circular basin. Behind the columns is another pool, this one for the village washerwomen: a cleverly conceived arrangement, for every passing stranger must stop to stare at the fountain and this in turn affords the washerwomen the opportunity to stare at him.

Around two sides of the town curves the canal along whose placid surface the slow barges occasionally pass. They tell me that some very beautiful women go by on these canal boats, but I suspect that the reason that they seem so beautiful is just that they do go by—the lure of the unobtainable. At the south end of the town the canal disappears into a hill-side, four miles to the southwest it appears again; a rather remarkable, and in view of the fact that in the most piping times of peace the traffic on the canal never exceeded four barges each way a day, inexplicably extravagant feat of engineering. Every now and then a little crowd of ordnance boys will take a notion to walk through the tunnel which has a path cut at one side, an excursion which must be unspeakably dreary as the whole length is quite unlighted and the air damp and close beyond anything. More than once on these excursions a boy has fallen into the canal and had to be fished out again.

My hut-to-be is on the further edge of town in the centre of a beautiful open green field like a lawn. Just behind it is a large ruined stone house which the boys use as a background against which to take pictures "at the front" and on one side is a lovely tall wayside cross and a tiny chapel, the smallest I have ever seen, almost hidden in a little grove of bushes. The hut is a French recreation barracks; long, low, covered with black tar paper, the windows filled with grimy cloth, it is comprised of four walls, a roof, a tiny stage and a mud floor,—a good mud floor, the best mud floor, I am assured, in this part of France.

As for my billet, I am to lodge, it seems, with Monsieur le Curé. He was out when I called but the Major du Cantonment and Madame the Caretaker settled things between them. What Monsieur le Curé will say when he come home and discovers that *une demoiselle Américaine* is to live *chez lui,* I don't know, but as Monsieur le Major himself suggested it, it must be in accordance with the clerical proprieties.

The Curé's mansion is a rather stately, gloomy square house set back from the street with a rose-garden edging the path in front. My room has a Juliet balcony with a view of the Egyptian Fountain, the ancient church and a scrap of rolling hills beyond. Breakfasts I have arranged to take with Madame the Caretaker who lives several doors down the street, dinners and suppers I am to eat by courtesy of the C. O. at the camp.

When I returned tonight I told my landlady of my plans. Her eyes fairly danced with mischievous glee.

"Oh la la! You and the Curé!" she cried. "*Le diable avec le bon Dieu!* It will be necessary for you to become a good Catholic, say your prayers, and go to mass every morning. Who knows? Perhaps you may end by becoming a *religieuse.*"

Mauvages, November 2.

We are building. This proves to be a painful process, consisting largely of discovering what you can't have and what you will have to do without. For instance, it appears that there is not enough lumber to be had in France to furnish me a complete floor, and I had set my heart on having a nice, whole, *sweepable* floor! French barracks, one should note in passing, are constructed of sections; the upper part of the walls containing the window sections being vertical, the lower sloping outward at an angle of about thirty-five degrees. By a process of begging, borrowing and salvaging—nobody says *steal* any more these days,—I have visions of getting the floor in the centre all filled in, but for the edges, under the sloping sides, I am afraid there is no hope. But I'm not going to mind, I tell the boys; I shall start a series of war gardens in the little mud-plots, cabbages in number one, brussels sprouts in number two, and violets just for my own satisfaction in three. And the boys can take turns hoeing them.

For the rest, we have cut a door in the side for general entrance, the original one being reserved for cooks, colonels and K. P.s, and across the front end opposite the stage we have constructed our store-room, kitchen and canteen. A lattice is all that separates the kitchen from the counter; this is so, in order to facilitate social intercourse between the cook and the customers, and also to enable the secretary, no matter if she is engaged in

stirring the chocolate or washing the dishes, to keep a weather eye on what is going on outside. But the triumph of my hut-plan is the window-seat. Half-way down the hut we have a stove, a stove which looks as big as an engine-boiler, a stove which makes the eyes of all beholders fairly pop with admiration. "That's a real stove," say the boys. "That ain't no frog stove I'll tell the world!" And back of the stove we have a seat three sections long against the wall. Wonderful to say that seat is comfortable and what's more it has sofa-cushions. "What are those pillers for?" demanded one boy suspiciously. "Are they for the officers to sit on?"

"D'you know what this is?" asked a boy today as he luxuriously stretched his length on the window-seat. "This is the Lounge Lizard's Roost." So the Lounge Lizard's Roost it is.

The yellow curtains are already up in place. They give a rather stunning effect against the black tar paper when the æroplane camouflage curtains are let down. In each space between the windows we have tacked one of that gorgeous series of French railway posters, so my hut is brave with color, tawny orange, sharp blues, and shadowy purples.

Meanwhile the whole French populace has called, singly or in crowds, in order to see just what is going on. As for the children, I am sure they must have declared a school holiday in honor of us. The whole concern is evidently a bit puzzling to the French mind; but they have solved the riddle by terming the hut a *"coopératif,"* and so I let it rest.

But you will be wondering how *le diable* is contriving to live with *le bon Dieu*.

Monsieur le Curé is quite old. There is something stern and something tragic in his face, with all his urbane graciousness. He is a refugee from the devastated area and like myself a lodger in the house, whose owners have fled this zone of armies. Monsieur le Curé was a captive for six months with the Germans and the desolate confinement wrought a little on his mind; "At times he is absent," says Madame the Caretaker. This morning I stopped and chatted with him at his door downstairs, he called me in to show me "a souvenir of his captivity," a little dirty-white tin basin out of which as prisoner he ate. "I learned to smoke then," he told me. "There was nothing to do the whole day long but sit and smoke and wait for the clock to strike." Tonight I am going to take him a little gift of American tobacco.

I am planning a house-warming with which to formally open the hut.

Mauvages, November 6.

We didn't have that house-warming. Even as we were finishing the hut all hands came down with the flu. Curiously enough it hit the camp all in a heap after dinner. Thirty per cent of the boys, the two officers, the building detail and myself were all laid low between one and six o'clock. Fortunately it was the lightest sort of an epidemic, a mere *soupçon* as it were, in every case. I merely retired to my bed for a day and a half and refused to eat. On the third day, which was yesterday, I crawled back to the canteen. It was a case of pipe all hands on deck and stand to the counter. Two companies of engineers had arrived in the night. They were back from an advanced station just behind the lines and they were starved for chocolate and cigarettes. Two months ago they left Abainville, green troops, just over, now they are seasoned veterans, in proof of which they carry souvenirs salvaged from German dugouts. I heard all about these souvenirs, as I was taking breakfast, from the lips of an excited Neighbor Woman. From the list of unwarlike trophies which she rattled off I gleaned umbrellas and a wall-clock; but the best was reserved for me when I reached the canteen. One of the boys had met one of these same engineers toiling up the hill from the railroad with a large upholstered armchair on his back.

"You can't imagine," he complacently replied to his gaping questioners, "how nice it is, at the end of a hard day's work, to be able to sit down and smoke one's pipe in real comfort."

Up and down the street are heaps of pale-green cabbages. The field kitchens by the fountain are busy cooking them. The town is fairly steeped in the odor of boiling cabbages. These are the famous German cabbages captured in the Saint Mihiel drive, and for the past two months, the engineers, they tell me, have had them boiled for dinner, for supper and for breakfast, until it seems that they hate the Germans for those cabbages as much as they hate them for the rape of Belgium and the sinking of the Lusitania.

At the corner by the fountain this noon a lady stopped to speak to me. She was tall and white-haired and bore herself with gracious dignity. She had heard, she told me, that these men had just returned from Hattonchatel. She was very anxious to learn something of the fate of a nearby town, Haumont by the lakes, where her aged sister had lived. Since the German invasion four years ago she had heard absolutely no word of her. Was the town in such a state that it was possible her sister might still be there, or had the inhabitants been herded off to Germany? I questioned several boys, finally I found a lad who spoke French. Yes he knew the town to which she referred. He had often observed it from the height of a nearby hill,—it had been daily under shell-fire. Very sadly, but with her gracious sweetness undisturbed, the lady turned away.

Mauvages, November 9.

Life is just one breathless bustle now-a-days. Hardly had we got our minds adjusted to the engineers when a whole battalion of machine-gunners marched into town. From the moment they arrived it has been one interminable line from morning until night, demanding the Three C.s,—chocolate, cookies, and cigarettes. Luckily my closet was well stocked and so has stood the strain.

And speaking of closets, I have acquired a skeleton in mine. It came about through a sick soldier, an accommodating captain and an egg-nogg. The sick boy I discovered in Madame the Caretaker's stable while breakfasting this morning. He was very miserable, Madame told me, and had been quite unable to eat a thing for days. I stopped in at the stable and verified her words. The boy looked wretched.

"Come to the canteen at ten o'clock and I'll have something for you to eat," I told him. Then I begged a cup of fresh milk from Madame.

The Captain I discovered in front of my canteen counter, and knowing him to be a southerner and a gentleman, I summoned my courage and whispered a petition for a few drops of something, from the flask he carried in his pocket, to put in the egg-nogg for the sick boy. The Captain, who was corpulent and dignified, in some embarrassment replied that he was unfortunately without anything at present, but that the lack would be immediately supplied. He disappeared, returning to produce before my startled eyes, from beneath his coat, a life-sized bottle labeled cognac. Then he invited himself into the kitchen to help make the egg-nogg. He proved expert. I quaked fearing the customers would sniff the cognac through the lattice-work. The sick boy came, turned out to be one of the Captain's own men. The Captain cocked an unsympathetic eye.

"What's the matter with you, Smith?" he questioned, "been drunk again?"

"Captain," I scolded horrified, "I won't have any rough talk like that in my kitchen!"

Smith indignantly denied the charge. He drank his egg-nogg and left looking three shades happier.

"Captain," said I, "did you ever make an egg-nogg for one of your men before?"

"Never," replied the Captain with decision. He drained his own bowl and took his departure. "I will leave the bottle behind," he told me.

"But I don't want it!"

"You might need it again," he declared. And nothing could induce him to change his mind.

That bottle weighs on my conscience like a crime. I have hidden the guilty thing in a corner of the store-room shelf behind some perfectly innocent-looking bundles of stationery and a pile of safety razor blades.

But out of sight it continues to haunt my mind. I feel as if I were giving sanctuary to the devil. And, worst of all, I have a vision of coming into the hut some day to find that the bottle has been discovered and the whole Y. M. C. A. is on a jag.

Mauvages, November 11.

It isn't true. It isn't real. It can't be that the war is really ended.

This morning I awoke to the sound of the most tremendous barrage I have ever heard. At this distance however it was almost more like a sensation than a sound, a sort of incessant thrilling, throbbing vibration.

The question was on everybody's lips: "Do you suppose they really *will* sign the armistice?" "It don't sound much like peace this morning!" would come the dubious reply. We have heard rumours just since yesterday, but in rumours we have so long ceased to put any faith! As the morning wore on our skepticism grew. The almost unbroken reverberation frayed the nerves. As eleven o'clock drew near the tension became torture. Would the guns cease? Could they? It seemed as if they must go on forever. The clock in the old grey church tower began to strike the hour. I flung open the kitchen door. We all stood breathless, frozen, listening. Ding-dong, ding-dong; through the notes of the bell we could still hear the throbbing of the great guns. Eleven times the slow bell chimed, there was a heavy boom, one more, and then absolute silence. We stared at each other blankly incredulous. "They've signed," said a boy.

I walked down the little lane that leads to the ammunition dump and picked a bunch of orange-scarlet berries. I wanted to be alone, to listen. It was a day all pearl and lavender, a violet mist hung over the brown hill-sides. No one passed on the road, there was not a sound of any sort that reached me, the world seemed to be asleep. The stillness was terrifying. I waited, tense, not able to believe, expecting every moment to have the silence broken by the resumption of the cannonade. Then as the minutes passed and still my strained ears could not catch so much as a whisper, I turned back and entered the little roadside Chapel in the Bush. There in its dim blue and silver solitude I knelt down before the little statue of Jeanne d'Arc and prayed.

At noon someone started the old church bell to ringing, it jangled frantically for hours.

I think we are all a little dazed. I for one have a curious feeling as if I had come up suddenly against a blank wall.

Mauvages, November 12.

Last night we celebrated. The whole ordnance camp got out and set off flares and signal rockets from the dump, while two of the boys put over a barrage with the machine-gun on the hill. And there was much champagne. This morning the street is hung with flags,—I never knew before how thrilling the tricolor could be until I saw it like this, against the stone-grey of the old houses.

A company of French cavalry is just passing through town. They are very beautiful to look at, with their bright blue uniforms, their bright bay horses, and the long slim lances which they carry in one hand, each with a tiny pennant at the end. As each one comes into view down the street I think; "Thank God, for one more Frenchman left alive."

The boys have already begun to argue about the date on which they will reach home. But though the fighting may be over, there are long months still ahead of us here I am sure. And now with the strain and the excitement gone, France is bound to look greyer and muddier and more whats-the-use to the boys than ever before. May Heaven help us all!

Mauvages, November 17.

I want to make you acquainted with Bill and Nick, my two invaluable assistants. Bill is my official detail formally assigned. Nick is a volunteer, his services a free-will offering proferred at such times as he is not required in his regular capacity as guardian of the bath-house.

Bill is a lame tame giant six feet two and up. He slipped a cog in his knee one time while shuffling shells last summer and never got quite straightened out again. Bill is my salvation. He redeems what would otherwise be a desperate situation. For Bill has a Business Brain. If it weren't for that, I believe I should be driven to the mad-house trying to balance the francs and centimes at the end of each week. Besides having a head for figures, Bill is an all round handy man with a turn for inventions. When I come back to the hut after a morning expedition to Gondrecourt in quest of suppplies, I may or I may not find last night's dishes washed but I am pretty sure to find some wonderful new contrivance added to my hut equipment. Bill has made me a stove-pipe out of a German powder can. Bill has installed an automatic closing attachment for the main door, which consists of a rope, a pulley, a stove grate and an excruciating squeak; the chief advantage of this invention being the squeak which always betrays the sneak who tries to escape undetected in the middle of a prayer. Sometimes I think it hurts Bill's pride to have to take orders from a lady, especially one with such an unmathematical brain as I. Occasionally he lapses into a you're-only-a-little-girl-after-all sort of attitude and then I have to put on all my dignity and read the riot act to him. But when I hand in my weekly cash sheets at Headquarters and the cashier there tells me that my accounts are the best in the whole area, why Bill could have the whole hut and everything in it.

As for Nick, if Bill is right hand man, why Nick makes a quite indispensable left, and this in spite of the fact that the poor fellow is almost blind. He got a crack in the back of his head from the corner of a case of "75s," while unloading ammunition some two months ago, which affected the optic nerve. And though the doctor promises a partial restoration of his sight, at present he must grope about in dark glasses and semi-darkness. Nick has a history. An orphan, educated for the priesthood, he ran away at the age of sixteen and started on the career of a cowboy. After having broken every bone in his body in the course of his broncho-busting he rose to the heights of his profession and joined Buffalo Bill's Wild West Show. Here he met his wife, a lasso and pistol expert. While riding an "outlaw" in Madison Square Garden, he was thrown and had one of his legs badly smashed, which forced him to retire from public life. After this he spent a couple of years as a bar-tender in New York. In his spare moments, aided by his ecclesiastical Latin, he learned practical chemistry from an old German druggist who kept shop next door. Now in his civilian capacity Nick is consulting chemist for a Brooklyn laundry concern, while his wife conducts successfully a French millinery store in Flatbush. So much for romance!

Nick is, I am quite sure, the politest Irishman in France. Moreover he is the darling of the feminine portion of the town. Partly by reason of his blindness, which appeals to the quick sympathies of the Frenchwomen, and partly because of his unvarying courtesy, his kindliness and his quaint humour, he is the most sought-after man in Mauvages. He knows, I should judge, some six words of French, but with these he manages to "get by." And he is forever being invited out to supper.

Every morning between sweeping up and washing the dishes and waiting on the counter we hold a coffee party in the kitchen; Bill and Nick and myself and whoever else happens to be around. The party consists of coffee with plenty of sugar and canned milk,—always a treat in the army as in the messes you must drink it plain;—and K. P. cookies. Now K. P. cookies, you must understand, are cookies from the end of the package that the mouse didn't eat. As there is considerable activity on the part of the mice these days there are any number of K. P. cookies. And yet I have done my best. Pricked on by conscience I said to Nick day before yesterday, "Nick do you suppose you could get me a trap?"

"Certainly Ma'am, I'll buy one at the store."

"But wait a minute, do you know the word for mouse-trap?"

"Don't worry. That's not in the least necessary." And he set out for the *General Store Articles Militaire* down the street.

But for once his sign language failed him. He was offered everything in the store from a screw-driver to an egg-beater and only achieved the trap finally by stumbling over one on the floor. It was a French trap to be baited with flour and sewed up with thread; I looked at it skeptically, but the next morning we had caught a mouse. However today it was K. P. cookies as usual.

"Bill," I said, "you'll have to borrow Iodine." Iodine is the Medical Sergeant's cat.

"Aw shucks," says Bill, "Iodine is a frog cat. She wouldn't look at a mouse unless you served it to her on a platter dressed with garlic."

Bill says no home is complete without a dog. I quite agree with him. Only, I say, we must catch him young so we can bring him up in the way he should go. These French dogs for the most part seem to have neither manners nor morals. So Bill is keeping an eye out for a likely puppy.

"But," he said, "when we close up here, the only way we'll be able to settle it between us will be to make him into sausages."

If we ever do get a dog I think I shall call him "Tin Hat" just because every other dog in the A. E. F. is named "Cognac."

Mauvages, November 20.

Our relations to the French populace are enough to try a diplomat. Hardly a day passes in the hut but what some delicate social or ethical problem arises.

First, there is Louis, a most disreputable old scamp if there ever was one. He keeps the café across the street and so is my deadly rival. The other day the old rascal appeared at my counter grinning from ear to ear, and demanded "*bonbons pour le rheum*," producing, in witness of his urgent need, a feeble and patently artificial cough. When I answered that unfortunately we had none, he instantly substituted chocolate in his request. Unable to resist the rapscallion's grin I gave him a handful, whereat in beaming gratitude he immediately invited me over to the café to have a glass of wine at his expense. And when I hastily informed him that I didn't care for wine he genially amended the invitation so that it stood, "glass of beer." And now I am told by the boys that he has announced that I, forsooth, am his "fiancée!"

But chiefly there is Rebecca. We call her Rebecca because when Bill goes to the well to get a pail of water he usually happens to meet her there. Rebecca is thin and dark and lively. Her English vocabulary includes such phrases as "beeg steef" and "Mek eet snappee!" She is, as the boys put it, "full of pep." Rebecca has a little black and villainous-looking husband who occasionally appears in town from the trenches, but for the most part she is free to follow where her fancy leads. If it should ever lead her to confession I am afraid she would make the old Curé's eyebrows curl.

Bill's acquaintance with Rebecca is entirely on business lines he wants me to understand. She does his laundry for him. "It's all very well," I say, "to take her your washing, but why must you take her chocolates?" He knows I disapprove. When he lingers too long on the water detail I eye him severely on his return.

"Bill, have you been hobnobbing with Rebecca?"

Bill grins admission.

Rebecca lives in a white little one story door-and-window house just around the corner on the Rue d'Eglise which I must pass going to my canteen. And Rebecca keeps tab on the precise hour and minute at which I return to my billet under Bill's escort every night. Going home one stormy night I took Bill's arm. The next day Bill informed me that Rebecca had advised him that such conduct, according to French notions, was not quite *comme il faut*.

Bill, I find, is able to make an astonishing amount of conversation with his "nigger French" that takes absolutely no account of moods, tenses, conjugations, declinations or any of the other stuff in grammar books. And I am afraid he understands a great deal that it would be just as well he didn't.

"How did you learn it all?" I asked him.

He looked at me side-wise. "Rebecca gave me lessons," he answered grinning.

Last night, as we passed Rebecca's house, I noticed that her door was the least bit ajar.

As Bill left me at my gate I admonished him; "Now don't you stop to say good-night to Rebecca."

"Gosh, no!" said Bill, "if I did I'm afraid I might have to hurry or I'd be late for breakfast."

Whenever I meet Rebecca on the street she always bows to me most urbanely.

Nor is Rebecca all my concern in relation to Big Bill. There is also the pretty girl who lives down the street who undoubtedly would not be averse to accompanying him to America. Bill stops at her house every night in order to get a quart of fresh milk for the C. O.'s breakfast. I bid him be wary of these Franco-American alliances, citing horrible examples I have known, such as the machine-gunner, for instance, who, in order to be in harmony with his future family-in-law, felt it incumbent on him to appear at his wedding wearing a pair of wooden shoes; and of the doughboy who married a widow with two children, and, since he knew no French and she no English, persuaded his company commander to detail an interpreter to live in the house with them for the first three days after their marriage.

Not many days ago a girl came to my kitchen door in company with a soldier. She had a United States paymaster's cheque which she wished to have cashed. Afterwards I questioned Bill. It seems a lieutenant had married and afterwards divorced her. She was still drawing his allotment. She looked so thoroughly the peasant, bare-headed, in a shawl and shoddy skirt, with nothing to particularly distinguish her pretty but inexpressive face, that I voiced my wonder to the boys.

"Oh but you ought to see her when she gets dressed up!" they said.

"Fine feathers don't make fine birds," I remind severely. "Bill, be warned!"

"Yes, but there's Gaby," Bill suggests. "What about her?" Now Gaby is the little chauffeuse who has been driver for a French general three years and who turns up periodically in town. She is quaint as a wood-cut and solemn as an owl, with her shock of bobbed hair and her great staring child-like eyes. She sits at the mess table and never says a word but draws your glance irresistibly. Always she wears an odd little straight-cut dress hanging just below her knees and a *croix de guerre* pinned to her breast. Gaby killed a man with her car not long since and was held a prisoner at Ligny-en-Barrois for ten days in consequence. Gaby and one of the sergeants at the A. R. are undergoing all the woe and wonder of love's young dream.

"Oh well," I say, "Gaby is different."

This afternoon Rebecca appeared at the canteen and asked for Bill. She was so elegantly attired that at first I didn't know her. After a parley at the door, Bill, with an odd expression on his face, takes his second-best raincoat from the peg and hands it to her. I looked my inquiries. An old doughboy sweetheart of the lady's, it appears, had returned on leave and they were going travelling together.

"Going off on a honey-moon with another feller, in my raincoat! Gosh, it's a cruel war!" grinned Bill.

Mauvages, November 24.

Now that the time is drawing on toward Christmas the boys,—bless them!—are all wanting to send some remembrance to mothers, sisters, wives and sweethearts at home. But what to send has been the desperate question. One sort of goods and one only is offered for such purposes by the French stores in this locality, a line of flimsy silk stuff, handkerchiefs, scarfs and little aprons, machine-embroidered with gay flowers and each bearing the legend "Souvenir de France." They are fragile slazy things, absurdly high-priced, inappropriate and often hideous. But to the boys they are altogether beautiful. After many requests and inquiries I gave in. I went to Gondrecourt and purchased what I could find that was the least tawdry, the least exorbitant. I brought them to the canteen; they proved so popular that three days afterward I had to make another trip to town to buy some more. Now we carry a regular stock of fancy silk handkerchiefs and aprons in addition to the chewing tobacco and cigarettes. But here one is faced with a delicate problem. Each handkerchief is embroidered with some such specific legend as *To my Sweetheart, To My Dear Wife, To my Darling Daughter,*—I refused to consider the bit of lacy frippery marked *To my Dear Son!*—and this complicates matters immensely I find. Somehow we always manage to have a supply of Sweethearts on hand when a man is in quest of a Dear Wife and vice versa. In vain I artfully suggest that it would be a pretty compliment to call one's wife "Dear Sweetheart," to their minds there seems to be something essentially compromising in such a notion. Occasionally the reverse will work however, and a boy, grinning and abashed, will select a handkerchief marked "Dear Wife" to send to his sweetheart. Sometimes during these sales one's faith in the single heartedness of Young America receives a shock, as when an innocent-looking lad will blandly select half a dozen "Dear Sweethearts" and put each in a separate envelope to send to a different girl!

Speaking of souvenirs, there is a boy who acts as fireman on the dinky little engine that pulls the work-train on the narrow-gauge between Mauvages and Sauvoy. He belongs to a regiment of engineers who served with the British in Flanders for some eight months. While there he dug up enough dead Germans,—"You could always tell where they were buried because the grass grew so much greener there," he explained,—and picked enough gold fillings out of their teeth, to make a whole match box full. He was going to take it home and have a dentist put the gold in his teeth "for a souvenir," but unluckily in the spring drive he lost all his possessions and the match box with them. Now this, as Kipling would say, is a true story.

Mauvages, November 30.

Let me recount to you the gentle tale of the German prisoners and the Thanksgiving movies, an incident which I consider a sort of sermon in a nutshell and a Warning to the Nations.

Unluckily there is in this division a secretary who is a sentimentalist. He has an idea that an important part of his object in France is "to enliven the long evenings of the French villagers," and particularly does he consider it his Christian duty to do something to demonstrate how much we love the poor German prisoners, those gentlemen who wear the big P. G. for *Prisonnier de Guerre* on their backs and "ought," as the boys say, "to have an I in the middle." There are several hundred of them in a camp at Gondrecourt and they are, it is said, just as well housed and fed as our boys, and not made to work nearly as hard.

Now, as there was no other sort of entertainment available, I had set my heart on having movies in my hut on Thanksgiving. I had presented my request at the Headquarters office and understood the matter settled. But the Sentimental Secretary it seems had made up his mind that the poor dear German prisoners must have a treat and, other schemes falling through, he also put in a request for the movies. There was only one portable machine in working order. Through some misunderstanding or something in the office, the P. G.s got the movies. To enlarge upon my sentiments when the news was broken to me Thursday morning or to record the opinions expressed by the boys in regard to the matter, is not to the purpose of this tale.

Failing our show, all that I could manage in the way of celebration was a little box of nuts and raisins tied up with a bit of red, white and blue ribbon for every man in camp. The mess sergeant, however, outdid himself. Our Thanksgiving dinner was nothing less than a feast. For days the A. R. jitney had been scouring the country for poultry. At last the sergeant had succeeded in getting enough for all. He did this by assembling specimens of the whole feathered tribe; turkey, duck, chicken and goose. And I had a slice of each. But for all that I didn't enjoy that dinner worth six-pence. Those movies were on my mind. I tried to think of the touching gratitude of the German prisoners. Perhaps after all if one should pursue them with delicate attentions it might lead them to see the error of their ways. Perhaps giving them a movie show would inculcate, by example, a beautiful lesson of Christian charity and forgiveness. Who could tell what uplifting moral influence Charlie Chaplin or Mutt and Jeff might exert?

Last night was our regular movie-night. In the midst of preparing for the show, Georges, the French operator, who was getting the machine ready, Georges the little dandy, always nonchalant and blasé, came charging back to the counter, his eyes as big as arc-lights. He thrust his hands, which were full of cartridges, beneath my nose, fairly dancing on tip-toe in his excitement. He had found them in the carbide; when the carbide had gotten hot, "*Poof!*" he dramatized the wrecking of the hut with explosive gestures. "*C'est les Boches! Les cochons!*" Never again would he take his machine there, never, never!

As the machine had been left at the German Prison Camp after the Thanksgiving show and then brought directly from there to Mauvages there seems little room for doubt that the prisoners had placed the shells there. Of course, if there were any poetic justice in things, the Sentimental Secretary himself would have been blown up by the Germans' cartridges, but unfortunately in real life things don't happen that way.

Mauvages, December 3.

The French Army is in possession of Mauvages. A regiment of artillery moved in on us yesterday afternoon. There seemed a never-ending line of them as they crawled into town, the horses just barely able to drag the heavy pieces. There must have been a shocking shortage of fodder in the French Army; the poor beasts look wretched beyond words. The big guns are lined up all along the street. They look like great spotted lizards in their green and brown and yellow coats of camouflage. Each piece has a girl's name carved on the muzzle. The one in front of my canteen is Marthe, further up the street stand Lucile and Marie. We watched them as they brought the guns into place, unhitched the teams and made their preparations to settle down and stay. Once settled, our perplexities began. Immediately they started to trickle into the canteen in search of cigarettes. To the first comers in a weak moment I slipped a few packages. That was enough. Thereafter it was just like flies to the molasses jar, and then of course I had to harden my heart and say no. But they wouldn't take no for an answer. They begged, pleaded and cajoled. I posted a polite sign at the end of the counter explaining how the canteen supplies had been brought into France without payment of any duty, under the strict agreement with the French Government that they would be sold only to Americans. But they refused to read the sign. One handsome brigadier stopped me on the street in order to present his petition. And at the canteen a little poilu with a round cherubic face, after being refused some nine or ten times over at the counter, followed me out into the kitchen to urge his piteous plea. It was dreadful, it was harrowing. I have never felt quite so mean about anything in all my life.

In the evening we had billed a stereoptican lecture on London. Forseeing that the poilus would form a large proportion of the audience, I tried to get an interpreter to explain the pictures in French to them but at the last minute the interpreter failed me. Notwithstanding, the Frenchmen remained courteously quiet while the lecture lasted. But once it was finished the atmosphere of the hut underwent a change. The blue-coated figures who were swarming into the canteen now had evidently spent the earlier part of the evening in the cafés. I went out into the centre of the hut to see what was going on; all about me stretched a swarm of poilus in a genial mood. The door squeaked open, a little soldier came skipping into the hut. To my horror I saw he carried in one hand a tall tumbler and in the other a large bottle of Benedictine. The victrola was jigging out a rag on the counter. Posing for a minute in an attitude reminiscent of the great Isadora, the little poilu proceeded to dance in time to the music, pirouetting on one toe as he waved the bottle and the tumbler above his head with Bacchanalian gestures. Then suddenly he sat down at one of the tables and started to pour himself a glass. I swooped down upon him. It was *défendu* I explained, strictly and absolutely *défendu* to drink in this hut. He stared incredulous. I reiterated with emphasis. Finally he nodded sulkily and, slipping the bottle underneath his arm, turned away. Two minutes later I caught him offering a red-nosed friend a drink square in front of my counter. I flew to the attack again. I told him it was against the rules to so much as *bring* wine into the hut. He held his ground defiantly. I wanted to take the little wretch by his coat collar and march him out the door; I felt I could have done it. Instead I plead, expostulated and commanded. A score of grinning poilus crowded about us: it was evidently as good as a show to them. I entreated the little poilu please, *please* to carry the bottle out of the hut! "*Dehors! Dehors!* Outside!" they chorused gleefully. I exhausted my vocabulary, apparently without effect. The little poilu wasn't used to taking orders from a girl, especially one who spoke French so badly, but finally I won. "*Bon!*" he snapped explosively, turned on his heel and marched out. I fled precipitately to the kitchen and stayed there until closing time. I didn't feel equal to coping with any more tipsy poilus.

It's curious how the whole character of a dwelling-place can change. When the priest and the cat and I are keeping house together, the old mansion is the dimmest, most decorous place imaginable. At night I let myself in the dark front door, locking it carefully behind me,—Monsieur scolded me for leaving it unlocked once; I had left him, he said, at the mercy of the passersby!—then grope my way down the cold unlighted hall and up the steep stairs to my chilly room and to bed by one flickering candle's light. The place is as silent and lifeless as a tomb. Then new troops come into town and suddenly everything is changed. The lower floor is taken over for an officers' mess and often too, for Headquarters. Savory odors of cooking, warm smells mount up the dim stairway, candles gutter in niches in the passage-ways, smart-looking officers in khaki or horizon-blue as the case may be, meet and salute one in the hall. The tramp of booted feet, the ring of spurs, the clink of glasses, laughter, song, the piano played tumultuously sometimes late into the night,—everything from Madelon to Mozart—and most startling, and incredible of all, the jangle of a telephone bell, installed for the occasion; for a few days we live in a strange bustling vivid world, then on they move and we are left again to our silence and solitude.

Tonight as I was washing up for supper I was startled by a rap on my door. There stood Monsieur le Curé and a French officer. I had a bad moment wondering what the cause of such a visitation might be. Was he going to turn me out of my billet perhaps? Or was he going to complain about the treatment his men had received in the Y.? Monsieur le Curé was ambling through a long and elaborate peroration. At first I could make no sense out of it, then suddenly I caught on. Monsieur le Capitaine was a stamp collector. He wanted to know if I perhaps had some stamps *des États-Unis* which I could spare him!

Reports have come in tonight of friction between the French and American soldiers in town, resulting in a number of scrimmages. The whole trouble springs, I gather, from the eternal feminine and the native jealousy of the male; the Fair Sex of Mauvages having made quite evident to the poilus their decided preference for the doughboys.

Mauvages, December 6.

The theatrical season at Mauvages has been inaugurated. The carpenters were busy in the hut all day yesterday, hammering and sawing, making us a roll curtain out of roofing paper, manufacturing foot-lights from commissary candles and tin reflectors cut from the lining of tobacco cases. When the stage was done it was very gay. We had a red curtain across the back, bright yellow wings, red and yellow draperies around the proscenium arch, festoons of little flags strung across the top, and a large American flag draped centre back. It wasn't what we wanted, it was just what, by hook or crook we could get, and the effect really wasn't half as bad as it sounds.

The programme might be classed in two parts, rehearsed and impromptu. For a starter we dropped a tear over Baby's Prayer, that bit of ninety-nine one-hundredths pure sentimentality, without which no programme in the A. E. F. is complete these days; after which we were adjured to "Pray for sunshine, But always be prepared for rain,"—a quite superfluous admonition in this part of France at this season of the year!

"Put all your pennies on the shelf,
The almighty dollar will take care of itself."

"Humph!" grunted the boy next me, "I'll bet it was a Jew wrote that."

Following the songs we heard Barney, the Poet Laureate of the Camp, celebrate the deeds of the ordnance detachment in verse. At least we supposed that was what it was, for Barney has a brogue all his own and if you get one word in ten you're lucky. As the C. O. says, it is much easier to "*compree*" a Frenchman than it is to understand Barney.

After Barney we had a sermon, a burlesque darky sermon preached by a black-face comedian. As luck would have it, two real darkies from a labor camp up the line slipped in at the back of the hut just as the preacher began. They took it all in deadly earnest, and warmed, I suspect, by a glass at the corner café, they presently began to respond to the preacher's exhortations with genuine religious fervor.

"Dat's so! You tell 'em bruder! Hallelujah! Bless de Lord!"

The audience up front, hearing a commotion and unluckily not catching the comedy, hissed indignantly and the darkies, abashed, slunk out.

Of course at the last moment some of our headliners failed to come across. The mumps claimed our dramatic reader and our buck-and-wing dancer sent word, just as the curtain was going up, that in all the camp, no shoes outside of hob-nails, large enough for him could be found. But we made up for these defections by our impromptu acts. The most surprising of these was the Little Fat Poilu. He popped up suddenly from Heaven knows where, a round rosy dumpling of a man with a shiny nose and a fat black beard, and offered his services. On his first appearance he played the violin with vim and spirit. Then in answer to the applause he dropped his violin, seized the tall hat from the head of the darky preacher, clapped it on his own, and bounced back onto the stage. The transformation was amazing. In an instant, instead of a poilu he had become a jolly little bourgeois shopkeeper out for a stroll on the boulevard. He proceeded to sing a comic song, a song with an interminable number of verses, unquestionably very funny and in all probability quite scandalous. The French portion of the audience was charmed, they joined vociferously in the jiggy choruses, and when he had done they insisted on another and another. For a while it looked as if France was going to run away with the programme, but finally the little poilu came to the end of his repertoire,—or of his breath maybe, and America once more took the stage.

Today we are living in an atmosphere of theatrical enterprise. Already there are three or four "bigger and better" rival shows in process of incubation. What's more, Barney is writing a play. He sits at one of the canteen tables surrounded by a group of admiring would-be actors and each sheet, as he finishes it, is gravely handed around the crowd. So far it seems to contain just three characters; Rose the beautiful stenographer, the villain landlord and the office boy. I am waiting in suspense to see whether Barney's masterpiece is going to turn out a melodrama, a problem play or a dramatic treatise on the social and political wrongs of Ireland.

The French troops are moving tomorrow. Tonight the Little Fat Poilu came to bid us good-bye. When no one was looking I filled his pockets up with cigarettes.

Mauvages, December 9.

A very regrettable incident occurred last night. The day being Sunday we were due for a religious service at seven-fifteen. At seven-ten the Reverend Gentleman, who was to instruct my flock in the way wherein they should go, arrived in company with the Business Manager from Gondrecourt. Now it happened that the Reverend Gentleman on this occasion was none other than my friend the Sentimental Secretary. He surveyed the congregation; there were nine boys in the hut. He sat down and waited for the audience to arrive. But the audience didn't. Instead one wretch surreptitiously sneaked out the door. At last I felt it necessary to come forward with apologies and explanations; my flock at present was small to start with, the sheep had all gone to Domremy on an excursion, the goats were deep in an after-payday poker game.

"Do you wish me to hold the meeting?" the R. G. questioned grimly.

"If you will."

The Reverend Gentleman, a bit tight about the lips, laid on. It was a cold night; we gathered by the fire. I tried to make myself look as large as possible, but stretch the congregation as you might, we only reached two-thirds of the way around the stove.

"Well," said the Business Manager when it was all over with, "how soon will you be ready to close out this hut?"

I reminded him that after all it would have only taken ten righteous to save Sodom, so might not eight save Mauvages?

Of course just as soon as the Reverend Gentleman and the Business Manager had shaken our dust off their feet and disappeared, a whole crowd of boys came streaming into the hut. I accused them of having waited just around the corner until they had seen the Religious Service depart. As for Big Bill I consider him nothing short of a slacker, he sat in the kitchen all evening and wrote a letter to his girl. I tell him that as hut detail it is obviously his duty to attend all services but he explains that "it makes him homesick."

In a town on the road between Mauvages and Gondrecourt there is a labor camp of Chinese coolies. These are the laziest folk in Europe I am sure. They are supposed to be working on the road, which needs it badly enough, resembling, as one boy declared, "the top of a stove when all the lids are taken off." All day long they squat by the roadside, or stand idle watching the traffic go by. "They'd rather be caught dead than caught working," as one boy said. The story goes that if one of them dies the French Government must pay the Chinese Government thirty francs. They come dear at that. Moreover, they are unconscionable thieves. Up on the hill back of the town where they are billeted there is an American aviation field. The camp was abandoned after the armistice, but twelve boys from the air service were detailed to stay and guard the property. These boys find that the chief end of their life is to chase the Chinks out of the stores; they are quite persistent and perfectly unabashed. More than that, if the Chinks catch one of the guards by himself, they are likely to attack in force armed with sticks and as our boys are not allowed to carry weapons, such an attack is no laughing matter. The trouble began, the boys tell me, in the days when the camp was populated; two mechanics had once thought it a good joke to give one of the Chinks a bath by ducking him in the horse-trough.

One of these heathen, I am told, came to church here at Mauvages yesterday and almost broke up the meeting. It pleased him to sing all the way through the service, a wierd sing-song chant all his own, and as if that were not bad enough, in the middle of a prayer he had turned square about and started to play with the rosary of the scandalized Madame behind him! The most pious-minded could scarcely keep their thoughts on the priest's dissertation. There was "*beaucoup distraction*" as one Mademoiselle phrased it.

This morning I went down to Gondrecourt.

"Well, and how are your eight men?" asked the Business Manager.

"One of them has gone to the hospital with the mumps," I answered. "So now I have seven."

Mauvages, December 12.

I have been A. W. O. L. I have been on a joy ride. For the first time since I came to France I have taken a real day off. I got a chance to go up to the old battle front on a "speeder." I didn't mention the matter to the office, but I took the chance. I knew I could safely trust the hut to the management of Bill and Nick for one day.

We started out shortly after six A. M., on the narrow-gauge bound for Mont Sec. There were five of us on the speeder which is, you must know, a little flat car something like a hand-car, only that instead of being propelled by hand power, it is run by a gasolene motor. Speeders are the jolliest possible way of travelling and they can go like the wind: they possess just two disadvantages, their propensity for having engine trouble, and the ease with which they jump the track at the slightest provocation. It is told how in Abainville the other day a speeder jumped the rails, the engineer, after turning a half a dozen somersaults, picked himself up, squared off, demanded; "Who in hell put the pebble on the track?"

From Mauvages we followed the A. and S. to Sorcy. There we switched onto the line which the boys at Abainville used to declare "ran through the trenches." They would tell me wonderful tales of the trips they had taken on this line; the smoke-stack of the engine protruded over the top, they explained, and "Gosh, you could hear the bullets just splatterin' against it!"

A short ways out from Sorcy we passed the last inhabited village. Ahead of us we could see the barren sinister outline of Mont Sec, that little Gibraltar of the land which the Germans had captured and fortified early in the war, which the French had endeavored to retake in 1915 with the most fearful losses, but which had remained impregnable, commanding, looking down in contempt on our men in their muddy lowland trenches of the Toul

Sector, until, on September twelfth, the American Army had taken it along with the rest of the Saint Mihiel salient.

As we neared Mont Sec we began to pass devastated villages, some of them mere formless ruins, others from a distance holding the shape and outline of habitable dwelling-places but on approach revealing themselves as mere groups of riddled house-shells. Across the open places stretched interminable grey swathes of rusting tangled wire, "barbed-wire enough to fence Texas," as one boy put it. On sidings we passed long lines of cars full of salvage, all the junk of war tossed carelessly together. Along the tracks were scattered empty shells and here and there piles of unexploded ammunition. In a shell-hole by the roadside, half filled with water, lay a hob-nailed shoe,—prosaic but pitiful witness of some tragedy. It was the loneliest land, the most forsaken I have ever seen. Far and wide as one looked over the empty plain there was no living, moving creature anywhere.

At the foot of Mont Sec we stopped. There in the woods were the remains of a German camp; it had been a jolly little place fixed up like a beer garden underneath the trees, with fancy "rustic" work and chairs and tables. We left the speeder there, and tramping across the fields, climbed Mont Sec. Near the top we found the entrances to the dugouts. The hill was tunneled through from side to side, all the corridors and rooms walled, roofed and floored with the heaviest oak lumber. Everywhere through the passage-ways ran a perfect network of electric wires. Long stairs led to the different levels. No furnishings were left except the bunks and some rough tables. We ate our luncheon of bread, jam and corn willy in what had evidently been the officers' quarters; the room was nicely finished with cement, there was a fancy moulded pattern in bas relief over the doorway, a pipe-hole showed where a stove had been.

After lunch we inspected the concrete machine-gun pill-boxes which dotted the hill-top. Then we went down the steep eastern slope to the village of Mont Sec. About the town, to judge from the ploughed and pitted vineyards, the fighting must have been the fiercest. The village was a village of the dead. We went inside the church; part of the tower, some of the walls, a little of the roof was left, beyond that nothing. Near the door a French officer had scrawled *"Maudite soit le boche qui détruit les églises,"*—cursed be the Hun who destroys the churches. In this church, Madame the Caretaker tells me, the Germans commanded all the male inhabitants of Mont Sec to assemble. Here they were kept prisoners for three days and nights. On the fourth day they were marched off at the bayonet's point into Germany, and no one has ever heard a word from them since.

Just outside the village in the little cemetery, ploughed with shell-holes, we found French, American and German graves. The German inscriptions all commemorated "heroes dead for the Fatherland;" one of them vowed, with the help of God, vengeance on the enemy.

We went back to the speeder. As it was early in the afternoon we decided to go on. Rounding Mont Sec, we passed into German occupied territory. We saw the famous cabbage patches which fed our soldiers after the Saint Mihiel drive, and, on a hillock beside the road, one memorable scarecrow dressed from head to foot as a German soldier, "feldgrau" uniform, cartridge belt, helmet and all. At Hattonchatel we looked down on the German barracks from the hill-side but didn't have time to stop. It was growing late, so we must turn about-face. Once headed for home our troubles began. The rain which had been teasing us all day as a faint drizzle, settled down to business. A few hundred yards down the hill-side the speeder jumped the track. Fortunately we weren't running fast and the speeder jumped on the right side, if it had jumped on the left we might have gone over the edge of the mountainous hill-side. As it was no real harm resulted beyond a violent bumping and shaking up; I jumped and got a lame wrist. "The chances are, that whatever happens, she won't turn over," the boys told me, "so hang on after this." So I hung tight. The engine, which had worked like a charm all the way up, began to sulk and balk by fits. Presently it grew dark. We had one lantern, we lighted it and the boy who sat at the front end held it so the light would fall on the rails. Every now and then the wind would blow it out. At each station along the track we would stop and ask the engineer operators whether the block ahead was clear. When we came to the last station before the long forest stretches about Mont Sec the operator who came out to speak to us was quite angry; there were three trains, he said, somewhere on the track ahead; we were doing a very dangerous thing, running after dark. We went on, straining our eyes as we entered the woods in order to discern the dark mass on the track ahead which would mean a train, for the trains, in memory of war days, I suppose, carry absolutely no lights. A week ago a speeder ran head-on into a train at night just above Sauvoy; of its three passengers, two were killed, the other fearfully injured. We held ourselves tense, ready the moment we had made out a train, and the speeder slowed down, to jump, and, lifting the car, push it to one side off the tracks until the train had passed. Once we were lucky enough to make a siding just at the critical moment. Sometimes we ran at the edge of high embankments, sometimes we would cross, on a trestle, a wide marshy stream; then the thought would come to me, *What if the speeder should jump here?* And she did jump twice more on the way back, but luckily both times in well-selected places. The worst feature of these acrobatics was that the jar had an unhealthy effect upon the engine and after each occasion the mechanics in the crowd had to delve and tinker before the speeder could be coaxed to speed again. Also it was wet. The rain soaked through my raincoat, through my sweater, into my leather jacket; my skirt was a dripping rag, the water oozed from my gloves, raindrops dripped from my nose, my "waterproof" shoes were like sponges. You felt, as one of the boys put it, exactly like a figure in a fountain.

Between Mont Sec and Sorcy we got a tow. In the dark we came upon the rear end of a salvage train, tied ourselves up to it, and bumped merrily along behind until the train turned off on a branch line and we had to cut loose and make our own way with the increasingly contrary engine. Fortunately, from that point most of the way was down hill; on the up-grades we got off and walked; the last part of the way the boys simply had to push the car. We reached home at half-past ten, tired, soaked to the skin, but happy.

Mauvages, December 16.

After this, Mauvages is going to be on the map! Mauvages is to be headquarters for the — Artillery Brigade, with seventeen hundred men in town and thousands more in the villages about. Wonderful to say, this is the very brigade to which my two batteries from the Artillery School belong and though neither of these will be here in town, still they will be near enough so I can get a glimpse of my old boys, I am sure.

Already we have an ammunition train and a crowd of "casuals" waiting here for their outfits. The hut, which has of late been rather empty mornings, is now filled all day. These casuals are for the most part replacements, shipped here directly from the ports, after a ten days' residence in France. They have nothing to do at present but sit in the hut and think how miserable they are. It is funny to hear them talk. Their opinion of Mauvages is inexpressible in polite terms. They are quite convinced that they have come to the Very Last Hole on Earth. In vain I assure them that Mauvages is quite a fine town, as French towns go, in vain I draw their attention to its beauties and advantages. They are absolutely certain that nothing could be worse!

Meanwhile I have been busy making frantic trips into Gondrecourt to demand, in view of the coming crowds, a new hut, an electric lighting system, an addition to the old hut, anything or everything, except a man secretary! But Gondrecourt takes the situation very calmly.

Just to pass the time away, one of the new arrivals went fishing in the canal yesterday. He bestowed his catch on me; it measured about six inches by one and a quarter. As it was still wriggling faintly I put the poor thing in the water-pail, only to find later that Big Bill in disgust had thrown water and fish out into the back yard. Whereupon I raised such an outcry that Bill must go out in the dark and feel through the wet grass for that fish until he found it. I carried it down to camp, inviting the K. P.s to prepare it for the C. O.'s dinner. At dinner it appeared elegantly garnished with parsley in the center of a huge platter. Just to pay me back they made me eat it, while the rest dined on steak.

"How do you suppose he caught it?" asked the C. O. I said nothing. Fishing with hand-grenades is strictly against the law.

Mauvages, December 18.

Mauvages is in disgrace. Mauvages is the black sheep in the Y. fold. Mauvages is in wrong all the way around. And it's all because of one Old Gentleman and his ill-timed opinions.

The Old Gentleman came out to talk to us yesterday evening. We weren't expecting him. We were expecting a lecture on the Man Without a Country,—whoever that may be, Jack Johnson or the Kaiser! as the boys say,—by the Educational Department. But then we have almost given up expecting to get what we expect. This is only the third time we have been fooled on the Man Without a Country who appears to be our Old Man of the Sea.

The Old Gentleman was brought out in state in the best Y. car by the Big Chief, the Entertainment Department and a driver. The Entertainment Department immediately ensconced himself by the cook-stove with a Sunday Picture Supplement; the driver retired to a secluded corner to play a game of checkers with one of the boys; while the Big Chief took his stand out front. I for once back-slid scandalously, and, instead of occupying a front seat with a deeply interested expression spread upon my countenance, sat in the kitchen and ate jam and waffles, the waffles which were heart-shaped and crisp and heavenly, having been brought by Nick from his latest supper party.

The Old Gentleman stood out by the stove, the stage proving too chilly. There was a crowd in the hut. He put his foot in it at the start. He announced himself as an intimate friend of ex-President Roosevelt. The boys, sniffing politics, grew suspicious, even hostile. He began on the scandal of America's unpreparedness, from that passed by degrees to the view that Germany was not yet defeated and as a climax called upon the boys to rise and put themselves on record as being willing to stay in France until Kingdom come, if necessary, in order to do the job up brown. The boys did not rise. Instead they heckled the Old Gentleman until he grew as red as a turkey-cock and so indignant as to fairly wax speechless. One of the ammunition train boys, a husky lad who, they tell me, is an old guard house standby, led the opposition. Out in the kitchen you could have heard a pin drop. The Entertainment Department and I sat and stared at each other.

The whole trouble as I saw it, was that the Old Gentleman had slipped up on his dates. He was giving them a Before-November-Eleventh speech when it was after the eleventh. It was as if he had quite failed to comprehend that at eleven o'clock on that date the whole psychological outlook of the American doughboy underwent an instantaneous change. His entire mental horizon became forthwith concentrated to one burning point,—the desire which he expresses simply but adequately in the words; "I want to go home!" And not ex-President Roosevelt, nor President Wilson, nor General Pershing, nor anybody else could make him interested in anything that was not remotely, at least, related to that issue.

At last the agony was over. The Old Gentleman came back to the kitchen mopping his brow. When he had finished expressing his opinion of Mauvages, the driver went out to crank the car. The car was gone. Of course then, everyone remembered having heard a car drive off in the middle of the lecture,—every one that is, but I, I had been too interested in the waffles,—but of course no one had really thought that it could be, etc. A search party was recruited which scoured highway and byway. The M. P.s at Gondrecourt were notified by 'phone. Meanwhile it was ten o'clock, a bleak night and four indignant gentlemen were stranded six miles from home. An ambassador was elected to go and lay the case before the A. R. C. O. The C. O. on his way to bed, instructed the emissary where billets for the night might possibly be had. But the Old Gentleman, upon receiving the information, flatly and finally refused to stay in any billet in town; he would sleep in his own bed or no other. After a nervous interval the ambassador again approached the C. O., this time suggesting the loan of his car and chauffeur. The C. O., aroused a second time from bed, acceeded shortly, the ambassador returned to despatch the unfortunate Bill to camp to break the news to the chauffeur. The chauffeur, who was in the midst of an after-hours poker game, when he recovered from his astonishment, replied (expurgated) that he'd come when he got good and ready, and settled back to his game.

In the meantime my four guests by the kitchen-stove discussed in part the peculiarities of the Japanese language, but chiefly the shortcomings of Mauvages. The Chief, however, showed himself a gentleman. He washed the dishes up! And considering that he was a man and a minister and that the light was dim and the water cold, he washed them pretty well.

At a quarter to eleven the A. R. chauffeur having presumably forced all the others into bankruptcy, or gone bankrupt himself, drove up to the door and I said farewell to my friends.

This morning a rescue expedition was sent out from Gondrecourt. It finally discovered the lost car, none the worse for its joy-ride, in a ditch half-way to Sauvoy. Information has reached me on the side that it was a little group of "hard-boiled guys" from the ammunition train who stole the auto. They were displeased with the Old Gentleman's opinions, and they made up their minds that he should walk home.

So this is how matters stand: I and my hut are in discredit at Headquarters, because my boys stole their car. The Old Gentleman has openly declared that Mauvages is the most unpatriotic spot in France. The A. R. C. O. is disgusted because he was routed twice out of bed in one night. The chauffeur is so incensed at me and mine at having to drive into town at eleven P. M. that he persistently forgets to stop for my daily papers. And the boys are all sore and touchy on account of the opinions expressed by the Old Gentleman in and after his lecture. Such is the happy lot of a hut secretary.

Mauvages, December 23.

The Big Push is here. Our lawn has turned into a gun park with limbers and caissons elbowing each other under our very eaves. All day the little hut is crowded to its capacity and at night it becomes so full that I am literally afraid it will burst out at the seams. Colonels and captains are forever bobbing up like so many Jack-in-the-Boxes in my kitchen which I was used to consider as a refuge and a sanctum. They have the best intentions in the world; they offer me advice on every subject under the sun from the building of new shelves in the canteen to the frequency with which I should require Big Bill to shave. And quite unsolicited they have given me a detail,—a detail of such proportions that I am swamped. I don't know how many there are. They never stand still long enough for me to count them. Sometimes there appear to be ten and sometimes twenty. Like the Old Woman who lived in the shoe, I have so many details I don't know what to do. They are the nicest boys that ever were, if only they didn't take up quite so much room! Now when I am minded to sit down for a moment to think, my only course is to go into the store-room and sit on a packing-box, and the store-room is very cold. And the worst of it is that they all, from colonel to K. P., have the beautiful idea in their heads that I am not to do any work, but just to be a sort of parlor ornament, and a sweet influence; that I will, in short, like the old man who was afraid of the cow, "sit on the stile and continue to smile," while the army runs my hut. Which is not at all my notion of things.

In the meantime we have been busy making such preparations for Christmas as we could. Chiefly we have decorated the hut. I begged two boxes full of lanterns, flags, tinsel and festoons, from the office, then I merely mentioned the fact that I wanted a tree and lots of branches to trim with and the boys did the rest. I don't know where those greens came from, I don't want to know. But there is one spectre that keeps haunting me; the apparition of an indignant Frenchman at my canteen door, with a bill half a metre long for damages.

This new outfit has brought a heathen custom to town with them. The band plays for Reveille! We had been so peaceful, so unmilitary here in town with not so much as a bugle note to make a ripple in our slumbers! But now at some unimagined hour before daylight a brazen clangour bursts suddenly forth. Down the street and past under my window in the dark they go, making the grand tour of the three streets in town, thumping and tooting as if their lives depended on it. I never knew a band could make such an amazing racket, nor could sound quite so joyously impudent. A bucketful of cold water couldn't dispel sleep any more effectively. I feel like jumping out of bed. But I don't, for it is pitch dark and cold and very damp. There is a fireplace to be sure in my room but after one or two fruitless attempts at making it produce a little heat I abandoned the idea and decided to spend all my time between my bed and the canteen. But when I desire to view my countenance in the mirror, I have to take a towel and wipe off the moisture that collects on it to trickle down in little streams.

I have received my first Christmas present. Bill and Nick—the dears!—have presented me a beautiful silk umbrella. I think they did it largely for the honor of the family. As long as my old faithful only had its handle gone, they could overlook it, but when the ribs took to parting company with the covering, they evidently thought that something should be done about it. Nick went to Gondrecourt to buy it; coming back, he managed to fall off the truck, was picked up and given first aid by a kindly Frenchwoman, and reached home in slightly damaged shape but with the precious umbrella safe. I have been suggesting to Bill that he set a two franc piece in the handle and then I will have his and Nick's initials carved on it, but he doesn't wax enthusiastic.

Mauvages, December 25.

We sat up half the night packing Christmas boxes,—seventeen hundred of them, one for every man in Mauvages. Two packages of cigarettes, a cigar, two bars of chocolate and a can of "smoking" went into each little cardboard box labelled in red "A Merry Xmas from the folks at home through the Y;" that is, theoretically they went in, practically it was discovered that no human ingenuity could so arrange the pesky things as to make them fit the box. So finally we decided to treat the "smoking" as a separate affair. I wanted badly to have Santa Claus hand the boxes to the boys underneath the Christmas tree, but the boys finally convinced me that the difficulties, including the danger of "repeaters" ad lib, were too great, so we fitted the boxes into packing-cases and shipped a case to each company and let each of the top sergeants play that he was Santa Claus.

It was half past twelve by the time I passed the church on my way back to the billet. They were celebrating midnight mass. The light of the altar-candles illumined the old windows with a soft radiance. They were Y. M. C. A. candles. Monsieur le Curé had begged them from me in the afternoon; he could get no others, he said, and was in great distress.

Chez nous there was much activity. I stopped inside the door to chat with the cooks. They were up plucking the Colonel's goose and expected to make a night of it.

Sounds of gaiety were ringing from the dining-room. A young lieutenant, slightly touseled, thrust his head out of the door. I wished him a Merry Christmas; in return he asked me in to partake of an anchovy sandwich. I took one look inside the door at the array of empty bottles, declined with thanks, and climbed the stairs to bed. For a long while afterwards someone downstairs kept mewing like a cat. It might have been the slightly touseled lieutenant.

Today it has been raw and damp and chill and grey and drizzly. I had a notion that I might ask the French kiddies in this afternoon to see the tree and receive some little gifts of cookies and chocolate but when I reached the hut this morning and saw how packed it was I quickly gave up the project. Not for all the children in ten villages would I turn the boys out into the rain.

Tonight there is to be some sort of show, arranged by the entertainment officer.

Just before dinner time the Second Lieutenant from the A. R. came in, looking full of mysterious importance. "The C. O. leaves this noon," he said. "He's ordered to report at Souilly by twelve tonight. I'll tell you all about it later." Later I learned. Inspectors had been visiting the dump. They had found it in a very dangerous state indeed. The wet weather has affected the explosives so that should the sun come out for a day or two the chemical change ensuing would in all probability cause an explosion which would set off the whole dump with its millions of dollars worth of high explosives. In which case little Mauvages would of course go higher than Halifax. The C. O. has been removed and the Second Lieutenant left in charge. The work of destroying the dangerous explosives is to be pursued at top speed. In the meanwhile we will pray for continued rain.

I received two gifts today that touched me deeply. One was a pretty pink embroidered scarf from the boys at the aviation field. The lad who brought it to me had walked twelve miles, into Gondrecourt and back again in the sleety rain, to buy it! The other was a package labeled; "Wishing you a Mary Xmas from the Operators at A. S. No. 9, and may the next one be in the States." Inside were two boxes of chocolates, their Christmas candy issue!

As for me, I am ashamed—I have been so busy and so bothered that I just couldn't seem to manage a gift for anyone, not for Bill nor Nick nor even Monsieur le Curé.

Mauvages, December 28.

Neddy has come back! His battery has just arrived at Rosières and last night he got off and walked over here to see me.

We sat and talked by the kitchen-stove and I found him just the same shy, slow-spoken dreamy lad. The long months at the front have seemingly instilled nothing bitter in him, nor left any scars on his spirit, no matter if he is wearing a wonderful belt quite covered with German buttons all "cut off of dead ones." He dug out of his pockets for me two odd little picture frames made cleverly out of rings from German fuses, with pieces of celluloid cut from the eye-holes of German gas-masks for glass, and held together with surgeon's plaster. Then of course there were the latest pictures of his girl to show me.

He told me about the battery. On the whole their casualties have been light. Jones was gassed, and is in hospital somewhere; it seems just like Jones, somehow, to get gassed! The boys, he told me, had been fairly homesick for the little old Artillery School Hut,—most of all, he said, they had missed my hot chocolate.

Then just to make the occasion perfect, who should walk in but Snow! Snow's battery is at Delouze, two towns away; but Snow has been on leave down on the Riviera, having the time of his young life.

"I never could see what there was in this country worth fighting for," he told me, "until I went down there. But now I know."

He had just returned from his furlough this very afternoon. He hadn't a thing to eat all day, being of course, "dead broke." I got the best impromptu supper I could and we all three sat in the kitchen and ate it. The menu was: crackers and canned milk; sardines and crackers; cracker-pudding and cocoa; crackers and jam. The boys gossiped and swapped yarns like two old veterans. Neddy related how the gunners at the front when loading would pat and even kiss a shell as they adjured it not to be a dud! Snow told me how —, the talented, the brilliant, had gone to pieces at the front and had been sent back to the S. O. S. This must have been hard on Snow for the two were close friends. "I said to him one day," recounted Snow, "—, you must have done something awfully wicked in your life to make you so afraid to die." Undoubtedly the poor fellow's failure was due, not so much to lack of courage, as to over-sensitiveness and too much imagination. The pity of it is that this will surely prove a bad blow to his self-respect.

When it was time for Neddy to go I saw there was something he wanted to say to me. At last it came out. Around his neck, it seems, he is still wearing the chain with the little cross which I gave him when he went to the front. And he has the unshakable notion in his quaint head that it was the cross which kept him safe!

Mauvages, December 29.

Tonight we gave a party: hot chocolate and cookies for the whole camp. Every Sunday before the Big Push came I had been serving hot chocolate free but I had been staggered by the thought of trying to make chocolate for seventeen hundred men on my little stove that is just big enough to sit on, over a fire which has to be coaxed with German powder sticks and candle ends before it will burn, and serving it in our sixty odd cocoa bowls. This morning, however, I had an inspiration. I consulted the detail, they approved. Accordingly we sent requests to three of the battery mess-kitchens, asking that they should each furnish us, at five-thirty, the largest container they possessed full of hot water. Then we asked the mess sergeants to announce the party at supper and tell the boys to bring their mess-cups. The sentry at the street corner was also instructed to let no one pass without his mess-cup. Then we started in, heating all the water we could manage, making chocolate paste, opening whole cases full of canned milk.

At six o'clock the fun, per schedule, began. The boys lined up from the counter to the stage. But instead of a single line, it soon became evident we had two, one coming and one going, which together formed an endless chain like a giant wheel which kept slowly but surely revolving. After the second or third time around a boy would begin to acquire a slightly sheepish look and endeavor to avoid my eye, but when they found that all they got was a grin and "I'm glad you like it!" they grinned back unashamed.

"I can't stop," joyfully explained one lad to me, "I'm in the line and I can't get out; I just gotter keep on coming round."

"Oh boy! but that's the best thing I've had in France!" declared another.

While a third announced; "Gee, but I'm full all the way up! If I drink another drop I sure will bust"—a confession which may have contained more fact than fancy, for some of the boys did drink so much that they got sick right then and there. It was an orgy. And when the last of the four huge containers had been drained to a drop, why everyone, I believe, for once had had enough.

"You've got all the business in town right here tonight," one of the boys informed me. "I just took a look in at the cafés. Every one of them is empty."

Personally I feel that the party was a Great Success. We shall have to have one just like it every Sunday.

Mauvages, January 1, 1919.

Mes meilleurs voeux de Bonne Année! or, as the boys say; "Bun Annie!" We welcomed the new Year in *con molto giubilo*. Downstairs at my billet there was music until late and after that sounds as of a repetition of the Christmas party. At twelve o'clock by the old church bell, the band, which I had imagined long since safe and sound in bed, burst forth into music and straggled down the street playing *"There'll be a hot time in the old town tonight,"* and all the rest of the most rakish airs in its repertoire. I stepped out on my Juliet balcony. The boys were setting off pyrotechnics of all sorts "salvaged" from the dump; flares, colored lights, and rockets. The street burned out of the darkness in rose-colored mist against which showed black silhouettes of soldiers who waved their arms and shouted and sang; while from the edge of the village sounded a sharp tattoo of rifle shots. Just as the light was beginning to fade out I heard an emphatic bang of the front door below me and looking down saw two figures; a little brisk bustling one and a tall, lean one go hurrying down the path and out the gate. It was our Colonel and an attendant officer. Retribution, I knew, was bearing down upon the revellers. Sure enough, this morning I learned that the Colonel, sallying forth, had struck right and left, leaving a trail of arrests all over town.

But even with the Colonel's sortie, quiet did not descend on Mauvages for some time. The party below-stairs was not confined to the mess-hall this time but was also being celebrated in the kitchen. At about one o'clock a K. P. stumbled up the stairs and knocked on the door of the Curé's chamber just across from me. He had some champagne for the Curé, he explained in thick and execrable French. The Curé must drink it in honor of the New Year. It was good champagne. I could hear the Curé replying from his bed in rapid deprecating sentences, but the K. P. held to his point; he had set his heart on the old man's joining the celebration. *"Champagne bun,"* he kept repeating, *"Vous camarade. Bun annie."* For a long time they carried on the argument, but finally, as the priest implacably refused to open his door, the genial K. P. gave up in disgust, confiding to his friends as he reached the floor that the Curé was, after all, nothing but a dried up old fish.

This morning I went down to Headquarters to turn in my accounts. Alas, for the vanity of human intentions! At Christmas I had sent little boxes of fudge to several of the men at the office, hoping thereby to curry favour for my canteen and counteract any bad impressions which our delinquencies in the matter of attending Sunday Services and appropriating other people's autos might have caused. Now I find I have made more enemies among the ones that I left out, than I made friends of the ones I favoured.

In spite of this sad condition of affairs I managed to tease one driver into agreeing to take me to Vaucouleurs. At Vaucouleurs I had been told that there was a commissary where one could purchase candles, and the boys are desperately anxious for candles. At first I did not quite understand so burning a desire as they exhibited, but now I am wise. They want them—poor wretches!—so they can "read their shirts," before they go to bed! I stayed down in Gondrecourt, missing dinner, and then set out for Vaucouleurs with my heart full of hope and my pockets crammed with currency. It was a long, cold trip in the driving, drizzly rain. Arrived at Vaucouleurs we found that, being the first of the month, the commissary was closed for inventory.

Mauvages, January 3.

Everybody has a little pet trouble of his own these days. The A. R. has its share and more of them. Lieutenant C. recounted some of his tonight. He had been carrying the dangerous explosives over beyond the woods to the west of the town where they were being blown off. Then the French Town Major had called.

It wouldn't do, he said, to blow off the ammunition there any more; there were sick people in the town and the explosions fairly made them jump right up out of their beds. And really one couldn't blame them. So then the Lieutenant had switched to the north, over beyond the narrow-gauge, only to be promptly visited by a furious delegation of engineers. Whether it was because proper precautions hadn't been taken or what I don't know, whatever the case, in the course of the explosions a large rock had made a gaping hole in the roof of A. S. No. 9 and narrowly missed one of my good friends the operators. The complaint of the engineers was shortly followed by an indignant ultimatum from the Captain at Abainville who is in charge of the railway. Unless the explosions were forthwith stopped, he threatened, no more trains would be run on the road. On top of all this the Colonel of artillery must call the Lieutenant to account. The boys whom he arrested New Year's night had been shooting off their rifles. The shells must have come from the dump. Since it was Lieutenant C.'s dump, it was his business to keep his shells in their proper places. Therefore Lieutenant C. was responsible for the shooting.

I don't know just how the matter has been arranged with the Captain at Abainville, but the explosions beyond the tracks have been going on all day. Latest reports testify that that roof of A. S. No. 9 is riddled like a sieve with stone-holes and that the cook, who never was known to be a religious man, spends all his time beneath the table praying.

Two of the ordnance boys have been badly burned while setting off the explosions, and the whole detachment is sore and disheartened because they are being worked so hard in the mud and rain and their Sunday holiday denied them. Special details from the artillery are being sent to work at the dump every day in order to hasten the work of destruction, but these boys, too, are sullen and rebellious. They have been used to handling shells at the front, they say, and they consider it an indignity to have to handle them here in the dump as if they, forsooth, belonged to the ordnance! And so the work goes none too quickly. Everyone has been instructed to keep a particular lookout for German delay fuses, those deadly little infernal machines, which can be set, according to the strength of the acid which eats through the spring, to explode any time between a week and six months. They are disguised cleverly to look exactly like ordinary percussion fuses, the only betraying mark being a tiny six pointed star on the nose. Several have already been found planted in dumps which contained captured German ammunition, and the tale runs through camp that some have been discovered here, although this I rather suspect is just another army rumor.

Tonight one of the ordnance boys hobbled into the hut, his left foot swathed in bandages; a shell had fallen on a toe and crushed it. I attempted to sympathize.

"Don't waste any of your sympathy on me," he retorted, "I'm the luckiest feller you know. There ain't a man in camp who don't envy me."

As for me, I am having a few pet troubles too. One of these is concerned with the army dentist at Gondrecourt. And this is all in consequence of the kind operators at A. S. No. 9 and their Christmas chocolates, for among those chocolates was a caramel and,—well that candy was made in Switzerland and so was probably pro-German anyway.

Yesterday I had to witness the harrowing spectacle of a stalwart doughboy being separated from a tooth. When the ghastly business was over he shook himself.

"I've been over the top," he declared, "and got filled up with machine-gun bullets,"—he was wearing two wound stripes,—"but I'll tell the world them bullets weren't nothin' to that tooth!"

But the chief of my troubles is the hut lighting problem. So far, I have not been able to get any response to my petition for an electric lighting system. Our fine carbide lamps are a frank fizzle, our candles are all gone, we have nothing but a few lanterns and small oil lamps. Every day someone breaks my heart by breaking another lamp chimney, and new ones, alas! are not to be had for love or money in this part of France. Moreover the boys have developed a most inconvenient habit of walking off with the lamps. At first I said in exasperation; "Well, let them take them! As soon as the oil burns out they'll find the lamps aren't any use to them." But I didn't reckon on their Yankee ingenuity. They are smart enough, it seems, to bring back the empty ones, and exchange them for filled ones, every evening!

Mauvages, January 5.

Mauvages is in a state of mind for mutiny, and it's all over a little piece of cloth about two inches square. The case is this; the — Artillery Brigade, having served six months continuously at the front, having participated in all the big offensives, and having won an enviable reputation, was attached, on coming to this area, for the sake of military convenience, to the — Division already stationed here, a draft organization which had never been to the front at all. The artillery were far from pleased over the arrangement, but they managed to swallow their pride and put a good face on the matter. A few days ago, however, the order came out that they were to abandon the insignia of their old division and appear—every last man of them,—with the insignia of the new division on his arm. The men were furious. The batteries stationed at Rosières made a bonfire and burned the detestable insignia publicly, for which they got two weeks restriction to camp and a new set of little red patches. One boy sewed his "clover-leaf," as they call them, to the seat of his breeches. Raincoats have become all the wear, even in the best of weather, for under these the hated symbol is hidden. Indeed the feeling was so intense that in some places both officers and men tore off their service-stripes before putting on the new insignia.

I alone in the town am wearing the insignia of the old division and this is a wonderful and weird affair cut out of turkey red bunting and pinned to my sweater sleeve in a moment of reminiscent loyalty by my indignant detail. But the band keeps on lustily proclaiming the brigade's undying allegiance, for every morning for Reveille, as it makes the grand tour of the town it brays forth defiantly the war march of the old division.

"We haven't got orders to stop *that!*" says the leader.

Since the spirit of rebellion is abroad I have been managing a little mutiny of my own. It came about in the matter of Sunday movies. Up till the present we had been accustomed to having a service every Sunday night, but since the artillery moved in we have been furnished with a full-fledged morning service by the regimental chaplain, in view of which I had set my heart on having movies in the evening rather than a second service. I based my position on the grounds that, since to my notion at least, the main end of the work over here is simply to keep the boys away from the things that would hurt them, on Sunday night, the most dangerous night of all the week, this could best be done by drawing them to the hut with a movie show; always provided that their "religious needs" had been supplied earlier in the day.

The movie machine was at the hut, I had found an operator in one of the batteries, a little Jewish boy who bragged of long experience in the states; all I wanted was a film. I went with my request to the office. My logic it seemed to me was unassailable. But the office couldn't see it that way. After much debate we agreed to disagree in theory. In practice I carried off my film. But I did it with a sinking of the heart. My relations with the office have always been quite cordial, this was the first incident to cast a gloom over them. Anyway, I thought, we're going to have those movies! I advertised the show extensively.

Sunday night came. The hut was thronged. I was feeling rather particularly pleased with things. We had ministered to the boys' souls in the morning, fortified the inner man with free hot chocolate at six o'clock, now we were going to finish out the day by satisfying their romantic cravings with a film drama of love and adventure.

But oh! for the pride that goes before the stumbling-block! When it came to the test it seemed that the little operator, for all his bragging, couldn't make the movie machine go. Perhaps it was because the lad didn't understand the foreign make, perhaps it was because the machine needed to be talked to in French, or perhaps it was just because the project had been unblessed from the beginning; I don't know. We had half the camp ganged around the machine, offering to take a hand. Everybody was criticizing and advising, which, I suppose, added the last touch to the little operator's confusion. After waiting an interminable time in the dark we witnessed a few feeble flickers on the screen and then darkness once more. The audience dribbled disgustedly away. They probably made up for their disappointment in the cafés.

This morning the driver stopped at the hut to take the machine away. "Have a good show, last night?" he asked.

"Umm hm," said I, grinning cheerfully.

I am praying that the truth about that show never reaches the office!

Mauvages, January 10.

Tonight I leave Mauvages. Two weeks more and I shall be "homeward bound." I am so tired that it has seemed to me for some time that the only thing I can do is to go home. There isn't any room in France these days for anyone who isn't perfectly strong, perfectly rested. A week ago I went to Nancy and persuaded the lady in charge of the women workers of this division, after some argument, to let me go. I have already overstayed my contract by eight months. Now they have telegraphed from Paris that they have a sailing for me. The man secretary is here to take over this hut.

Because I hate leave-takings I tried to keep the fact that I was going dark until the very last minute but at the end word got around. The boys came flocking into my kitchen with messages and missives for the states. Boys whom I had never to my knowledge seen before pledged me to call up their wives on the long distance telephone as soon as I should land. One boy gave me two German fuses weighing a number of pounds apiece to carry home. If I would take one for him, I might keep the other one, he said.

"Say hello to the Statue of Liberty for me!"

"Give my regards to Broadway."

"Say Lady, can't you take me in your trunk?" they chorused.

As for Nick, he has instructed me to go to Brooklyn, pick out the best hat in his wife's millinery store, "And tell the missus it's on me."

I have taken my last agonized inventory, turned in my last accounts,—balanced by Big Bill. This afternoon I went to take my last look at the little hut. It is all torn to pieces, they have begun to build that addition which I started begging for a month ago; I slipped one of my canteen tea-cups into my bag just for old times sake.

Neddy came in to say Good-bye. At the last moment he shyly placed a little box in my hand. In it was a pretty gilt Lorraine cross. He had walked all the way into Gondrecourt to get it. He would have bought me a chain too, he explained with a flush, only he was "pecuniarily embarrassed." Dear little Neddy! If he only knew how much better I liked it without the chain.

My luggage is all packed and Bill has strapped it up for me. I have said adieu to the Curé and the Colonel. Madame the Caretaker has kissed me on both cheeks and dropped a tear over me. Now I am waiting for the A. R. jitney to come and take me to the station.

A horrid thought has just occurred to me. The captain's cognac must be still in the corner of the store-room shelf. What *will* the secretary think?

CHAPTER VII
VERDUN—THE FRENCH

Paris, January 12.

It is fortunate that the world looks tolerantly on a certain instability in the feminine mind. When I left Mauvages there was just one thought in my head,—to go straight home. I have been twenty-four hours in Paris; already my resolution is wavering. It's all on account of what they said to me at the Headquarters office.

Paris is truly a different city from the one I last saw in September on my way back from Saint Malo; the streets thronged with people, and brightly lighted at night, the shop windows gay and inviting, freed from their patterned lattices of paper strips which formerly protected the glass from the concussions caused by shells and bombs. In the Place de la Concorde the statue representing the City of Strasbourg, divested of the mourning wreaths which it has worn ever since 1870, now smiles triumphantly above a mass of flags and flowers; and, most thrilling of all, the crouched grey guns of Germany, like so many dumb impotent monsters, throng the Place de la Concorde, stretch in a double line along the Champs Elysées all the way to the Arc de Triomphe.

Everywhere the shop windows display a picture; a woman's form, heroic, bearing a great sword, with wide spread wings which are at the same time wings and American flags; before her the bent and cowering form of the Emperor; while beyond, a sea of khaki, illimitable hosts of warriors melting away in waves against the horizon; and underneath the words:

"But what tremendous fleet could have brought hither such an army?"

"The *Lusitania*."

The Patisserie shops are full of enticing little cakes once more; but, sad to say, the quality one finds has depreciated while the prices have gone sky-rocketing. I thought I would economise this noon and, instead of eating a five franc luncheon at the hotel, substitute a cup of cocoa and some little cakes at a tea-shop. When I came to pay my bill it was seven francs fifty! While I was partaking of my frugal repast a French Red Cross nurse came into the shop leading two blind poilus. She bought them each some cakes as if they had been two little boys and they stood there eating them. The poilu nearest me, a tall fine-looking fellow, tasted his, "*Ah!*" he exclaimed, "*c'est une vrai Madeleine!*" He lied. It was no more like a pre-war Madeleine than chalk is like cheese, but if it had been made of India-rubber I suppose he would have said the same thing, and said it with just the same grave and gracious courtesy.

Now that the war is over, one feels sorrier than ever for the French officers who haven't medals.

"The Frenchies are issuing the *croix de guerre* with their rations now," the boys used to say. And indeed when one sees a French officer without some sort of decoration one feels instinctively that something must be the matter with him.

To go or not to go? I am thinking of a compromise. I will postpone my sailing, take the furlough that is due to me. At the end of two weeks I can calmly make up my mind.

Cauterets, January 20.

"There's only one poor feature about this place;" declared a boy today, "they won't let you stay long enough."

This is a representative but not a universal sentiment. Some of the boys don't like the snow, for Cauterets being high in the Pyrenees, is deep in snow at present. A few complain that they don't get enough to eat. It is the breakfasts chiefly that fail to satisfy. The French having been used, time out of mind, to a *petit déjeuner* of rolls and coffee, utterly fail to comprehend the American need for heartier sustenance. When the contracts with the hotels were made it was carefully stipulated that eggs, meat or fish should be served at breakfast in addition to the continental menu, but the quantities were not stated and to a hearty doughboy on a cold morning *one* egg is a mere tantalization, if not an insult. Every morning you may see them flocking in swarms to the Y. in order to round out their unsatisfactory breakfasts with hot chocolate and bread and jam. Yesterday I overheard some indignant splutterings from a little crowd at one of the canteen tables.

"What's the matter, boys?"

"They gave us fish this morning for breakfast!"

"They did?"

"Yep! One sardine to each man!"

Yet in spite of a few such inharmonious notes, Cauterets, like Saint Malo and Aix-les-Bains, is instinct with the spirit of the American soldier on leave. And the American soldier on leave is the Playboy of the Western World. When the last doughboy has walked up the gang-plank of the last west-bound transport, I think the railway officials, gate-keepers, station agents, and train conductors all over France will settle back in their chairs and draw a deep breath of relief.

The French poilu and the English Tommy have both questioned often and bitterly why it was that while they must ride third class, the American soldier habitually traveled second and first; the answer being that you simply can't keep the doughboys out! It is the idea of the social distinction implied by the *classes* I fancy that makes half the trouble. However that may be, it is absolutely against the rules of the game for any doughboy to ride third class if there are any second class coaches, and equally disgraceful to ride second class if there is a first. I myself have seen an American buck private with third class transportation in his pocket stretching his legs in a luxurious first class compartment seat, while a French general stood up outside in the corridor! At another time I took a journey in a first class compartment built for six, in which three English officers, an English titled Lady, her companion, two muddy doughboys and myself were all crowded. This was an anxious trip for me, for not only was I worried lest an indignant conductor should eject the doughboys, but I was also guiltily conscious of having paid only a second class fare myself!

One joyous company of eight lads on leave whom I encountered on the way down here counted in their number one sergeant with a well-worn second class pass. Things arranged themselves very simply. In the line-up at the gate or in the car, the sergeant, heading the file, presented his pass first, then, as it was handed back to him, slipped it behind his back to the next man and so on down the line. Once in a second class compartment it was usually an easy matter to transfer to first. This same crowd related to me how, when locked out of an empty first class compartment by an irate conductor they merely waited until the next stop, then getting out climbed through the window on the off side of the train into the forbidden seats.

"Golly, but that old frog got a shock when he looked in through the glass door and saw us sitting there!"

They were overcome with chagrin because at the last change one member of the party allowed himself to be bullied by a hard-boiled M. P. into leaving the first class car.

"He's broken our record," they mourned; "he's disgraced the family!" And half their pleasure in the remainder of the trip was spoiled it was evident.

Irrepressible, curious of all things, awed by nothing, the doughboy cares not a snap of his fingers for the whole of French Officialdom. An officer told me how, when standing on a station platform the other day, an irate and husky doughboy sailed by him, headed for the baggage-room in search of somebody's luggage.

"If you hear a noise, Major," he remarked in transit, "you'll know that I'm stepping on a frog."

The French railway system affords him a never-failing topic for amusement. And truly it has its quaint points. On the trip down we passed over one line where the heating system for the cars consisted entirely of long flat metal cans filled with hot water which were shoved in under our feet, so that, no matter how chilly the rest of us might be, our toes at least could travel in comfort; while on the walls of each coach, we observed with glee, was an official notice requesting the passengers to refrain from throwing objects such as *empty bottles* out the windows as numerous casualties among the employees had resulted from this practice!

The doughboy passes everywhere by virtue of the magic words, "*no compree*." Traveling he develops a stupidity that is absolute and unshakable.

"I never understand anything they say," chuckled one youngster joyously, "until they begin to talk about something to eat".

Wonderful tales are told of escapades and adventures; such as the story of the boy who started out to spend his leave at Aix-les-Bains and traveled half over Italy before he came back, all on the the strength of the pass-word "onion-stew" and an unidentified document that happened to have a red seal attached. Common rumour has it that the official report records sixty thousand A. W. O. L.s at the present date in the A. E. F. in France. I don't know whether this is correct, but I rather hope it is. Now that the war is won I am glad that in spite of Provost Marshals and M. P.s some of the boys at least are on the way to discovering that there is something more to France than just "mud and kilometers."

Paris, February 7.

I'm going to stay. If I went home now I would feel like a quitter all the rest of my life. I don't know where I'm going. They asked me if I would like to go to Germany but I said no, I didn't want to look at Germans. I shall have to stay here in Paris for a week or so anyway in order to get that wretched business of a broken tooth, which the Christmas caramel at Mauvages began, straightened out. In the meantime, I am doing what I can in a perfectly amateur and impromptu way to help young America see Paris.

Paris is the lodestar of France for the A. E. F. From every part of the country it draws them like a magnet. When on leave, no matter from what portion of France they may have come or what corner they may be bound for, they always contrive to get there by way of Paris. If the R. T. O. instructs them to change to another line before they reach the city, they arrive there just the same, to explain blandly to the M. P. that they went to sleep on the train: "and when I woke up, why here I was in Paris!" What dodges the doughboys haven't worked in order to circumvent the M. P.s and get into Paris without official permission, or once in Paris to stay longer than the short time allotted them, would be beyond human imagination. There is one story current, for whose truth though, I cannot vouch, of an American private who passed a week in the forbidden city in the uniform of his cousin, a lieutenant in the French Army. At the time of the signing of the armistice, for several days the M. P.s' vigilance was relaxed and boys from all over France swarmed to the city to participate in the festivities, but since then the penalties for the unlucky ones who are caught have grown more and more severe.

Yesterday by request I took two boys to the Louvre. We wandered through the galleries of Greek and Roman sculptures. One boy, looking at the yellowed and discolored surfaces, declared himself bitterly disappointed. He had heard that the statues were all real marble here, but it was perfectly plain that they were nothing but plaster imitations! The other boy asked naïvely if the mutilated statues were "meant to represent people who had had their heads chopped off." After about half an hour they consulted their watches, announced that we had just time to get to a movie show, and wouldn't I go with them?

But if the finer points of Greek art are lost on many, there are plenty of other things which they do appreciate.

"Can you climb to the top of the Eiffel tower?"

"Where is the church that the shell struck on Good Friday?"

"What would you advise me to buy to send home to Mother?"

"How often does the Ferris Wheel go?"

"Is there any place in Paris where one can get ice-cream soda?"

These are some of the questions that they ask you. Some go to the Opera, sitting invariably in the best seats to the amazement of the French people. Yesterday I stopped at the box-office to buy some tickets. A boy standing just inside the door spoke to me.

"I beg your pardon, were you going to buy a seat for this afternoon?"

"No," I said; "for Saturday."

"I have an extra ticket. I'd be glad to have you use it."

He went on to tell me that he was taking the six o'clock train, that he had bought tickets for himself and a friend for the matinee as a last pleasure, but that his friend had failed him. I hesitated, uncertain. "What's the opera?" I asked, just because it was something to say.

"It's La Bohème," he said. I fell.

"I'm mighty glad," he told me, "I was just about to go out and pick up a chicken on the street, when you came in."

The opera was a dream of loveliness. I felt as if I must have done something very good indeed in some previous existence to be thus rewarded.

Today I encountered two boys who told me how they had "done" Paris.

"We stopped at a store and bought a bunch of post cards, all the famous buildings and everything. Then we got a taxi. After that all we'd do was to show the chauffeur a post card and he'd drive us to it,—then we'd show him another one, and so we kept a-goin' until we'd seen most all of Paris. But gee! That taxi bill was a fright!"

This afternoon, coming down the "Boulevard de Wop," as the boys call the Boulevard des Italiens, I paused beside a fiacre, attached to a particularly wretched looking old nag, which was drawn up by the sidewalk. Into it were piling merrily some eight or nine doughboys, the cabman fairly dancing on his seat as he uttered frantic but perfectly unheeded expostulations. Finally as the cabby appeared to be developing apoplexy, I spoke up.

"Boys, you know that *really* that broken-down old beast never *could* pull all of you!"

Whereupon half of them immediately piled out again. One of the remaining ones leaned out of the fiacre.

"Say Lady, can you talk French?" he demanded earnestly.

"Why a little."

"Well tell that old guy for me, will you," he indicated the still disgruntled *cocher* who, like the rest of his tribe, was crowned with an ornamental "stove-pipe," "that I want him to lend me his hat."

Tonight I met a girl I know who is in the Hut Equipment Department. She has just returned from an extended tour of inspection. I told her I didn't know where my next assignment was to be.

"Why don't you go to Verdun?" she asked. "The conditions about there are worse than any other place in France. Men are commiting suicide there every day."

So I wrote a note to the Office asking that I be sent to Verdun.

Bar-le-Duc, February 16.

Somewhere here in Bar-le-Duc there is an extraordinary thing. It is the Mausoleum of René of Chalons, prince of Orange, and designed in accordance with his wishes. Against an ermine mantle, under a rich armorial crest, stands a skeleton or rather the rotting carcass of a man, half bone and half disintegrating tissue, holding aloft in one ghastly hand, his heart, an offering, so the story goes, to his lady wife.

Every time I am in Bar-le-Duc, even if it is only an hour between trains, I go hunting for that skeleton; but the nearest I have come so far, is to find it on a picture post card. Once I thought I had surely run it to earth when I came upon a strange old church built so as to bridge a narrow moat-like canal, and so low that it seemed as if the water must ooze up through the stone slabs of the floor, but no.

I am here at Bar-le-Duc for a few days because it seems that after all it isn't quite certain whether I had better go to Verdun or to Souilly. While my fate is being decided, I am acting as a sort of errand-girl, special messenger and Jack-of-all-jobs here at Headquarters.

This morning I went out in a flivver to do an errand. The driver told me how, a few days ago, he had carried a young French girl all over the country-side looking for her aviator-lover's grave. Finally with the help of a French officer they had found it. The girl had placed a wreath on the grave, said a little prayer and turned away. He showed me the place, three grey wooden crosses, one with a china wreath on it, marking the field where a large aviation camp had once been and now quite the loneliest and most deserted spot in the world.

Coming back, I was sent to the Provost Marshal's office to telephone. While I waited for my connection two M. P.s brought in a prisoner. He belonged to the — Division which reached France in September. Two days after he landed he went A. W. O. L. and had been missing ever since. By some unknown means he had managed to acquire a typewriter and all winter, it appeared, he had been living in the woods supporting himself by typing faked travel orders and selling them to the soldiers. He was a heavy-set fellow, sullen and taciturn under their questioning. They went through his pockets and turned out the collection on the table; chewing gum, tobacco, a shaving-set, old newspapers, screws and nails, buttons and string and matches and pins, pencils, and post cards, a knife and three toothbrushes.

Bar-le-Duc I understand does a thriving business in A. W. O. L.s. One of the M. P.s told me of a lad who, when asked for his papers, took to his heels and was promptly pursued.

"I chased him all over town, and finally I ran him into the canal," he narrated joyfully. "He stood out there with the water up to his waist while I stood on the bank and shied stones at him. And he had on a serge uniform too."

"How did it end?" I asked.

"Oh I let him go; I figured if he wanted to get away that bad he had a right to."

Up this same canal a few weeks ago came a flotilla of French submarines bound for the Rhine, the sailors startling the inhabitants by their sudden appearance in the streets in their naval uniforms and their casual references to their ships close at hand. Somebody was unkind enough to declare that the subs had started their journey from the coast on Armistice Day, but I am sure this must be a libel.

This afternoon I asked if I might work in the canteen. This is in a French house, a few doors beyond the beautiful Officers' Club, the home of one of the wealthy manufacturers of the *Confiture de Bar-le-Duc*, lent by him, rent-free for the use of the Americans during the war. In the course of the afternoon I became the possessor of a puppy-dog presented me by a motor-truck driver, who, following some careless remark of mine about wishing I had a puppy, dropped the scared little black thing in my arms and fled. As soon as I could collect my senses I flew around the counter and out the door after him, calling on him to take his dog back. But when I reached the street, motor-truck and driver both had vanished. I would have loved to keep the little beggar, but here I am, a transient traveller bound for nobody knows where; what could I do? I explained my dilemma to the grinning crowd in the canteen. One of the boys spoke up.

"I'll take him and give him to my French girl," he said. I relinquished the little fellow regretfully. I hope Mademoiselle makes him a good foster-mother.

A little while later I noticed a boy at the counter who wore three service stripes and two wound stripes. "What's your division?" I asked. He told me. He belonged to my old regiment! He had been in the Milk Battalion at Goncourt, and he remembered me. He was a Class B man now and in the post office at Bar-le-Duc.

"What of the rest?" I asked.

"They're mostly dead," he answered, and he told me how, after one charge, out of the whole Company M six men and the captain had come back.

I broke down and cried; I couldn't help it. The boy, embarrassed, drew away. He is the only man I have seen out of my regiment since last March, and all he could say was, "They're mostly dead!" Dead at Château-Thierry, dead on the Marne, dead by Soissons, dead in honor, dead with glory. America, will you ever forget?

Bar-le-Duc, February 18.

Everyone here is incensed this morning over the action of the French troops in the matter of the theatre. It seems that the Americans had arranged a schedule of movies and shows to be given at the local theatre a month in advance. A soldier show was billed for tonight, the company had reached town, the audience was beginning to gather from the nearby villages, when the French troops who began to arrive in town yesterday announced that they had their own exclusive and immediate uses for the building. All efforts to arbitrate the matter have so far failed. And now word comes that a French lieutenant in order to be ready to repel any possible move on the part of the Americans to take possession of the theatre for the night has had his bed made up in one of the boxes!

It is the greatest of pities that there should be this wretched element of friction between the two allies. If every American could have been miraculously whisked out of France the day after the armistice was signed the doughboy would likely have been to this day a bit of a popular French idol. It is this hanging about with no ostensible end in view that frays nerves on both sides and leads to a mutual stepping on each other's toes. No two nationalities I am convinced could be thrown into such an intimate and trying relationship and produce perfect harmony. There must inevitably be a clash of temperaments. The case in this instance, as I see it, is complicated to an extraordinary degree, with human foibles and failings a-plenty on both sides.

We Americans have undoubtedly been guilty of bad manners. Quite openly and persistently the doughboy has called the Frenchman "frog" to his face and this the French have by no means enjoyed. The odd part of the thing is that the doughboy can give no explanation of the nickname.

"But why do you call them frogs?" I ask the boys. Usually they look quite blank.

"It's 'cause they sound like frogs when they talk," explained one lad.

"'Cause they jump around like frogs when they get excited," offered another.

Not one of them suspects that this nickname is a curious survival of the old term of contempt "Frog-eaters" applied to the French by the English in the days when they were enemies instead of allies!

Undoubtedly too the feminine factor, leading as it has to jealousy, has played its share in arousing antagonism.

"The chief victories of the Americans in France," declared a French officer bitterly the other day, "are his conquests over the feminine heart!"

Indeed from the start it has been an open secret that the "Mademoiselles" have taken a prodigious fancy to the American soldier. This is partly because he possesses the charm of novelty, partly because he has money and can procure chocolate and cigarettes and partly just because he is himself.

"There are three thousand men in this town and three girls," ran a postal addressed by a joyous youngster on leave to his lieutenant; "I'm going with one of them and Abe has the other two."

And who can blame the poilu for a certain amount of resentment, when, coming back from the trenches he has discovered that a dashing American stationed at an engineering camp in his home town has supplanted him in the affections of his sweetheart?

On the American side there is of course the old grievance of the overcharging.

"D'you know why you don't see any Jews in France?" asked a lad of me the other day, "It's because they couldn't make a living."

In part, this sense of grievance, as I see it, is justifiable. An officer told me not long ago that he had recently been left behind when his outfit moved out from a village, as "Mop Up Officer" to settle the claims of the townspeople for damage done by the soldiers during their stay,—a pane of glass, a truss of straw, the tine of a pitchfork. Hearing a commotion in the town square he looked out; the town crier was announcing to the populace that now the Americans had gone the price of wine would be cut from five francs a bottle to two. But in part this sense of grievance is unjustifiable, for the American has in no small measure brought this state of affairs upon himself. From the start the doughboy's disgust with the flimsy paper bills and the puzzling tricky scheme of the francs, sous and centimes engendered a carelessness toward French money which the tradespeople took as a delightful indication of unlimited wealth. "But everyone is rich in America!" I have heard them declare with childish conviction. So prices began to rise and presently, with the prices, the doughboy's resentment, and then the poilu's; for the rise automatically put all luxuries out of the French soldier's reach and this of course he in turn blamed bitterly on the "rich" American. Indeed the sending of a large body of men paid at the rate of a dollar a day into a country where the native troops were paid at the rate of five cents a day was a social-economic error which somehow, say by some system of reserve pay such as the Australians have, should have been avoided.

Then too, the American won't haggle. The Frenchman, as a rule, won't buy unless he can. Prices are fixed with the expectation of a compromise after bargaining. Not easily shall I forget a dramatic scene witnessed at the "Rag Fair" at the Porte Maillot in Paris between a prosperous householder and a "rag" seller over a second-hand padlock. The seller remained firm in demanding six cents for the padlock. The householder was equally determined not to pay more than five. Finally the householder with great dignity withdrew, only to be called back by a despairing yelp from the seller. He had capitulated. To the American such a performance seems both tedious and undignified; he either takes the article at the first price asked or leaves it.

Nor can it be denied that the doughboy tends to be a bit of a prodigal. Chief of his spendthrift weaknesses are two; he will pay almost any price for sweets, sink almost any sum in a present for his girl. Then too the universal custom of gambling in the army, leading to swollen fortunes for the favoured ones, has helped to establish standards of extravagance. An officer in charge of a company belonging to a negro labor regiment told me of seeing two of his boys in a café sit down to a twenty-five franc bottle of champagne and then, the taste for some reason not quite suiting their fancies, walk out leaving the bottle practically untouched behind!

In the light of such incidents as this, who can blame the French people for regarding the American as a sort of gift from God beneficently allowed them at the time of their greatest national impoverishment, for the replenishing of their depleted pocketbooks?

Verdun, February 20.

The little narrow-gauge train pulled us in here from Bar-le-Duc at ten o'clock last night, a thirty mile run and six hours to make it! When I asked for a first class fare at the station I noticed an odd expression on the ticket-seller's face. "They're all the same," he said; "all second class." Arrived at the train I understood. The coaches were filthy and furnished with straight-backed wooden benches; a heap of rubbish surrounded the rickety stove in the centre. Shortly after we crawled out of Bar-le-Duc it began to rain. Half the windows were innocent of glass. The rain beat in through the empty sashes. Presently it grew dark. Several of the passengers, American, reached in their pockets and brought out a few grimy candle-ends. We made little grease-spots on the benches and stuck the candles there, but the gusts of wind from the empty windows kept blowing them out, so half the time we jogged along in darkness.

Among the passengers was a little old Frenchman with one arm. He was returning to his native village in the devastated area the other side of Verdun, after an absence of four years. With him was his young son, an immature lad of seventeen.

"J'ai tine passion," declared the old man with startling fervour; *"j'ai une passion véritable de revoir le village de ma naissance!"*

In all probability he was returning to nothing but a crumbled heap of stones.

"You are very brave," I told him.

Ah but it was for them, the old, to set an example for the young! It was they who should lead the way! It was they who should rebuild France! His frail old body fairly shook with the strength of his emotion. What a strange, thrilling, tragic pilgrimage!

Verdun resembled nothing but a ruin mercifully wrapped in darkness as we passed through the gate and made our way up the hill. We had found, luckily, a guide who had a lantern; nowhere else in all the city was so much as a gleam of light to be seen. In places, as we passed, the shells of houses still stood, staring down with empty eyes at us, in other places there were nothing but rubble mounds with here and there a narrow jagged bit of wall or a naked chimney standing out like a lonely monolith.

Headquarters offices are at the Château on the summit of the hill close to the Cathedral, one of the few buildings left undamaged in this part of town, a rambling, ungainly, rather gloomy structure. The second story consists almost entirely of a series of great empty barren loft-like store-rooms. In one of these, known as the Ladies, Cold Storage, I have my habitation. Supposed to be a sort of one-night-stand dormitory for female tourists,—nurses chiefly,—who are touring the battle-fields, the Ladies, Cold Storage is a large dusty garret with grimy rough-plastered walls, without a window or as much as a crack to let in any light or air except for a few small slits in the roof where the rain leaks in. A stove, a long row of cots and a tin basin on a shelf surmounted by a broken piece of looking-glass are its only furnishings. However, the L. C. S. boasts one luxury, it is equipped with electric lights. This helps—when the current is turned on!—when it isn't, we light a candle stub and stick it in an old milk can. The electricity is generated underground in the Citadel. When the Americans first came to Verdun some enterprising electricians tapped the wires and had forty lights working before the French knew anything about it. Upon discovery the French cut off the Americans, only to find shortly afterwards that another connection had been made. This absurd performance was repeated no less than seven times. After the seventh time the French gave up.

We were fairly frightened out of bed this morning by a most horrible hubbub,—a Klaxon gas-alarm which is used to call the guests to breakfast. Having heard it I am quite convinced that if Gabriel wishes to do the job efficiently on the last day, he will scrap his trumpet and take a Klaxon.

After breakfast we newcomers hurried out to get a glimpse of the town. There were plenty of others likewise occupied as Verdun is a veritable magnet for A. E. F. tourists. The Cathedral is closed to visitors but we happened upon two French officers who kindly took us through. The roof is badly damaged and the stained glass of the windows shattered to bits, but beyond that the Cathedral is comparatively unharmed. I was much embarrassed when the officers informed me that the *sacrés pierres*, the sacred stones from the altar, had been stolen and presumably sent as souvenirs to America. At first I pretended not to understand, but they took such pains to explain, finally taking me to the altar and showing me where the little marble slabs had been dug out, that I finally had to admit I understood. The two nurses who were with us were anxious to climb the clock-tower, but this, we found, was strictly *défendu*. All through the war, we learned afterwards, the clock in the tower had been kept going by the faithful verger who refused to leave his post, and what's more, it had kept time. But a short while ago the clock had started "skipping." A party of American boys had just visited the tower. Upon investigation it proved that one of the wheels was missing! Sometimes I think the French are very patient with us.

Everywhere we went we came upon German prisoners engaged in the most leisurely fashion in cleaning up. There are several thousands of them here and more to come. Verdun is to rise from her ruins and live once more. Yet she can never be in any sense the stately city that once she was; for while the business and poorer portions of the city below the hill are not irreparably damaged, the finer part with its stately mansions and exquisite specimens of mediæval architecture is wrecked beyond repair. The most serious obstacle in the way of making at least some small portions of the city habitable at present lies in the great difficulty of obtaining window-glass.

From the Cathedral we went to the Canteen-in-the-Convent. How the nuns would stare, I thought, if they could see their virgin precincts in possession of a mob of boys in khaki, white and black, interspersed with the blue-coated poilus! Across the back of the building runs a wide terrace, once worn by pious feet of patient sisters engaged in holy meditations. Here among the lounging boys stand life-sized carved and colored images of saints and angels. Their size of course prevents them from traveling to America as souvenirs, but even so they must stand witness to the irreverence of young America, for the Angel Gabriel is hideous in a German gas-mask!

After dinner we went on a trip through the Citadel, that vast underground soldier-city with its miles of corridors and rooms enough to harbor a whole army, a little world deep underneath the earth. We saw the bakery which bakes bread not only for the whole garrison but for all the troops in the vicinity; the Foyer, a writing and recreation hall, named in honor of President Wilson; the movie theatre; and the hospital with its wards and operating room,—what a nightmare horror I thought to be sick in those damp and dimly-lighted subterranean caverns! But we were not allowed to see more than the outer door of the chapel which they say is sumptuous, since it is enriched by all the costly furnishings and precious images moved there for safety's sake from the Cathedral. Nor were we shown the underground café where, I have been told, an unusually good brand of beer is sold.

From the Citadel, rumour has it, tunnels lead out to the circle of forts that form the defences of Verdun, but if you ask a Frenchman if this is so, he only looks wise and keeps mum.

Verdun, February 25.

I don't believe there is another canteen quite like my canteen in the whole of France. It is a canteen for French civilians. The one-time inhabitants of Verdun and the devastated area beyond are allowed by the government, it seems, just twenty-four hours in which to visit their former homes, after which they must return as there is no food for them here and very little shelter. In return for many favours the French authorities asked the Y. to co-operate with them in running a sort of rest-room for these refugees; they supplying a detail, and we supplying the materials to make hot chocolate which is given away, and a secretary to take charge. The canteen is in the Collège Buvignier at the foot of the hill. There is a *dortoir* in the building also, in charge of the man who was once manager of the principal hotel in the city; two long halls full of cots with straw mattresses where the refugees may pass the night. My assignment to this canteen is only to be temporary.

The room where my canteen is must have once been quite beautiful, high-ceilinged with wainscot panelling below and embossed leather covering the walls above. Even now in its state of dingy disrepair, with half the panes in the tall arched windows replaced by dirty cloth, it keeps something of its old dignity and charm. Beyond the main room is another smaller one, connected by two doors, in which the detail lives and in which we make our chocolate.

When I took over the canteen from the man who had been in charge of it, it was absolutely bare except for four tables and some backless wooden benches. My first act on assuming charge was to clean house, my second was to persuade the detail to make the very watery chocolate richer. After that we proceeded to refurnish and adorn. We ran a frieze of war-pictures in color, taken from a child's pictorial *Histoire de la Guerre* around the top of the wainscoting, hung French and American flags from the chandeliers, teased the French authorities into bringing us some nice upholstered armchairs for the old ladies to sit in, and, finally, put a little pot of primroses or snow-drops, dug with a broken tile from a ruined garden, in the centre of each table. Then a kind secretary bound for Bar-le-Duc was persuaded to go shopping for us and brought back an array of French magazines, hand-picked, and an assortment of toys to amuse the kiddies who must often wait here with their families between trains, though so far, it must be confessed, it is chiefly the detail who have been amused by them. And now I am wondering what there is to do next.

Besides the hot chocolate, we carry on a trade in bread, a huge sackfull of which is brought us fresh every day from the underground bakery on the back of a little round-faced poilu; and we do a brisk business in checking parcels, without checks. Yesterday a rabbit was left all day in our care. I was sorry for the poor beast cooped up in the little box and wanted to give it a drink of water, but the poilus insisted that this would be fatal. Whether this might possibly be a zoölogical fact, or is just part of the national prejudice against water, I can't determine.

At first, remembering my difficulties with the French Army at Mauvages, I was a little apprehensive as to how my two poilus, Emil and Guillaume and I might get along. But though I am sure they think me the oddest creature in the world, and my presence here unconventional beyond words, yet their behaviour could not possibly be more courteous, considerate and deferential. They won't even allow me to wash the chocolate cups.

"Mademoiselle will soil her hands!"

And they are forever telling me that I am working too hard. "But Mademoiselle will be fatigued!" Which is so absurd as to fairly exasperate me.

Besides Emil and Guillaume we have four soldier friends-of-the-family, as it were, who also frequent the back room. The canteen is supposed to be a strictly civilian affair, but we make an exception in favour of the four *camarades*, and they repay us by helping chop the stove-wood which is stacked in a great pile outside the door and is nothing more or less than the stakes to which were once fastened barbed-wire entanglements. Each stake still bears two little rings of wire around it and every few days one has to clear out the accumulation of barbed-wire entanglements from the chocolate-stove. *Les défences de Verdun* the poilus call the wood-pile. The poilus are all artillerymen from a regiment of "75s." Guillaume has brought down three Boche planes, he tells me, and Emil five. One of the poilus is a handsome brigadier, or corporal, who wears wooden shoes. I said something about *sabots* the other day. But don't they wear *sabots* in America? The poilus were astonished to learn that wooden shoes were unknown among us! There is also a sergeant who is the aristocrat of our little circle, a dreamy looking lad, a student of architecture at the Beaux Arts. Yesterday he shyly proffered me an envelope; in it was a pretty pen-and-ink sketch of two little girls, one in the costume of Alsace, the other of Lorraine, proffering bouquets, and underneath was written, "Souvenir of a Frenchman who thanks America for having given the victory more quickly." Our poilu friends are constantly straying into the back room in order to read the newspapers here and to get a cup of hot chocolate. Every now and then they all get together and hold a *vin rouge* tea party. On these occasions it is evidently a mystery to them why, though I join them in eating bread and cheese, I always refuse the *vin rouge*!

The politeness of the poilus is equalled by that of the clientele. They are extraordinarily grateful for what little we do for them. Today an old lady, in spite of anything I could say, insisted on tipping me with a two franc piece! I spent it buying chocolates and cigarettes for the poilus at the Canteen-in-the-Convent. Every class of society flows into my little canteen from gently bred ladies under the escort of immaculate officers to old men who resemble nothing but the forlornest vagabonds. The cheerfulness and courage of the refugees in general is astonishing. One would think that a room full of people engaged in such a mournful mission would be a gloomy place, but on the contrary, although occasionally you see a woman quietly sobbing, at most times we fairly buzz with pleasant sociability. The women come in with faces bright with excitement. "Oh the poor Cathedral!" they cry.

"Did you find anything of your home?" I ask. For a moment the tears swim in their brave eyes. "*Rien*" they answer shaking their heads. "Nothing!"

Today an old man in a long white apron smock was the centre of attention here. He was busy searching the ruins of his house for buried treasure. Every little while he would come back to the canteen with the fruits of his pathetic salvaging,—a few silver spoons, some paint brushes, a bolt of black velvet ribbon,—place them in a basket and then return to look for more. Two German prisoners were digging for him. Finally he came back with six unbroken champagne glasses and a face scored with tragedy. He had been hoping against hope to recover the treasures in his wine cellar but he was too late, not a bottle was there left!

Verdun, February 28.

This morning I went out on a truck to Fort Douaumont. This is the fort which was captured by the Germans, held by them for five months, and then retaken by the French and marks the enemy's nearest approach to the city. Oddly enough the French were the gainers through this occupation to the extent of a splendid electric lighting system introduced by the Germans into the fort!

A modern fort does not resemble in the least the idea that one has of a "fort." Viewed from outside it is nothing more or less than a hole in the ground. Once inside we had the sense of being in a monster ant-hill as we followed our guide through a network of tunnelled corridors. We saw the room of the Commandant with its wonderful relief maps both French and German of the Verdun hills, we saw the war-museum, the Foyer, the store-rooms and engine-rooms, the magazine rooms where the big shells were stacked like cord wood, and we climbed up into the turrets of the disappearing guns. In this strange fort which has been both friend and enemy we looked through one empty doorway into a pit of ruins open to the sky, under the wreckage sixteen Germans lay, they said; it was here that a French shell had broken through. We passed by another door which bore a sign on it announcing that this was the tomb of five French mitrailleurs who had been killed by a German shell in the room within; instead of burying the bodies they had simply sealed up the door and left them. Then we ducked through a little low door and climbed up over the hillock which forms the roof of the fort as it were. All about us stretched the abomination of desolation of the battle-fields, wracked tortured earth, seared and scarred into a yellow-grey desert waste. Here and there lay bones, human bones, sometimes scattered loose, sometimes gathered in a little heap with a rusty helmet and a broken rifle lying close beside them. Only a few hundred feet from the road, the man who guided the party told us, he came yesterday upon two unburied bodies.

To the northeast we could just discern a large wooden cross. A French officer who was stationed at the fort pointed it out to us. Here, he said, lay buried no less than twelve hundred French soldiers. They had been given a line of trench to hold, the officers were taken from them, they were to expect no reinforcements or relief. They were left there knowing it was only a question of days or hours. When the French finally reached the line again every man was dead. So they left them where they lay and filled the trench in over them, but each man's rifle they took and planted upright in the earth beside him. There is a heroic theme for a poet!

When I reached the canteen again I found a ragged disconsolate old soul occupying one of the benches. On seeing me he began a sad recital of sore feet, ending with the petition that I procure him a pair of rubber boots and emphasizing the point by taking off his shoes then and there and exhibiting his troubles,—which weren't pretty,—to me. I was perplexed, not knowing what to do, when the friendly M. P. on the beat happened in; so I put the case up to him. He told me that there was a salvage dump at the station. We set out together and succeeded in finding an enormous pair of rubber overshoes, and, what's more, in getting away with them. The old man was pleased as Punch, put them on and hobbled off in them. Tonight someone told me a melancholy tale. An M. P. stationed upon the hill had spied an old Frenchman going by in a pair of American overshoes and had straightway held him up and ordered him to relinquish what was Government property. And the old man perforce had to sit down in the street and take off his shoes.

Speaking of boots reminds me of the tale told me by a doughboy the other day; a tale of a pair of tan shoes, handsome, shiny, new tan shoes which was sold to every man in turn in his whole company only to be finally purchased as a bargain at thirty-five francs by an unsuspecting Frenchman. They were beautiful shoes, the boy assured me, the only trouble was that they both happened to be for the left foot.

CHAPTER VIII
CONFLANS—PIONEERS, M.P.'s AND OTHERS

Jarny, March 2.

I am living in a hospital. Being in the occupied territory, the hospital has been for the last four years, of course, a German hospital. Over the doorways are painted such pious mottoes as "*Gruss Gott!*" and the theatre, for there is an amusement hall in the building, is adorned with a back-drop on which a Siegfried-esque hero overlooks an ideal German landscape wherein a picture-book castle perches on the top of an impossible mountain. At the other end of the hall is painted an enormous iron cross. The masterpiece of the collection, though, is on the wall of the basketball court and is, naturally, a portrait of His Late Imperial Majesty, although one indentifies him rather by inference than recognition, for the countenance having recently served for a pistol target is battered almost out of human semblance. The main part of the hospital is occupied by the Y.; in the wings some two hundred ordnance boys are quartered; we ladies find comfortable lodging in the operating room. There are five of us here at present, two American girls, besides myself, and two Englishwomen. These latter are ladies of high degree, I gather, being related to bishops and other such personages. They go under the unvarying title of the "British Army, First and Second Battalions." According to report they were sent over here from England to do propaganda work, that is, to create a pleasant impression on young America and thus help to forge another link between the two nations etc., but this they indignantly deny. However that may be, the boys derive a rather wicked joy from teasing and arguing with the good ladies, and particularly from filling them full of amazing tales about "The States." Even the Secretary can't resist the temptation to "rag" them, and though they are usually very patient under his plaguing, today at dinner we received a shock. In response to one of his more daring sallies, the Bishop's sister, fixing the Secretary with an icy eye, lifted one patrician hand to her august nose, and thumbed it! Which only goes to show that even an English Lady of Quality has human moments. And if we on our side must laugh a bit at them, it is plain to see that they, in their turn, find us infinitely amusing. In fact I half suspect, since they spend hours every day covering sheets of paper with close, fine handwriting, that the good ladies are engaged upon writing a book concerning the peculiarities of their American cousins when seen at close range. And in view of all the wonderful material the boys have furnished them, that book should make rich reading.

There are three Y.s here in a little triangle each a mile apart, all under the same management; Jamy, Conflans and Labry. Within this triangle, besides the ordnance detachment, there is a regiment of engineers, two companies of pioneer infantry, a telegraph battalion and a detachment of negro labor troops.

When the Americans came here last November, the town, they tell us, was an indescribable mess, the roads choked with abandoned military material and litter of all sorts. To the Americans as usual fell the pleasant task of cleaning up. Sometimes I think that if France doesn't come out of this war as clean as the classic Spotless Town it will only be because the Americans weren't here long enough. And yet, funnily enough, France being cleaned up by America has often provided a spectacle analogous to a little boy having his face washed against his will. At Bourmont, when the Americans sought to make the town sanitary by a liberal use of disinfectants, a frantic protest went up from the inhabitants: their wells, they claimed, had all been ruined! At Gondrecourt the Mayor presented a formal complaint; the Americans were wearing away the streets, he said, by too much cleaning! And on the other hand this sort of work proves none too pleasant a pill for American pride to swallow. Today a young New York Jew came into the canteen. He was a handsome fellow and in civilian life evidently something of a dandy. He belonged to the pioneers and he had been engaged all day, I gathered, in following about at the tail of a dump cart, picking up tin cans and rubbish.

"My God!" he suddenly burst out. "If my wife could see me now! My God! if she could see me!"

One day last fall going down a street I passed a boy who was engaged in a particularly dirty sort of cleaning. He looked up, caught my eye, stood grinning sheepishly at me a moment. Then he drawled, half humourously, half-bitterly:

"And my mother thinks I'm in the trenches!"

Conflans, March 10.

After so many weeks of wandering, I have settled down to a job again. The last six "huts" in which I have been were in a barracks, a casino, a private house, a convent, a college and a hospital. This "hut" is in a hotel. The hotel is situated directly back of the Conflans-Jamy railroad station. Before the war the hotel was a prosperous and pleasant place, judging from the photograph which Madame showed us; its windows filled with real lace curtains all matching! as she pointed out; the broad terrace in front on sunny days filled with little tables and crowded with well-dressed people. Now, after four years of German occupation, it is a melancholy spectacle; ragged, dingy, half the panes gone from the windows, its front painted over with staring German signs. There are two entrances, one into the hall leading to the rooms given over to the Y. the other into what we call the "Annex," a little café kept by Madame and Monsieur, the proprietors of the place. Next to our red triangle sign stares a board announcing brazenly in red and yellow *Vin et Bière*; but the irony of the juxtaposition is quite lost on the French; indeed yesterday Madame asked me if I couldn't get her the loan of a truck to go to Nancy for a load of beer!

Madame and Monsieur have been here all through the German occupation. The Germans weren't bad, Madame told me, if one were very meek and never said a word, but did just exactly as they said,—she had had some difficulty to be sure, reducing her more temperish spouse to the proper attitude of meek submission!—but they had made a clean sweep of everything of value; all her linen that she had carefully hidden, her copper utensils, everything.

The Y. consists of a canteen room, a reading and writing room, store-room, kitchen and office. When I first saw the place it was as uninviting as anything could well be; dark, dirty, ill-smelling, the walls covered with soiled ragged paper. But now it is very nice; the dirty cloth in the window frames has been replaced by vitex, the windows hung with pretty curtains, new electric lights have been added, and best of all, the walls entirely covered with German camouflage cloth and decorated with bright posters. This camouflage cloth is a Godsend; woven of finely twisted strands of paper, it comes in three colors, a soft brown, a yellowish green and a dark blue, resembling, when on the walls, a loosely woven burlap. It was used by the Germans to conceal and disguise military objects and was left here in large quantities when they evacuated. The Americans hereabouts use it for every imaginable purpose; for covering unsightly walls, for curtains, for officers' mess table-cloths. Then there are the ammunition bags made of paper cloth which the boys use for laundry bags. "When in doubt, camouflage," is the motto. I chose brown for my canteen and now it is on the walls I feel that no millionaire could ask for anything prettier. Only I wonder; will they ask me to join the paper-hangers' union when I get home?

Besides running the dry canteen, we serve hot chocolate free every night for all comers here, filling up their canteens so the boys can take it away with them, and run a free lodging-house. Every day we have boys coming into the canteen asking for a bed. So after nine-fifteen we stack all the chairs and tables at one end of the writing-room, and bring out canvas-cots and blankets from the store-room for our lodgers. There is only one unfortunate feature of this scheme; the lodgers become so attached to their blankets that they are all too apt to carry them away with them the next morning!

A man secretary and I are to run the hut together; a minister in the states, here he answers to the unvarying title of "Chief." The "Chief" I find at present chiefly remarkable for his trousers. These are garments with a past apparently and a present of such a sort that in the company of ladies he is only rendered at ease by assuming a sitting posture. If compelled to rise he backs out of your presence as if you were royalty or goes with the gesture of the little boy who has been chastised. Outside the house, no matter how fine the day may be, he goes discreetly clad in a raincoat.

"I must," declares the Chief at least six times a day, "go to Toul and get a new uniform."

"Amen," say I under my breath.

Besides the outfits stationed in town there are some twenty more in the neighborhood which draw their rations here at the railhead and then there are the leave trains on their way to or from Germany, whose passing, like a visitation of locusts, leaves the canteen stripped and bare. The negro labor troops in the vicinity supply quite a new element. Sometimes this takes the form of a bit of humour. Last night I had drawn several cups of cocoa ahead of the demand when a darky lad came shyly up to the counter and pointed to one.

"Please ma'am," he asked, "am dat cup occupied?"

There is one fat and genial little darky who is a constant customer, always he comes in munching a sandwich or an orange or some other edible bought from a street-vendor.

"Eating again, Jo?" asked the Chief today.

"Why Boss," expostulated Jo, "I only eats one meal a day! But dat," he grinned, "am all de time!"

"Shines" the boys invariably call them.

Tonight we were amused to see a negro corporal, who, not content with the chevrons on his sleeve, had sewed an additional pair on his overseas cap!

Conflans, March 14.

My family at the hut consists of the Chief, Harry, Jerry and Slim. Harry and Jerry are as nice lads as one could find anywhere, but Slim is the bird that hatched out of the cuckoo's egg. Lean, uncouth, according to his own claim, "the tallest man that Uncle Sam's got in his army," with an inordinately long neck and an Adam's apple so prominent as to give him the appearance of an ostrich in the act of swallowing a perpetual orange, "Slim Old Horse" as the boys call him, seems to me at times more like an animated caricature of the middle west "Long Boy" than a being of flesh and blood and bone. How he ever became attached to the Y. is a point on which nobody seems certain, but here he is and here he sticks in spite of every effort to dislodge him. I fancy his "Top Kick" was only too glad to get rid of him and when he discovered Slim's inclination toward the Y. simply let him go and washed his hands of him. Slim's health is uncertain. Most of the time he only feels well enough to sit in the office and eat or "chaw."

"I started in ter chaw terbaccer,"—he talks with a nasal twang which is impossible to reproduce,—"when I was a kid four years old; when my daddy an' my mammy found it out, they sure did start ter raise hell with me, but I says to 'em; 'All right, have it your way, but then it will be whisky and rum fer mine, when I'm twenty-one!' So my mammy says 'Let 'im chaw.' An' I've chawed ever sence."

"I've only got one lung," he remarked the other day, "and that's a little one."

"Slim," I urged, "I'm worried about you. You oughtn't to be here. You ought to be in the hospital where you could be properly cared for. Go to your medical officer and tell him from me that he must send you to the hospital."

Slim reluctantly departed. I dared to hope we had seen the last of him. But before the afternoon was over he was back on his old perch. He had brought some little pills back with him. Just wait, I thought, until I meet that medical officer!

Slim seldom feels attracted to the meals at the mess-hall. So he sits in the office and lives chiefly upon cheese, Y. M. C. A. cheese purchased to make sandwiches for the canteen at a cost of a dollar and a quarter a pound. Sometimes he fries himself eggs, taking whatever mess-kit, Harry's or Jerry's or mine, happens to be handy and never, in spite of anything I can say, will he wash it up after him! Sometimes Harry and Jerry and I decide that instead of going to mess we would like to have a supper-party at the canteen ourselves, and then the question is, how to get rid of Slim?

"Slim, it's getting near chow-time," we say, "I'll bet they're going to have mashed potatoes and brown gravy tonight. Isn't that 'Soupy' I hear going now?"

But Slim refuses to budge any more than a bump on a log, so we usually have to end by inviting him. But if I find Slim a burden, how must the Chief feel toward him? For Slim has appropriated the extra cot in the office, which also serves as the Chief's bed-room, and so has fairly camped down on him. And the Chief is a gentleman of nerves and delicate perceptions.

"He gets up in the middle of the night," confided the Chief to me today in an almost awe-struck voice, "and he goes for the water-bucket and drinks a half a pail without stopping. He makes a noise just like a horse swallowing it."

I have given up trying to do anything with Slim. Nothing that I can say seems to make the least impression on him. Slim is a married man, yet yesterday I caught him embracing Louise, Madame's cross-eyed maid of all work, in the passage-way. I undertook to reprove him.

"Why that ain't nawthin!" he turned a blameless and unabashed eye upon me. "That's jest a man's nature."

This is the first time that I have eaten regularly from a mess-kit and I am learning things. I have learned that the aluminum mess-cup draws the heat from the hot coffee so that it is impossible to drink out of one until the liquid has become half-way cold, and that it is most unappetizing to have to wash one's mess-kit afterwards in a pail of greasy soap suds in which a hundred odd other mess-kits have already been bathed. I used to tease the boys with their mess-cups in the chocolate line by telling them that I could tell just how recently they had had inspection by the shine on their mess-cups, but now whenever I look at the state of my own cup I think I won't have the face to ever tease them that way again! I have also learned that cold "gold fish" or "sewer carp," as the boys call their canned salmon, is just as bad as they say it is, and that slum made of hunks of bacon, potatoes, onions and unlimited water is no easy thing to swallow. But this sounds ungrateful and I don't mean to be, for the cooks are nice as can be and never say a word no matter how late I may be. While as for the boys, they put on all their company manners for me.

Here at the hut we are busy building an addition in order to enlarge our restaurant business. This is in the shape of a room on the terrace. The Germans had kindly built a roof over one end, a detail from the ordnance detachment at Jarny is enclosing the sides; we are to have three real glass windows looking out onto the street and a door connecting the terrace-room with the present canteen. This afternoon the detail ran out of lumber; the Chief managed to get the loan of a truck to fetch some more. He asked Slim to go with the truck. The afternoon wore away, neither Slim nor the truck appeared, the detail, disgusted, sat and twiddled their thumbs. Nobody could understand what had happened as the lumber yard was just around the corner! Jerry went out to search. There was no trace of Slim or the truck to be found. About five o'clock he turned up. He had gone to Mars-la-Tour he told us coolly. We had been talking of going to the commissary at Mars-la-Tour for canteen supplies, and that great goose had gotten into his head that the *lumber* was to be obtained there! At least that is his explanation. But Harry and Jerry insinuate darker things:

"We didn't know you had a girl in Mars-la-Tour before," they tease. "Oh Slim, you old devil, you!"

I wonder now, just what *was* he up to in Mars-la-Tour all afternoon?

Conflans, March 19.

Why is it that all the world loves a rascal? What is the secret of the fascination that outlaw and free-booter have exercised from Robin Hood down to Captain Kidd? Is it because each one of us, in our secret hearts, would like to go and do likewise, if we only dared? Of all the minor piracies committed by the A. E. F. in France, none, I think, are so picturesque as those of the — Engineers.

The — Engineers are a railroad regiment. My first acquaintance with them was last summer. A company of these engineers was located at a station on the Paris line just north of us. It was a point at which supplies for the American front were transferred from the standard gauge to the American narrow gauge; in order to effect these transfers the — Engineers had a switch of their own. Now freight trains in France are quite unguarded and so at the mercy of marauders. Indeed the losses in transit have been so serious that since the armistice it has been the custom to have cars containing American goods "convoyed" to their destination by soldier guards. Last summer of course the men could not be spared for convoy duty. So it was the easiest thing in the world for the — Engineers to "cut out" a Y. or a Red Cross car, side-track it, and lighten the load at their leisure.

"I went through their company store-house while I was there," a Q. M. sergeant told me, "and it was as well stocked with delicacies as the store-rooms of a big hotel back in the States."

No wonder there was such a dearth of supplies at Abainville last summer!

But it was after the — Engineers moved into the occupied area here following the armistice that they performed their most notorious exploits. Assigned to run a stretch of railway in cooperation with the French, a certain amount of friction was inevitable from the start, the red tape in the French railway system exasperating the Americans as much as our more direct methods scandalized the French. Finally the French protests at the Americans' disregard for the formalities of railroading moved the engineer officers to stricter discipline. "I'll *hang* the next man of you who runs a train out of the yards without a pilot!" declared one captain. After that things went more smoothly,—on the surface. Then came the Dance.

Now unfortunately for the — Engineers there is an extra large M. P. force here at Conflans under a Major whose greatest delight in life is the detection and punishment of both major and minor infractions of the law.

The Dance was quite an affair over which the — Engineers had spread themselves and to which the French fair sex was generally invited. When the party was about to begin, however, it became evident that the feminine partners afforded locally were all too few. Some bold soul had a bright idea; a train-crew forthwith hurried down to the yards, commandeered an engine and a couple of cars, and, in spite of the horrified protests of the French railroad men, ran it to a nearby town. Here they filled up the train with girls from the village and were about to start back again when a detachment of M. P.s, rushed up in autos from Conflans, broke in upon the scene. A sanguine scrimmage ensued, resulting in a victory for law and order.

In the meanwhile, back at the dance hall the engineers were waiting in impatient expectation for partners. Among the invited guests were two friendly M. P.s, old soldiers, with genial dispositions and several wound stripes to their credit. When word reached the party that the M. P.s had prevented the arrival of the "Mademoiselles" the engineers were furious. "Kill the M. P.s!" went up the cry. Catching sight of the red-arm bands on their two innocent guests the crowd started for them with the evident intention of making a beginning then and there. Heaven only knows what would have happened if the two M. P.s, by affecting an exit at the double-quick, hadn't immediately made their escape, unharmed but badly scared.

The most notable exploit of the — Engineers occurred not long afterwards. It is referred to as the Affair of the Serge Uniforms. One fine day, not very long ago, it was noised abroad that a car full of tailored serge uniforms, consigned to and paid for by officers of the Army of Occupation in Luxembourg, was standing down in the yards. The idea of going home in an officer's serge uniform from which, of course, the braid on the cuffs had been discreetly ripped, made a strong appeal to the boys' imaginations. When the time came for that car to be sent to Luxembourg it was found to be quite empty. But for once the Engineers had gone too far. The M. P. Major took the war-path. Word flew around the camp that a strict search was being conducted. The possessors of the incriminating uniforms must get rid of them and get rid of them quick. Some hid them in out-of-the-way places, between the floors and ceilings in the half-ruined houses; others frantically ripped the uniforms to pieces and burned them in the barracks stoves. The camp, they tell me, was full of the stench of scorching woolen. Still others got rid of them by planting them among the possessions of their innocent neighbors. One company postal clerk, a most upright and blameless lad, to his horror discovered one of the fatal uniforms stuffed in a mail-bag lying at his feet. Before the search party had made its rounds most of those serge uniforms had been safely disposed of; a few, a very few were found.

But now, having been baulked in his attempt to bring the culprits to justice, it is common rumour, that the M. P. Major is lying low, waiting to "fix" the — Engineers.

Conflans, March 23.

The — Engineers have left. They are on their way to Le Mans, presumably the first stage of their journey home. Their departure was not unmarked by incident. At the last moment, when they had all entrained and were ready to pull out of the station, the M. P. Major sallied forth, court-martials in his eye, to search the trains for contraband. But he had reckoned without the Colonel of the engineers who flatly refused to allow any such procedure. Being outranked by the Colonel, the M. P. Major was seemingly helpless. Then, however, the Colonel made a bad mistake. There were two train loads. The Colonel left with the first. The second, being left without any protector of sufficiently high rank, fell an easy prey to the Major. He searched to his heart's content, discovering several articles of unlawful loot and, one unfortunate clad in one of the notorious serge uniforms! The train was held in the yards while the M. P. Major indulged in an orgy of court-martials.

On the morning of the departure the captain of the motor unit where we had messed stopped in to speak to me. He came by request of the boys to bring an apology for any careless language which might have been uttered unwittingly in my hearing! Then the captain of another unit called to tell us, sub rosa, that, forced by shortage of transportation, he was leaving behind an over supply of rations which would be ours for the fetching. We fetched accordingly and found that we had fallen heir to dozens of loaves of bread, sugar, coffee, canned meat, canned tomatoes, hard bread, soap and unlimited beans. What to do with these surreptitious stores is now the embarrassing question. One simply can't offer the boys hard bread, tomatoes plain or scalloped, in the canteen, no matter if one should dress them with all the sauces of Epicurus and serve them on gold-plate. Yet they mustn't be wasted. What's more, the fact that they are in our possession must be kept absolutely dark, lest we get the kind captain into trouble. I feel something like the man who was presented with a million dollar check and then found he couldn't cash it.

With the — Engineers went Harry, Jerry, and Slim. I couldn't believe until the last moment that Slim was actually going. His departure almost compensated for the loss of Harry and Jerry. But though gone, he is not forgotten. This morning a lad came into the canteen. He would like his watch please, he said. I looked blankly at him. He explained; several days ago, just as he was leaving on a long truck-trip, he had broken the strap of his wrist watch. Happening to be in front of the Y. just then, he had brought it in and left it for safe-keeping "with the Y. man in the office." The Chief knew nothing of it.

"What did the Y. man look like?" I questioned.

He described him. It was Slim. We have searched every nook and cranny of that office, hoping to come upon the missing watch, in vain.

"I'll come in again," said the boy. "Perhaps by that time you will have found it."

But personally I am sure that that watch is now on its way to Le Mans, en route for the States. Was there ever anything more wretchedly embarrassing?

Conflans, March 27.

This is a curious world. Six "Relief Trains" pass through here every day bound east, loaded with food for Germany. Meanwhile in the little half-ruined hamlets within a stone's throw of the tracks the French villagers, for whom no provision has been made, are famine-stricken.

Lieutenant A. came in from the little town of Pierrefond which lies between Conflans and Verdun yesterday.

"They have nothing to eat there," he told me, "but the weeds they dig up in the fields for *salade* and the frogs they catch in the marshes. When the days are cold the frogs bury themselves so deep in the mud that they can't be caught. There is one old gentleman who told me today that he had existed for weeks entirely on a diet of turnips. They come to me and beg pitifully for a bite of something from the mess-kitchen, but I don't dare let them have it, as that would be, of course, strictly against regulations."

I thought of those bushels of beans in the store-house. It was taking a chance of course, because after all it was government property and nothing else, but I told the Lieutenant that if he was willing to run the risk, I was; then I put it up to the Chief.

This morning the Lieutenant came in with a flivver. We drove over to the store-house and loaded it up with army beans, issue coffee, sugar, rice, onions, potatoes and soap. Then we filled a special sack with canned soup, "gold fish," corn meal, canned tomatoes and corn syrup for the old gentleman who had lived on turnips. I felt he had a special claim on our sympathy.

We reached Pierrefond after a long drive in a stinging rain. It was a quaint pathetic village with a pretty little church whose tower had been sliced off as neatly as by a knife. Was it a German or a French shell which had done it, I wondered. We drew up in front of the Mayor's house. He came out to greet us, showed me a list of the seventy-three inhabitants of the town; men, women and infants in arms. All the supplies were to be duly weighed and measured and distributed, so much per capita. While they were unloading the flivver we stopped in at Madame C.'s for coffee and compliments, and to dry out by her hospitable fire. Everyone made pretty speeches, of course, and Madame bestowed on me a delectable bouquet of wall-flowers and daffodils. Poor things! It's little enough one can do for them. This will keep the wolf from the door for a short while perhaps, but after that, what then?

Pierrefond, like Conflans, was occupied by the Germans for four years. Now there is a young half-German population growing up, even as many as three to one family. The villagers accept the situation with tolerant humour; "Souvenirs Boches," they call the children.

As for the rest of the rations, I made jam sandwiches with the bread and bestowed them together with hot chocolate on a hungry leave train. What to do with the "Charlie Horse," as the boys call the canned roast beef, was a puzzle. Finally I made a paste of it mixed with bread crumbs, tomato soup, a few weenies and some ham scraps, pickles, parsley, onion and an egg,— we had six assistants in the kitchen and each added an ingredient,—put it between slices of bread and christened the result "Liberty Sandwiches. Guaranteed to contain neither Gold Fish nor Corn Willy." The boys ate and wondered and came back for more.

Conflans, March 30.

In our back yard a detail of German prisoners is busy cleaning up; already they have made quite a transformation. Madame must have a garden. I wonder, as I watch them, what their state of mind may be; their phlegmatic faces give no hint. Did some of these very ones, perhaps, make merry in this self same café, only six months ago, when they were conquerors?

Madame tells me how, when the German officers were living here at the hotel, they ate off priceless old French plates, which, apparently quite ignorant of their value, they had carried off as loot. Madame, coveting these treasures, tried to arrange an exchange with the mess orderly, offering a number of modern dishes in return for one antique; but the mess orderly, fearing that some officer might notice the substitution, hesitated and before they could come to an agreement the precious plates, with the rough handling accorded them, had all been broken to bits.

Some of the boys seem to think that the French don't give their prisoners enough to eat. The Germans, they say, when they get the chance, will wait outside the mess-hall door and seize eagerly the leavings in the mess-kits that the boys are about to throw away.

"Maybe it's just because they're greedy," I say. "Surely they look fat enough!" And then a picture comes back to my mind, the picture of a Red

Cross train seen while waiting at Pagny on my way to Paris last January, a train full of French prisoners who were being brought back from Germany, so weak from starvation that they lay on stretchers or sat pressing against the windows faces as wan and white as spectres.

The German prisoners, according to the boys' repeated stories, are by no means a humble or repentant lot. They're not beaten for good, the prisoners invariably declare. Just as soon as the Americans have gone and things have calmed down a bit, they are coming back to France again, they say, and this time they will settle matters with the French for good and all!

Last night a train load of German prisoners in box cars pulled into town. When the doors of the cars were opened it was found that one of the prisoners had died on the way. The dead man was wrapped in a blanket and left lying on the freight station platform. A "shine" from the labor battalion happened along in the dark, tripped and fell flat over the body. He came into the canteen in a state of nerves, quite prepared, evidently, to see a ghost in every corner.

Conflans, April 2.

The latest member of our household is something quite new in the way of details. He is a Salvation Army man and a very nice fellow indeed. A year or so ago he was beating a big drum in front of Gimbel's Store; then he was drafted to come to France with the pioneers; now he has applied for a discharge in order to join his organization over here; and while waiting for his release he is proving himself an invaluable aid in the canteen. Now more than ever, since The Salvation Army, as everybody calls him, has joined our force, I have been longing to realize a dream which I have cherished ever since I came to France,—to make doughnuts for the A. E. F. I have the recipe, I can get the materials, the stove is the sticking-point. At present our cooking equipment consists of a hot water boiler and a wretched German range which is really fit for nothing but the scrap-heap. As the boys say, I have lost more religion than I ever thought I had over that stove! So while we hope and hunt for a doughnut-stove we are specializing in sandwiches and puddings. The puddings are my special pride as I worked out the ideas for them myself and, as far as I know, they are served in no other canteen. There are four of them; Coffee Jelly, Raspberry Jelly (made with the "pink-lemonade" fruit juice) Chocolate Bread Pudding, and Blackberry Bread Pudding. The bread-puddings are baked for us, by kindness of the cooks, at a nearby mess-kitchen. The only trouble with the puddings is, that there never is enough! But lest anyone should think that I take this as a compliment to my culinary skill, I must explain that the boys would eat anything you offered them, I believe, just as long as it was sweet and was a change. And then there is perhaps a quaint psychological factor too.

"A man don't like to eat food that's cooked by a man," a lad confided to me the other day. "Anything that's cooked by a woman tastes better."

So if a boy does leave any scraps of pudding on his plate it bothers me unreasonably.

"Somebody didn't like his pudding," I remark mournfully to the S. A. as I pick up the dishes. This amuses him. Last night as we were clearing up before we closed he marched up to the counter, deposited a tiny wad found on one of the tables in front of me.

"Somebody," he declared in a tragic tone, "didn't like his chewing-gum!"

Nor can I boast, as a cook, of a record of unvarying success. On more than one occasion I must admit to having scorched the cocoa, and once, not many days ago—to my shame be it said!—I ruined a ten gallon can by putting in salt instead of sugar!

Here at Conflans we have an unusual amount of competition in the light lunch line. The other day a French fried potato booth, like a hot-dog booth at a country fair at home, established itself on the terrace just outside our door. Now a hungry doughboy can take the edge off his appetite with a paper full of hot French fries in return for a franc at any hour of the day.

Also in the street below the terrace are many little stands where oranges and sandwiches made of rolls and slices of sausage are on sale. The rivalry between these stands, it appears, is acute. Yesterday, hearing a hubbub, I looked out to see a comic battle in progress, the proprietors of two neighboring stands, a fat frowsy old woman and a little ragged man like a weasel, pelting each other for all they were worth with rotten oranges while half the A. E. F., it seemed, stood around and cheered. Nor did matters settle down to calm until a gendarme and intervention appeared on the scene.

This morning I stopped in at the little French store around the corner to buy half a dozen eggs to make a custard sauce for my chocolate bread pudding. When the man gave me my change I noticed he had overcharged me by twenty-five centimes.

"Why's that?" I asked.

"That," returned the shopkeeper, "is because you picked them out by hand."

Some canteen ladies can cook and wait on the counter and open milk-cans and wash the chocolate cups and yet keep spotlessly and specklessly clean. But I have come to the conclusion that as long as I live in Conflans, with its air full of smoke and soot from the train yards, and its water so hard that it curdles the soap,—and sometimes the milk in the cocoa too, that I will have to content myself with being godly and leave the cleanliness till a happier day. We have been having a regular plague of inspectors and investigators of late. Last night just as I had my final bout with the last chocolate container, a major and a lieutenant colonel wandered in, evidently in search of scandal. The lieutenant colonel fixed a piercing eye on me.

"So you are the only 'white woman' in this part of the world at present?"

"Well," I said looking at my fingers smudged with cocoa, "tonight I should say that I was a pale chocolate-colored woman."

"I noticed that your face was dirty," coolly returned the gentleman. I hurriedly excused myself in order to consult a looking-glass. Sure enough, there on my nose was a large smudge of soot! I must have got it the last time I stoked the chocolate-stove.

Conflans, April 7.

The M. P.s live in the hotel next door. Naturally we see a good deal of them. I try to treat them extra nicely because I feel sorry for them. They can't help being M. P.s any more than they can help being unpopular. And though many of them go about with a chip on their shoulders and an attitude of I-don't-give-a-tinker's-damn, still to know that you are anathema to the major portion of the A. E. F., to be publicly referred to as Misery Providers, Mademoiselle Promenades, and Military Pests, besides being made the subject of songs such as; *Mother take down your service flag, Your son is only an M. P.*, must be galling to the most insensitive.

Just as soon as the armistice was signed the doughboys started in to pester the M. P.s with the classic taunt:

"Who won the war?—The M. P.s!"

For a long while the M. P.s could think of no more crushing rejoinder than the time-honored;

"Aw, go to hell!"

But lately some bright soul has hit upon a bit of repartee that goes far to salve the M. P.s' self-respect. Now if a soldier is so rash as to jeer; "Who won the war? The M. P.s!" the response comes instantly:

"Yep! They chased the doughboys up front!"

There are two M. P.s from the detachment next door who have lately joined themselves to our family. Like Slim, they came unsolicited, and like Slim, they stick. They are known respectively as the Littlest M. P. and the Fattest M. P.

The Littlest M. P. is a pest. I feel sorry for him because he is so young and has no mother; otherwise there would be no tolerating him. He hangs about the canteen from morning until late at night under pretence of assisting us, and eats and eats and eats and eats. The other day I heard him proudly averring that he hadn't taken a meal in the mess-hall for two weeks, and I believed him. Yet when you ask him to do any particular piece of work, like filling up the wood box or fetching a pail of water, in return for his board, he always has some perfectly good reason for not doing it. Besides which, he has no morals. The other day he confided to me triumphantly that the reason that they didn't put him on guard work was that they knew he would take money to let men into cafés at prohibited hours. He went on to tell me about the town of S.

"That was a good place, you could get twenty-five francs for lettin' a feller into a café out of hours there."

I have tried to find out what he does in return for Uncle Sam's dollar a day and have discovered that his job is sweeping out the halls in the M. P. Hotel.

"But I skip about twenty feet at each end every time, so it don't take me more'n ten minutes."

Yesterday morning he came in with an air of righteousness rewarded.

"I told 'em I'd got to have help on that job," he announced, "so they put another feller on too."

This morning I got so exasperated with him that I told him in unmistakable terms that we could dispense with his company. He disappeared, and I congratulated myself that we were rid of him. But at supper-time he bobbed serenely up again.

"Some fellers would have got sore if you'd spoke like that to them," he told me with a magnanimous air, "but I just took it as a joke."

Now what is one to do with anybody like that?

The Fattest M. P. is the most unleavened lump of good-nature I have ever known. He is, I understand, a notorious poker-player and his breath, to my embarrassment, betrays the fact that he has a weakness for Conflans beer. Besides which, he really takes up quite too much room behind the counter. Yet in spite of all this, he is such a simple soul and is so anxious to help that one hasn't the heart to send him away.

Yesterday I thought I was going to be arrested by an M. P. I had gone over to Verdun in an army flivver to get some stock. Turning the corner into Conflans on our way home we were halted by the upraised billy of the M. P. on duty.

"Sorry, Buddy!" he called to the driver, "but you can't do that!"

Then, approaching, he got a closer view, turned red as fire and stammered;

"Beg your pardon, Miss. Made a mistake. That's all right, driver, you can go on."

Later he sent apologies to me at the canteen. It is, of course, against regulations to allow civilian women to use army transportation. The M. P., catching sight of a skirt, had taken me for a Mademoiselle on a joy-ride.

Conflans, April 7.

We must start an Orphans' Annex here, the boys tell me. Three nights ago as it was drawing on toward closing time the Chief called me into the office. By the table stood two young boys, about fourteen and sixteen I judged them; each carried on his shoulder a little sack which evidently contained all his worldly possessions. They were German boys from Metz; they had just come in on the train. Why had they come? we asked them. They had come to join the American army. But they were too young! He was eighteen, declared the elder. He dug into his pockets and produced documents. I looked at two of the papers, they appeared to be the birth certificates of his father and mother. Had his parents given their consent? He nodded. "And you really are eighteen?", *"Ja! Ja wohl!"* It was hard to believe,—he was so small. We stared at them a bit helplessly. Then, finding our German not quite adequate to the occasion, we called an interpreter. But to all the interpreter's questioning the boy returned the same unvarying answer. He had come to join the American army! As for the younger one, he merely stood and smiled and looked as guileless as a young angel. Whatever the elder one's intention might be, I was sure I could divine the younger's. *He*, I am certain, had set his heart on being an American "mascot." And he, for all his innocent and engaging air, had most patently run away from home!

We told the boys that we would put them up for the night. I busied myself in getting them some supper and then—another waif appeared! A little French lad of thirteen, with a peg-leg and a crutch, he came shyly hobbling into the office, and the face he lifted to us was one of the sweetest, the most sensitive and appealing that I have ever seen. Silently he tendered us a letter. It had been written by an American lieutenant; the bearer, it stated, was an orphan of the war; he had been shot by German machine-gunners near Verdun; his right leg had been amputated at the thigh. I looked at the crippled child in apprehension. How would he take the presence of the Germans? But my question was already answered. The little German lad and the French *mutilé* had drawn close together, seemingly drawn instantly to each other by a bond of childish understanding. Although neither could speak the other's speech they appeared to be communicating in some shy wordless way. Later, as we were getting the cots ready for the lodgers, passing the empty canteen room, I glanced inside. Somebody had started the victrola on the counter to playing a waltz, and to its music the German boys were dancing while the little French lad gaily kept time with his crutch!

We fed the three of them and put them up for the night. The next morning the French lad took his leave. Later he came back to see us dressed in a little American uniform; he had been adopted by one of the companies here. The German lads stayed with us, or rather, they slept and ate with the M. P.s next door and spent the rest of the day with us in the canteen. They loved to help about the counter; they were quick and deft and willing. The only trouble with the arrangement was that I fairly went distracted trying to talk three languages at once!

Two days afterwards, the M. P.s having taken the matter in hand, the German boys were sent back to Metz. But the French lad comes in often to visit us. We see him playing ball with the soldiers in the street in front of the hotel. This morning the S. A. and I stood watching him.

"I wouldn't mind it so much somehow," the S. A. remarked, "if he didn't have that wrap-legging wound so tight around that pitiful little peg-stick!"

The tenderness toward little children which the war has shown forth so vividly has been a revelation of an inherent sweetness in the boys' natures; this fondness for children other than their own, being, I believe a distinctive characteristic of our American men. Any number of companies have mascots, little French boys, orphans usually, whom they dress in miniature uniforms, take about from place to place with them, and, of course, spoil quite shamelessly. And in every unit that possesses a mascot you find boys whose dearest wish is to adopt the little fellow as his own and take him back home; but this the French law forbids.

"That's the best part of France, the little kids," remarked a boy to me as we passed a group of little tots by the roadside.

Unfortunately though, this petting has another side. Spoiled by the soft-hearted soldiers, the French gamins have developed into a brood of brazen little beggars. They have come to regard all Americans, it seems, as perambulating slot machines for "goom" and chocolate with whom, however, the purchasing penny is quite superfluous. I shall never forget being held up, as I was walking with a doughboy through the streets of Lourdes, by a tiny lad who demanded pathetically;

"Une cigarette pour moi, et une pour Papa, et une pour Maman qui est malade!"

Nor the fifteen year old conductor on a suburban tram line near Paris, who took up our tickets with a forbidding scowl, and then, his rounds made, hurried back down the car to confront us with the wistful childish plea: "'Ave you goom?"

For some while there has been a red-headed urchin of perhaps thirteen years hanging about the hut. As he was dressed in an O. D. blouse, breeches and leggings, I concluded that he was somebody's mascot. He kept coming into the canteen to buy gum and cigarettes; presently I discovered he was purchaser for a little gang of ragamuffins who would wait for him just outside the door. I asked the boys in the canteen if they knew anything about the red-head, but no one seemed to know who he was or to what outfit he belonged. The boy himself seemed stupid and sullen when I questioned him. Finally I told him that I could sell him nothing more. Tonight my friend the M. P. Sergeant asked casually;

"Do you remember that red-headed kid that used to hang around? Well we've got him and eight others."

"Why, what for?"

"They're Propaganda Kids. They came over here from Germany; they've been stealing American uniforms and smuggling them to the German prisoners so they could escape in them."

Conflans, April 15.

Of all the roads over which I have ever passed, the road from Conflans to Verdun will remain, I think, most sharply etched upon my memory.

Leaving Conflans, as one passes through the occupied territory, the predominant impression made upon one's mind is of signs. German military signs. These are everywhere, painted in great staring letters on the sides of buildings, covering bill-boards set at the road's edge, or hung suspended from the branches of trees over the truck drivers' heads. Here in this German sector behind the lines every movement was timed, ordered and regulated. No one could possibly go astray, no one could lose a moment in hesitation as to where he should go, in what manner and at what rate. Half-way between Conflans and the lines you come upon two great bill-boards at the highway's edge, one duplicating the other, in order that, marching past, what might have been missed on the first board, could be supplied by the second. They are headed "Under Enemy Observation!" and give in strict detail the order of procedure from that point forward, both by day and night, just what strength the marching groups should be and how many metres should intervene between them. The German thoroughness, the German system! Everything has been thought of, everything provided for, everything possible done to reduce the individual to an automaton, a mere senseless cog in a vast machine. And yet among all these signs there is one that lacks, a sign that is notable by its absence; it is the sign that should read *Nach Verdun*.

Once across the lines on the French side you are struck by the startling difference; here the only signs that one sees are two, poignant in their simplicity and directness. They are *Poste de Secours* and *Blessés à Pied*.

Every time I approach Verdun by this road I thrill when I think of the enormous energy that poured along it, directed, it must have seemed, irresistibly, over-poweringly against the city in the hills; a thrill only surpassed by the emotion that one must feel when he traverses the *Sacra Via* on the other side of Verdun, the "Holy Way" over which men and munitions flowed incessantly to the defense of the beleaguered city.

Everywhere one sees the ineffaceable scars of struggle, the aftermath of destruction. The stately trees bordering the roadside, the trees that Napoleon ordered planted along the highways of France, are barked with great ugly gashes where mines had been placed, the exploding of which would have felled the great trees across the road, blocking the pursuer's way. Others bear platforms high up in the branches where machine-guns were placed. Rotting camouflages of every sort, paper strips woven like lattice, curtains of branches woven through wire which once screened the road for miles from the enemy's observation, now lie disintegrating in the ditches. Shell holes pit the fields, concrete "pill-boxes" lurk in unsuspected places, every mound is shelter for a dugout, walls are riddled with ragged holes cut for machine-guns. Further on, one comes to the trenches zigzagging in what seems erratic and aimless patterns and the interminable barbed-wire entanglements, like the devil's brier patches.

Half across the open plain that lies before the hills of Verdun you come upon a German tank defence, a long line of heavy concrete pillars with enormous cables, once highly electrified, looped between. A little farther and the road crosses an impromptu bridge thrown hastily over the great gaping crater torn by an exploding mine. And always here and there over the plain, little heaps of glimmering whitish stones which mark the places where once were villages. Starting to ascend the hills, one looks down upon a ghost city, a city where many of the walls still stand, making you think of nothing but a huddled host of tombstones, a city chalk-white, naked, as if the flesh were all picked away from its dead bones; the most haunted, the most wraith-like, the most desolate of any.

Climbing the hills, sweeping around one slow curve after another, one beholds suddenly before him, a lesser hill ringed by higher ones, Verdun, scarred, wounded, but victorious, like the Winged Victory of Samothrace, mutilated yet triumphant!

When I first made the trip from Verdun to Conflans there were still good pickings for the souvenir-hunter by the way; shell-cases, helmets, gas masks lying along the roadside; but lately it has looked as if these trophies had been thoroughly gleaned. Nor does one wonder where they have gone when one sees the flivvers piled high with homeward bound souvenirs pulling in at the post office around the corner. But will they reach home, is the question? Ominous rumours are abroad that salvage plants have been established at the base ports for the particular purpose of confiscating shell-cases on their way to America, and thereby saving the Allies a fortune in brass. Some of the boys are inclined to try to carry their trophies with them rather than entrust them to Uncle Sam's mail service, but this entails some trouble to prevent their seizure during inspections. Nowadays, passing by, one can tell when an inspection is in progress within, by all the junk which is hanging out of the barracks windows! Homeward-bound troops have already discovered a use for gas masks not mentioned in the Drill Manual: the cases provide an excellent receptacle in which surreptitiously one may carry photographs and post-cards! When I first came to Conflans, camouflaged German helmets were a prize so rare as to be much sought after by the souvenir enthusiast; but now camouflaged helmets may be had for the asking; an enterprising bugler possessed of a knack with a paint-brush has gone into the business of camouflaging them while you wait.

Yesterday, after having returned from Verdun, I noticed a post-card in a Jarny shop. It showed a black cat and a white cat silhouetted against the moon, perched on the skeleton beams of a half-demolished house, peering disconsolately about them. Underneath the sentence ran; *Où est-il le toit de nos amours?* Where is the roof of our love? Could any nation but the French thus make light of such tragedy?

Paris, April 21.

I am on my way home at last. I am waiting here for my sailing. This time I am really going all the way through. Now that I am on the brink of the *retour au civil*, as the French say, it seems very odd. For eighteen months I haven't worn white gloves, or silk stockings, or a veil, no, nor even powdered my nose. And the worst of it is, these things don't seem to matter any more. Even a uniform, and a homely uniform at that, has tremendous advantages as part of a working scheme of life. As one girl remarked;

"You don't have to spend any time thinking: Shall I put on the pink or the blue tonight? The only question is, Do I or do I not need a clean collar?"

Somehow I feel a little unfitted to go back to a civilian existence once more. The same feeling one finds expressed continually among the boys.

"When I get back home, if I see a line anywhere I'll go and stand in it just from force of habit," remarked one boy, grinning ruefully.

But most often this feeling takes the form of a pathetic and wistful fear.

"I'm afraid I'll shock Mother when I get home."

"They won't know what to make of us, back home, the way we'll behave."

"I reckon I've forgotten how to act civilized."

And over and again they confess to a shame-faced apprehension lest they should unguardedly relapse into the language of the army and so frighten their women folk!

A famous French surgeon confided to my friend, the English Lady:

"In that first year of the war when we were allowed no *permissions* we became like savages. The first time that I returned home I was afraid. I was afraid all the while, afraid before my wife, before my children,—afraid that I would act the beast."

If by coming to France, we women who have had this privilege have discovered the American doughboy, the American doughboy, by coming to France, has discovered America. I don't know who first said; "After I get back, if the Statue of Liberty ever wants to see my face again, she'll have to turn around," but whoever did, uttered a sentiment which has been echoed and re-echoed all over France. The doughboy has been to Paris, "the City of Light," he has amused himself in the playgrounds of princes along the Riviera, he has visited the châteaux and palaces of kings and queens. And though he admits it is all mighty fine, in the face of everything he holds staunchly to his declaration of loyalty; "I'll tell the world the little old U. S. A. is good enough for me!"

At times perhaps his patriotic enthusiasm has outweighed his manners. Again and again a French villager, evidently echoing some doughboy's dissertation, has asked me a little wistfully;

"America *bon,* goode! France *pas bon,* no goode! *Hein?*"

"Anyway the war has done one good thing," I used to say to the lads in the canteens, "it has taught you to appreciate your homes."

"I used to want to get away from home," confided one boy to me, "but when I get back there again I'm just going to tie myself so tight to Mother's apron-strings that she'll never get the knot undone."

"Say, when I get back," declared another lad as he helped me wipe the dishes, "my mother's going to find I'm just the best little K. P. she ever knew."

"When I get home, I'm going to lock myself in the house and then I'm going to lose the key and stay right there for a month," announced another.

"Who's in your house?"

"Just Mother. She's good enough for me."

Sometimes I have thought that three things have stood as concrete symbols of all that was desirable to the American boy through his ordeal over here: a dollar-bill, the Statue of Liberty, his mother's face. And only a shade less touching than the doughboy's realization of all that is implied by "Mother;" is his attitude of chivalrous idealism toward the American girl. Once I ventured to say something in praise of the women of France.

"But they're not as fine as our girls!" came the instant jealous rejoinder.

"No *Mademoiselles françaises* for me, thank you. I've got a little girl of my own back home!"

"Our American girls, they're as different from these French girls," declared a tall Virginian, "as day is from night!"

"I've laid off of lovin' while I've been over here," confided one little engineer, "but, oh boy! my girl's goin' to get an awful huggin' when I get home!"

The most pitiful and hopeless cases that I have seen over here were boys who had taken to drink because their girls at home had proved inconstant. "That man never touched a drop," confided the buddy of one of these to me, "until he got that letter from his girl telling him that she was married to a slacker."

Not that the doughboy's conduct has always been above reproach. "Single men in barracks," as Kipling once remarked, "don't grow into plaster saints;" and he has been sorely tempted. But in his heart he has kept an ideal. It has stood between him and utter darkness. In this ideal he has put all his faith. If he loses it, he loses everything. Those women back home, I wonder, do they really understand?